GROWTH AND STRUCTURE
OF THE ENGLISH LANGUAGE

Andrew Linn

Emmanuel College, Cambridge 1987

GROWTH AND STRUCTURE OF THE ENGLISH LANGUAGE

OTTO JESPERSEN

With a Foreword by
Randolph Quirk

Basil Blackwell

©Otto Jespersen 1938

Foreword © Randolph Quirk 1982

Tenth edition with a Foreword by Randolph Quirk
First published 1982 by
Basil Blackwell Publisher
108 Cowley Road
Oxford OX4 1JF
England

First edition first published 1905 by
B. G. Teubner, Leipzig, London and New York

Fourth edition first published 1923 by
Basil Blackwell Publisher

Ninth edition first published 1938 by
Basil Blackwell Publisher

Reprinted 1948, 1954, 1958, 1960, 1978, 1985

British Library Cataloguing in Publication Data

Jespersen, Otto
  Growth and structure of the English
  language—10th ed.
  1. English language—History
  I. Title
  420'.9   PE1075
ISBN 0-631-12986-3
ISBN 0-631-12987-1 Pbk

Printed and bound in Great Britain by Billings and Sons
Limited, Guildford, London, Oxford, Worcester

Contents

Foreword

Our scholarly tradition has a long and distinguished line in popular one-volume treatments of English linguistic history. Jespersen's great little book of 1905 was, for example, preceded in 1904 by Henry Bradley's *Making of English* and followed in 1907 by Henry Cecil Wyld's *Growth of English*. And succeeding generations of philologists have contributed their own distillations in similar-sized vessels down the years. One that comes close to Jespersen's work in profundity and interest is the *Esquisse d'une histoire de la langue anglaise* (1947) by another non-native 'amateur' of English, the late Fernand Mossé.

Each has had its day, enjoyed a fair hearing, been duly tried out with the latest crop of sixth-formers and undergraduates. Each in turn has yielded place, not only (unremarkably) to its successor, but also to that excellent predecessor of 1905, for — alone in the long list of such studies — *Growth and Structure of the English Language* has retained its appeal. I have been challenged in this Foreword to explain why.

Let me begin by considering two possible reasons that must, I think, be rejected. First, it has not maintained its value by constant revision and updating. True, in the nine editions during the author's lifetime, Jespersen carried out some useful adjustments. In the Preface to the fourth edition of 1923, he summarises the changes made since 1905 — and they chiefly involve the chapter on Grammar (then chapter 8), in which he had for example reflected his own profound monograph on negation (1917) by adding a magnificently succinct additional page. In the Preface to the ninth edition (written in retirement at Elsinore), this prince of philologists confesses to further modest expansion, reorganisation and revision. For example, statistics on the current use of English in the world, updated to 1912 in intermediate editions, subsequently to 1926, now in 1938 reflected the figures given by Mencken two years earlier.

But for the most part, the book remained word for word as originally published: Jespersen knew when to leave well alone.

The second reason we must reject is that the work retains its appeal and its authority because it was far ahead of its time and therefore continued to seem satisfyingly 'modern'. True (again), Jespersen's work derives some of its permanence from the fact that he had thought more profoundly about general linguistic theory than most of those who have written popular histories of English. But the tenor of his outlook is far more Victorian than the cautious scepticism of post-behaviourism which colours (or rather un-colours) the scientific writing on language in this latter part of the twentieth century. Far more than any Whorfian, Jespersen believed in the reciprocal influence of language and the personality of its speakers. Thus, in §19:

The English language is a methodical, energetic, business-like and sober language . . . . As the language is, so also is the nation,

For words, like Nature, half reveal
And half conceal the Soul within. (Tennyson)

He had the nineteenth-century romantic love of those manly and forthright characteristics that were thought to typify the Germanic peoples. English monosyllables and blunt consonant clusters seemed to him emblematic. So too English was, importantly, a Germanic language for all its French and Latin superstructure: Jespersen chose to emphasise, if not somewhat to exaggerate, the medieval influence of Scandinavia:

> An Englishman cannot *thrive* or be *ill* or *die* without Scandinavian words; they are to the language what *bread* and *eggs* are to the daily fare (§78).

Above all, he had the optimistic Victorian's deep faith in progress, and saw the history of English as a steadily progressive 'gain in clearness and simplicity' (§188). What survived was the fittest and the most efficiently fitting. Appropriately enough, Darwin is one of the authors combed for significant observations (cf§172), for in this as in everything else, Jespersen was not representing casual or fashionable views, but views profoundly his own, acquired through intellectual investigation. Already in 1894 he had published a monograph entitled *Progress in Language*, replacing the 18th-century view of language change as a story of decay: rather, English like Chinese evinced 'a progressive tendency towards a more perfect structure' (quoted from a lecture to the British Academy in November 1928).

Of course, in stating the reasons that must be rejected, we see glimpses of the positive contrary. Jespersen's continuing appeal lies in the sheer scholarly quality of the man: our awareness in reading him that we are engaged with a supremely learned and cultivated mind. He is indeed the most distinguished scholar of the English language who has ever lived, in my view: no small claim when we reflect on the distinguished scholarship that has for centuries been devoted to our language. .A further and related reason is this. While being a deeply serious theoretical linguist to whom such daunting labels as phonetician and grammarian pre-eminently apply, Jespersen was above all a *philologist* in the older senses of this word, a lover of language and of the arts that are realised in language.

Among his papers, there is the farewell lecture given in 1925 when he retired from his Copenhagen chair at the age of 65 — protesting himself 'an old fogey', though English studies were fortunate that so youthfully creative a 'fogey' was to go on writing for almost a further two decades. In this splendid apologia, he explained that for him 'linguistic investigation' involved primarily 'understanding the texts . . . to penetrate into the innermost thoughts of the best men and women'. 'Speech is the noblest instrument to bind man to man, and . . . it is by speech as by literature, or best by both combined, that one comes to understand the people from whom they emanated.' First and foremost, of course, a student of *language*, he insisted on studying language *at its best*, and in that way he hoped, he says, 'to have imparted to my hearers some of my own enthusiasm for the great poets. My greatest enjoyment, and no doubt that of my hearers as well, has been in my Chaucer classes, partly because Chaucer has such a wonderful power of describing human beings.' So far from confining himself to expounding linguistic history for its own sake, he sees his work as 'combating the ghastly malady of our time, nationalism', 'the essential mark' of which 'is antipathy, disdain, finally hatred'. 'Especially now since the World-war this is a task of the very greatest importance, since it is necessary that the wounds of this gruesome time should be healed.' Thus he spoke to his students in 1925. Sadly, this noble friend of mankind was to see a still more gruesome manifestation of nationalism and to die in 1943 when his country had already suffered for some years the horrors of the Nazi occupation, when there was little opportunity 'to diffuse knowledge and love of what is best in other peoples' (from *Linguistica*, selected papers published in 1933).

His loving enthusiasm for literature and for people was

spelling of the First Folio (1623). The only point where, for the convenience of modern readers, I regulate the old usage, is with regard to capital letters and *u*, *v*, *i*, *j*, printing, for instance, *us* and *love* instead of *vs* and *loue*. To avoid misunderstandings, I must here expressly state that by Old English (OE.) I always understand the language before 1150, still often termed Anglo-Saxon.

As for the philosophy of speech underlying this book I may refer the reader to three recent books, "Language, its Nature, Development and Origin" (London, G. Allen & Unwin, 1922; German translation, "Die Sprache, ihre Natur, Entwickelung und Entstehung", Heidelberg, C. Winter, 1925), "The Philosophy of Grammar" (London, G. Allen & Unwin, 1924), and "Mankind, Nation and Individual" (Oslo, H. Aschehoug & Co., 1925). I have dealt with English grammar in the four volumes of "Modern English Grammar" (MEG., Heidelberg) and in the shorter "Essentials of English Grammar" (London).

The ninth edition has been carefully revised and brought up to date. The changes concern chiefly chapters VII (which has been made into two, VII and VIII) and VIII (which is now IX).

For some valuable suggestions I am much obliged to Professor R. Hittmair, of Vienna.

O. J.

Lundehave, Helsingør (Elsinore)
July 1938

Preface

The scope and plan of this volume have been set forth in the introductory paragraph. I have endeavoured to write at once popularly and so as to be of some profit to the expert philologist. In some cases I have advanced new views without having space enough to give all my reasons for deviating from commonly accepted theories, but I hope to find an opportunity in future works of a more learned character to argue out the most debatable points.

I owe more than I can say to numerous predecessors in the fields of my investigations, most of all to the authors of the *New English Dictionary*. The dates given for the first and last appearance of a word are nearly always taken from that splendid monument of English scholarship, and it is hardly necessary to warn the reader not to take these dates too literally. When I say, for instance, that *fenester* was in use from 1290 to 1548, I do not mean to say that the word was actually heard for the first and for the last time in those two years, but only that no earlier or later quotations have been discovered by the painstaking authors of that dictionary.

I have departed from a common practice in retaining the spelling of all authors quoted. I see no reason why in so many English editions of Shakespeare the spelling is modernized while in quotations from other Elizabethan authors the old spelling is followed. Quotations from Shakespeare are here regularly given in the so clearly bound up with his enthusiasm for language as to form a complex irradiating everything he wrote, not least the *Growth and Structure*. And he effortlessly communicates this nexus of enthusiasm to generation after generation of readers.

Time was when the curriculum for every student of English included the History of the Language. This wise provision may come back again. If it does, it will in no small way be due to the intellectual and aesthetic excitement which Jespersen gave to historical linguistic study and which is so limpidly demonstrated in this little masterpiece.

RANDOLPH QUIRK

University College London

Chapter I

Preliminary Sketch

1. It will be my endeavour in this volume to characterize the chief peculiarities of the English language, and to explain the growth and significance of those features in its structure which have been of permanent importance. The older stages of the language, interesting as their study is, will be considered only in so far as they throw light either directly or by way of contrast on the main characteristics of present-day English, and an attempt will be made to connect the teachings of linguistic history with the chief events in the general history of the English people so as to show their mutual bearings on each other, and the relation of language to national character. The knowledge that the latter conception is a very difficult one to deal with scientifically, as it may easily tempt one into hasty generalizations, should make us wary, but not deter us from grappling with problems which are really both interesting and important. My plan will be, first to give a rapid sketch of the language of our own days, so as to show how it strikes a foreigner—a foreigner who has devoted much time to the study of English, but who feels that in spite of all his efforts he is only able to look at it as a foreigner does, and not exactly as a native would—and then in the following chapters to enter more deeply into the history of the language in order to describe its first shape, to trace the various foreign influences it has undergone, and to give an account of its own inner growth.

2. It is, of course, impossible to characterize a language in one formula ; languages, like men, are too composite to have their whole essence summed up in one short expression.   Nevertheless, there is one expression that continually comes to my mind whenever I think of the English language and compare it with others : it seems to me positively and expressly *masculine*, it is the language of a grown-up man and has very little childish or feminine about it. A great many things go together to produce and to confirm that impression, things phonetical, grammatical, and lexical, words and turns that are found, and words and turns that are not found, in the language. In dealing with the English language one is often reminded of the characteristic English handwriting ; just as an English lady will nearly always write in a manner that in any other country would only be found in a man's hand, in the same manner the language is more manly than any other language I know.

3. First I shall mention the sound system. The English consonants are well defined ; voiced and voiceless consonants stand over against each other in neat symmetry, and they are, as a rule, clearly and precisely pronounced. You have none of those indistinct or half-slurred consonants that abound in Danish, for instance (such as those in ha*d*e, ha*g*e, liv*l*ig), where you hardly know whether it is a consonant or a vowel-glide that meets the ear. The only thing that might be compared to this in English is the *r* when not followed by a vowel, but then this has really given up definitely all pretensions to the rank of a consonant, and is (in the pronunciation of the South of England) either frankly a vowel (as in *here*) or else nothing at all (in *hart*, etc.). Each English consonant belongs distinctly to its own type, a *t* is a *t*, and a *k* is a *k*, and there an end. There is much less modification of a consonant by the surrounding vowels than in some other languages, thus none of that palatalization of consonants which gives an insinuating grace to such languages as

Russian. The vowel sounds, too, are comparatively independent of their surroundings, and in this respect the language now has deviated widely from the character of Old English and has become more clear-cut and distinct in its phonetic structure, although, to be sure, the diphthongization of most long vowels (in *ale, whole, eel, who,* phonetically eil, houl, ijl, huw) counteracts in some degree this impression of neatness and evenness.

4. Besides these characteristics, the full nature of which cannot, perhaps, be made intelligible to any but those familiar with phonetic research, but which are still felt more or less instinctively by everybody hearing the language spoken, there are other traits whose importance can with greater ease be made evident to anybody possessed of a normal ear.

5. To bring out clearly one of these points I select at random, by way of contrast, a passage from the language of Hawaii : 'I kona hiki ana aku ilaila ua hookipa ia mai la oia me ke aloha pumehana loa.' Thus it goes on, no single word ends in a consonant, and a group of two or more consonants is never found. Can any one be in doubt that even if such a language sound pleasantly and be full of music and harmony the total impression is childlike and effeminate? You do not expect much vigour or energy in a people speaking such a language ; it seems adapted only to inhabitants of sunny regions where the soil requires scarcely any labour on the part of man to yield him everything he wants, and where life therefore does not bear the stamp of a hard struggle against nature and against fellow-creatures. In a lesser degree we find the same phonetic structure in such languages as Italian and Spanish ; but how different are our Northern tongues. English has no lack of words ending in two or more consonants—I am speaking, of course, of the pronunciation, not of the spelling—*age, hence, wealth, tent, tempt, tempts, months, helped, feasts,* etc., etc., and thus requires, as well as presupposes, no little energy on the part of the speakers. That many suchlike consonant groups do not tend to render the language beautiful, one is bound readily to concede ; however, it cannot be pretended that their number in English is great enough to make the language harsh or rough. While the fifteenth century greatly increased the number of consonant groups by making the *e* mute in *monthes*, *helped*, etc., the following centuries, on the contrary, lightened such groups as *-ght* in *night, thought* (where the 'back-open' consonant as German *ch* is still spoken in Scotch) and the initial *kn-, gn-* in *know, gnaw*, etc. Note also the disappearance of *l* in *alms, folk*, etc., and of *r* in *hard, court*, etc.; the final consonant groups have also been simplified in *comb* and the other words in *-mb* (whereas *b* has been retained in *timber*) and in the exactly parallel group *-ng*, for instance in *strong*, where now only one consonant is heard after the vowel, a consonant partaking of the nature of *n* and of *g*, but identical with neither of them ; formerly it was followed by a real *g*, which has been retained in *stronger*.

6. In the first ten stanzas of Tennyson's *Locksley Hall*, three hundred syllables, we have only thirty-three words ending in two consonants, and two ending in three, certainly no excessive number, especially if we take into account the nature of the groups, which are nearly all of the easiest kind (-dz : comrades, Pleiads ; -mz : gleams, comes ; -nz : robin's, man's, turns ; -ns : distance, science ; -ks : overlooks ; -ts : gets, thoughts ; -kts : tracts, cataracts ; -zd : reposed, closed ; -st : rest, West, breast, crest ; -ʃt : burnish'd ; -nd : sound, around, moorland, behind, land ; -nt : want, casement, went, present ; -ld : old, world ; -lt : result ; -lf, himself; -pt : dipt). Thus we may perhaps characterize English, phonetically speaking, as possessing male energy, but not brutal force. The accentual system points in the same direction, as will be seen below (26–28).

7. The Italians have a pointed proverb : 'Le parole son femmine e i fatti son maschi.' If briefness, concise-ness and terseness are characteristic of the style of

men, while women as a rule are not such economizers of speech, English is more masculine than most languages. We see this in a great many ways. In grammar it has got rid of a great many superfluities found in earlier English as well as in most cognate languages, reducing endings, etc., to the shortest forms possible and often doing away with endings altogether. Where German has, for instance, *alle diejenigen wilden tiere, die dort leben,* so that the plural idea is expressed in each word separately (apart, of course, from the adverb), English has *all the wild animals that live there,* where *all,* the article, the adjective, and the relative pronoun are alike incapable of receiving any mark of the plural number ; the sense is expressed with the greatest clearness imaginable, and all the unstressed endings *-e* and *-en,* which make most German sentences so drawling, are avoided.

8. Rimes based on correspondence in the last syllable only of each line (as bet, set ; laid, shade) are termed male rimes, as opposed to feminine rimes, where each line has two corresponding syllables, one strong and one weak (as better, setter ; lady, shady). It is true that these names, which originated in France, were not at first meant to express any parallelism with the characteristics of the two sexes, but arose merely from the grammatical fact that the weak *-e* was the ending of the feminine gender (grande, etc.). But the designations are not entirely devoid of symbolic significance ; there is really more of abrupt force in a word that ends with a strongly stressed syllable, than in a word where the maximum of force is followed by a weak ending. 'Thanks' is harsher and less polite than the two-syllabled 'thank you'. English has undoubtedly gained in force what it has possibly lost in elegance, by reducing so many words of two syllables to monosyllables. If it had not been for the great number of long foreign, especially Latin, words, English would have approached the

state of such monosyllabic languages as Chinese. Now one of the best Chinese scholars, G. v. d. Gabelentz, somewhere remarks that an idea of the condensed power of the monosyllabism found in old Chinese may be gathered from Luther's advice to a preacher, 'Geh rasch 'nauf, tu's Maul auf, hör bald auf'. He might with equal justice have reminded us of many English sentences. 'First come, first served' is much more vigorous than the French 'premier venu, premier moulu' or 'le premier venu engrène', the German 'Wer zuerst kommt, mahlt zuerst' and especially than the Danish 'den der kommer først til mølle, får først malet'. Compare also 'no cure, no pay', 'haste makes waste, and waste makes want', 'live and learn', 'Love no man : trust no man : speak ill of no man to his face ; nor well of any man behind his back' (Ben Jonson), 'to meet, to know, to love, and then to part' (Coleridge), 'Then none were for the party ; Then all were for the state ; Then the great man help'd the poor, And the poor man loved the great' (Macaulay).

9. It will be noticed, however—and the quotations just given serve to exemplify this, too—that it is not every collocation of words of one syllable that produces an effect of strength, for a great many of the short words most frequently employed are not stressed at all and therefore impress the ear in nearly the same way as prefixes and suffixes do. There is nothing particularly vigorous in the following passage from a modern novel : 'It was as if one had met part of one's self one had lost for a long time,' and in fact most people hearing it read aloud would fail to notice that it consisted of nothing but one-syllable words. Such sentences are not at all rare in colloquial prose, and even in poetry they are found oftener than in most languages, for instance :

> And there a while it bode ; and if a man
> Could touch or see it, he was heal'd at once,
> By faith, of all his ills.
> > Tennyson, *The Holy Grail*

But then, the weakness resulting from many small connecting words is to some extent compensated in English by the absence of the definite article in a good many cases where other languages think it indispensable, e.g. 'Merry Old England'; 'Heaven and Earth'; 'life is short'; 'dinner is ready'; 'school is over'; 'I saw him at church', and this peculiarity delivers the language from a number of those short 'empty words' which when accumulated cannot fail to make the style somewhat weak and prolix.

10. Business-like shortness is also seen in such convenient abbreviations of sentences as abound in English, for instance, 'While fighting in Germany he was taken prisoner' (= while he was fighting). 'He would not answer when spoken to.' 'To be left till called for.' 'Once at home, he forgot his fears.' 'We had no idea what to do.' 'Did they run? Yes, I made them' (= made them run). 'Shall you play tennis to-day? Yes, we are going to. I should like to, but I can't.' 'Dinner over, he left the house.' Such expressions remind one of the abbreviations used in telegrams; they are syntactical correspondencies to the morphological shortenings that are also of such frequent occurrence in English : *cab* for *cabriolet, bus* for *omnibus, photo* for *photograph, phone* for *telephone,* and innumerable others.

11. This cannot be separated from a certain sobriety in expression. As an Englishman does not like to use more words or more syllables than are strictly necessary, so he does not like to say more than he can stand to. He dislikes strong or hyperbolical expressions of approval or admiration ; 'that isn't half bad' or 'she is rather good-looking' are often the highest praises you can draw out of him, and they not seldom express the same warmth of feeling that makes a Frenchman ejaculate his 'charmant' or 'ravissante' or 'adorable'. German *kolossal* or *fabelhaft* can often be correctly rendered by English *great* or *biggish,* and where a Frenchman uses his adverbs *extrêmement* or *infiniment,*

an Englishman says only *very* or *rather* or *pretty*.
'Quelle horreur !' is 'That's rather a nuisance'. 'Je
suis ravi de vous voir' is 'Glad to see you', etc. An
Englishman does not like to commit himself by being
too enthusiastic or too distressed, and his language
accordingly grows sober, too sober perhaps, and even
barren when the object is to express emotions. There
is in this trait a curious mixture of something praise-
worthy, the desire to be strictly true without exagger-
ating anything or promising more than you can
perform, and on the other hand of something blame-
worthy, the idea that it is affected, or childish and
effeminate, to give vent to one's feelings, and the
fear of appearing ridiculous by showing strong emotions. But this trait is certainly found more frequently
in men than in women, so I may be allowed to add
this feature of the English language to the signs of
masculinity I have collected.

12. Those who use many strong words to express
their likes or dislikes will generally also make an
extensive use of another linguistic appliance, namely,
violent changes in intonation. Their voices will now
suddenly rise to a very high pitch and then as suddenly
fall to low tones. An excessive use of this emotional
tonic accent is characteristic of many savage nations ;
in Europe it is found much more in Italy than in the
North. In each nation it seems as if it were more
employed by women than by men. Now, it has often
been observed that the English speak in a more mono-
tonous way than most other nations, so that an extremely slight rising or lowering of the tone indicates
what in other languages would require a much greater
interval. 'Les Anglais parlent extrêmement bas', says
H. Taine (*Notes sur l'Angleterre*, p. 66). 'Une société
italienne, dans laquelle je me suis fourvoyé par
hasard, m'a positivement étourdi ; je m'étais habitué
à ce ton modéré des voix anglaises.' Even English
ladies are in this respect more restrained than many
men belonging to other nations :

She had the low voice of your English dames,
Unused, it seems, to need rise half a note
To catch attention.

Elizabeth Browning, *Aurora Leigh*, p. 99[1]

13. If we turn to other provinces of the language we shall find our impression strengthened and deepened.

It is worth observing, for instance, how few diminutives the language has and how sparingly it uses them. English in this respect forms a strong contrast to Italian with its *-ino* (ragazzino, fratellino, originally a double diminutive), *-ina* (donnina), *-etto* (giovinetto), *-etta* (oretta), *-ello*, *-ella* (asinello, storiella) and other endings, German with its *-chen* and *-lein*, especially South German with its *-le*, *-el*, *-erl*, Dutch with its *-je*, Russian, Magyar, and Basque, with their various endings. Too frequent a recurrence of these endings without any apparent necessity tends to produce the impression that the speakers are innocent, childish, genial beings, with no great business capacities or seriousness in life. But in English there are very few of these fondling-endings ; *-let* is in the first place a comparatively modern ending, very few of the words in which it is used go back more than a hundred years ; and then its extensive use in modern times is chiefly due to the naturalists who want it to express in a short and precise manner certain small organs (*budlet*, Darwin ; *bladelet*, Todd ; *conelet*, Dana ; *bulblet*, Gray ; *leaflet*, *fruitlet*, *featherlet*, etc.)—an employment of the diminutive which is as far removed as possible from the terms of endearment found in other languages. The endings *-kin* and *-ling* (princekin, princeling) are not very frequently used and generally express contempt or derision. Then, of course, there is *-y*, *-ie* (Billy, Dicky, auntie, birdie, etc.), which corresponds exactly to the fondling-suffixes of other languages ; but its application in English is restricted to the nursery and it is hardly ever used by grown-up people except in speaking to

---

[1] Cf. my *Lehrbuch der Phonetik*, 15, 34.

children. Besides, this ending is more Scotch than English.

14. The business-like, virile qualities of the English language also manifest themselves in such things as word-order. Words in English do not play at hide-and-seek, as they often do in Latin, for instance, or in German, where ideas that by right belong together are widely sundered in obedience to caprice, or more often to a rigorous grammatical rule. In English an auxiliary verb does not stand far from its main verb, and a negative will be found in the immediate neighbourhood of the word it negatives, generally the verb (auxiliary). An adjective nearly always stands before its noun ; the only really important exception is when there are qualifications added to it which draw it after the noun so that the whole complex serves the purpose of a relative clause : 'a man every way prosperous and talented' (Tennyson), 'an interruption too brief and isolated to attract more notice' (Stevenson). And the same regularity is found in modern English word-order in other respects as well. A few years ago I made my pupils calculate statistically various points in regard to word-order in different languages. I give here only the percentage in some modern authors of sentences in which the subject preceded the verb, and the latter in its turn preceded its object (as in 'I saw him' as against 'Him I saw, but not her' or 'Whom did you see?') :

> Shelley, prose 89, poetry 85.
> Byron, prose 93, poetry 81.
> Macaulay, prose 82.
> Carlyle, prose 87.
> Tennyson, poetry 88.
> Dickens, prose 91.
> Swinburne, poetry 83.
> Pinero, prose 97.

For the sake of comparison I mention that one Danish prose-writer (J. P. Jacobsen) had 82, a Danish poet (Drachmann) 61, Goethe (poetry) 30, a modern German prose-writer (Tovote) 31, Anatole France 66,

Gabriele d'Annunzio 49 per cent of the same word-order. That English has not always had the same regularity is shown by the figure for Beowulf being 16, and for King Alfred's prose 40. Even if I concede that our statistics did not embrace a sufficient number of extracts to give fully reliable results,[1] still it is indisputable that English shows more regularity and less caprice in this respect than most or probably all cognate languages, without however, attaining the rigidity found in Chinese, where the percentage in question would be 100 (or very near it). English has not deprived itself of the expedient of inverting the ordinary order of the members of a sentence when emphasis requires it, but it makes a more sparing use of it than German and the Scandinavian languages, and in most cases it will be found that these languages emphasize without any real necessity, especially in a great many every-day phrases : 'dær har jeg ikke været', 'dort bin ich nicht gewesen', 'I haven't been there' ; 'det kan jeg ikke', 'das kann ich nicht', 'I can't do that'. In the usual phrase, 'det veed jeg ikke', 'das weiß ich nicht', *det* or *das* is often superfluously stressed, where the Englishman does not even find it necessary to state the object at all : 'I don't know.' Note also that in English the subject precedes the verb after most introductory adverbs : 'now he comes' ; 'there she goes', while German and Danish have, and English had till a few centuries ago, the inverted order : 'jetzt kommt er', 'da geht sie' ; 'nu kommer han', 'dær går hun' ; 'now comes he', 'there goes she'. Thus order and consistency signalize the modern stage of the English language.

15. No language is logical in every respect, and we must not expect usage to be guided always by strictly logical principles. It was a frequent error with the older grammarians that whenever the actual grammar of a language did not seem conformable to the rules

---

[1] Supplemental statistics are given by Curtis, Anglia Beiblatt, 1908, p. 137.

of abstract logic they blamed the language and wanted to correct it. Without falling into that error we may, nevertheless, compare different languages and judge them by the standard of logic, and here again I think that, apart from Chinese, which has been described as pure applied logic, there is perhaps no language in the civilized world that stands so high as English. Look at the use of the tenses ; the difference between the past *he saw* and the composite perfect *he has seen* is maintained with great consistency as compared with the similarly formed tenses in Danish, not to speak of German, so that one of the most constant faults committed by English-speaking Germans is the wrong use of these forms ('Were you in Berlin?' for 'Have you been in (or to) Berlin?' 'In 1815 Napoleon has been defeated at Waterloo' for 'was defeated'). And then the comparatively recent development of the expanded (or 'progressive') tenses has furnished the language with the wonderfully precise and logically valuable distinction between 'I write' and 'I am writing', 'I wrote' and 'I was writing'. French has something similar in the distinction between *le passé défini* (*j'écrivis*) and *l'imparfait* (*j'écrivais*), but on the one hand the former tends to disappear, or rather has already disappeared in the spoken language, at any rate in Paris and in the northern part of the country, so that *j'ai écrit* takes its place and the distinction between 'I wrote' and 'I have written' is abandoned ; on the other hand the distinction applies only to the past while in English it is carried through all tenses. Furthermore, the distinction as made in English is superior to the similar one found in the Slavic languages, in that it is made uniformly in all verbs and in all tenses by means of the same device (*am -ing*), while the Slavic languages employ a much more complicated system of prepositions and derivative endings, which has almost to be learned separately for each new verb or group of verbs.

16. In praising the logic of the English language we must not lose sight of the fact that in most cases where, so to speak, the logic of facts or of the exterior world is at war with the logic of grammar, English is free from the narrow-minded pedantry which in most languages sacrifices the former to the latter or makes people shy of saying or writing things which are not 'strictly grammatical'. This is particularly clear with regard to number. *Family* and *clergy* are, grammatically speaking, of the singular number ; but in reality they indicate a plurality. Most languages can treat such words only as singulars, but in English one is free to add a verb in the singular if the idea of unity is essential, and then to refer to this unit as *it*, or else to put the verb in the plural and use the pronoun *they*, if the idea of plurality is predominant. It is clear that this liberty of choice is often greatly advantageous. Thus we find sentences like these : 'As the clergy are or are not what they ought to be, so are the rest of the nation' (Jane Austen), or 'the whole race of man (sing.) proclaim it lawful to drink wine' (De Quincey), or 'the club all know that he is a disappointed man' (the same). In 'there are no end of people here that I don't know' (George Eliot) *no end* takes the verb in the plural because it is equivalent to 'many', and when Shelley writes in one of his letters, 'the Quarterly are going to review me', he is thinking of the Quarterly (Review) as a whole staff of writers. Inversely, there is in English a freedom paralleled nowhere else of expressing grammatically a unity consisting of several parts, of saying, for instance, 'I do not think I ever spent a more delightful three weeks' (Darwin), 'for a quiet twenty minutes', 'another United States', cf. also 'a fortnight' (originally a fourteen-night) ; 'three years is but short' (Shakespeare), 'sixpence was offered him' (Darwin), 'ten minutes is heaps of time' (E. F. Benson), etc., etc.

17. A great many other phenomena in English show the same freedom from pedantry, as when

passive constructions such as 'he was taken no notice
of' are allowed, or when adverbs or prepositional com-
plexes may be used attributively as in 'his then resi-
dence', 'an almost reconciliation' (Thackeray), 'men
invite their out-College friends' (Steadman), 'smoking
his before-breakfast pipe' (Conan Doyle), 'in his
threadbare, out-at-elbow shooting-jacket' (G. du
Maurier), or when even whole phrases or sentences
may be turned into a kind of adjective, as in 'with a
quite at home kind of air' (Smedley), 'in the pretty
diamond-cut-diamond scene between Pallas and
Ulysses' (Ruskin), 'a little man with a puffy Say-
nothing-to-me-or-I'll-contradict-you sort of coun-
tenance' (Dickens), 'with an I-turn-the-crank-of-the
Universe air' (Lowell), 'Rose is simply self-willed ; a
"she will" or "she won't" sort of little person' (Meredith).   Although such combinations as the last-
mentioned are only found in more or less jocular style,
they show the possibilities of the language, and some
expressions of a similar order belong permanently to
the language, for instance, 'a would-be artist', 'a stay-
at-home man', 'a turn-up collar'. Such things—and
they might be easily multiplied—are inconceivable in
such a language as French, where everything is con-
demned that does not conform to a definite set of
rules laid down by grammarians. The French language is like the stiff French garden of Louis XIV,
while the English is like an English park, which is laid
out seemingly without any definite plan, and in which
you are allowed to walk everywhere according to
your own fancy without having to fear a stern keeper
enforcing rigorous regulations. The English language
would not have been what it is if the English had not
been for centuries great respecters of the liberties of
each individual and if everybody had not been free
to strike out new paths for himself.

18. This is seen, too, in the vocabulary. In spite of
the efforts of several authors of high standing, the
English have never suffered an Academy to be in-

stituted among them like the French or Italian
Academies, which had as one of their chief tasks the
regulation of the vocabulary so that every word not
found in their Dictionaries was blamed as unworthy of
literary use or distinction. In England every writer is.
and has always been, free to take his words where he
chooses, whether from the ordinary stock of everyday words, from native dialects, from old authors,
or from other languages, dead or living. The consequence has been that English dictionaries comprise a
larger number of words than those of any other nation,
and that they present a variegated picture of terms
from the four quarters of the globe. Now, it seems
to be characteristic of the two sexes in their relation
to language that women move in narrower circles
of the vocabulary, in which they attain to perfect
mastery so that the flow of words is always natural
and, above all, never needs to stop, while men know
more words and always want to be more precise in
choosing the exact word with which to render their
idea, the consequence being often less fluency and
more hesitation. It has been statistically shown that
a comparatively greater number of stammerers and
stutterers are found among men (boys) than among
women (girls). Teachers of foreign languages have
many occasions to admire the ease with which female
students express themselves in another language
after so short a time of study that most men would
be able to say only few words hesitatingly and falter-
ingly, but if they are put to the test of translating
a difficult piece either from or into the foreign language, the men will generally prove superior to the
women. With regard to their native language the
same difference is found, though it is perhaps not so
easy to observe. At any rate our assertion is corrobor-
ated by the fact observed by every student of languages that novels written by ladies are much easier
to read and contain much fewer difficult words than
those written by men. All this seems to justify us in

setting down the enormous richness of the English vocabulary to the same masculinity of the English nation which we have now encountered in so many various fields.

19. To sum up : The English language is a methodical, energetic, business-like and sober language, that does not care much for finery and elegance, but does care for logical consistency and is opposed to any attempt to narrow-in life by police regulations and strict rules either of grammar or of lexicon. As the language is, so also is the nation,

> For words, like Nature, half reveal
> And half conceal the Soul within.
> Tennyson

naïve idolisation

Chapter II

The Beginnings

20. The existence of the English language as a separate idiom began when Germanic tribes had occupied all the lowlands of Great Britain and when accordingly the invasions from the continent were discontinued, so that the settlers in their new homes were cut off from that steady intercourse with their continental relations which always is an imperative condition of linguistic unity. The historical records of English do not go so far back as this, for the oldest written texts in the English language (in 'Anglo-Saxon') date from about 700 and are thus removed by about three centuries from the beginnings of the language. And yet comparative philology is able to tell us something about the manner in which the ancestors of these settlers spoke centuries before that period, and to sketch the prehistoric development of what was to become the language of King Alfred, of Chaucer, and of Shakespeare.

21. The dialects spoken by the settlers in England belonged to the great Germanic[1] (or Teutonic) branch of the most important of all linguistic families, termed by many philologists the Indo-European (or Indo-Germanic) and by others, and to my mind more appro-

---

[1] I retain the usual term *Germanic* for the whole branch of languages, though it is not very felicitous as it is liable to be mistaken for German by English-speaking people or to produce the impression that German is more important than, or even the source of, the other languages—a mistake which will not so easily happen on the continent, where other words are used for German (*deutsch, duitsch, tysk, tedesco, allemand, niemiecki*, etc.). Personally I prefer the term *Gothonic* and have used it in my book *Language* ; cf. especially G. Schütte's great work *Our Forefathers* (Cambridge, I, 1929; II, 1933).

priately, Aryan (Arian).[1] The Aryan family comprises
a great variety of languages, including, besides some
languages of less importance, Sanskrit with Prakrit
and many living languages of India ; Iranian with
modern Persian ; Greek ; Latin, with the modern
Romanic languages (Italian, Spanish, French, etc.);
Keltic, two divisions of which still survive, one in
Welsh and Armorican or Breton, the other in the
closely connected Irish and Scotch-Gaelic, besides the
now probably extinct Manx ; Baltic (Lithuanian and
Lettic) and Slavonic (Russian, Czech, Polish, etc.).
Among the extinct Germanic languages Wulfila's
Gothic was the most important ; the living are High
German, Dutch, Low German, Frisian, English,
Danish, Swedish, Norwegian, and Icelandic. The first
five are often grouped together as West-Germanic, but
Frisian and English seem more naturally to be con-
sidered a separate group intermediate between the
first three and the Scandinavian languages.

22. The Aryan language, which was in course of
time differentiated into all these languages, or as the
same fact is generally expressed in a metaphor of
dubious value, was the parent-language from which all
these languages have descended, must by no means be
imagined as a language characterized by a simple and
regular structure. On the contrary it must have been,
grammatically and lexically, extremely complicated
and full of irregularities. Its grammar was highly inflexional, the relations between the ideas being
expressed by means of endings more intimately fused
with the chief element of the word than is the case in
such agglutinative languages as Hungarian (Magyar).
Nouns and verbs were kept distinct, and where the
same sense-modifications were expressed in both, such
as plurality, it was by means of totally different endings. In fact, the indication of number—the three-
fold division into singular, dual, and plural—was

---

[1] Aryan is here taken in its purely linguistic sense and has nothing
to do with 'race'.

inseparable from the case-endings in the nouns and
from the person-endings as well as signs of mood and
tense in the verbs : one cannot point to distinct parts
of such a Latin form as *est* (*cantat*) or *sunt* (*cantant*)
or *fuissem* (*cantavissem*) and say this element means
singular (or plural), this one means indicative (or subjunctive) and that one indicates what tense the whole
form belongs to. There were eight cases, but they did
not, for the greater part, indicate such clear, concrete outward relations as the Finnic (local) cases do ;
the consequence was a comparatively great number of
clashings and overlappings, in form as well as in
function. Each noun belonged to one of three genders,
masculine, feminine, and neuter ; but this division by
no means corresponded with logical consistency to the
natural division into (1) living beings of one sex, (2)
living beings of the other sex, and (3) everything else.
Nor did the moods and tenses of the verb agree very
closely with any definite logical categories, the idea
of time, for instance, being mixed up with that of
'tense-aspect'. (in German 'Aktionsart'), i.e. distinctions according as an action was viewed as momentary
or protracted or iterated, etc. In the nominal as well
as in the verbal inflexions the endings varied with the
character of the stem they were added to, and very
often the accent was shifted from one syllable to
another according to seemingly arbitrary rules, just
as in modern Russian. In a great many cases, too, one
form was taken from one word and another from a
totally different one, a phenomenon (called by Osthoff
'Suppletivwesen') which we have in a few instances
in modern English (*good, better* ; *go, went*, etc.). An
idea of the phonetic system of the old Aryan language
may best be gathered from Greek, which has preserved
the old system with great fidelity on the whole,
especially the vowels. But of course, no one of the
historically transmitted languages, not even one of
the oldest, can give more than an approximate idea
of the common Aryan language distant from us

by so many thousand years, and scholars have now
learnt more prudence than was shown when Schleicher
was bold enough to print a fable in what he believed
to be a fairly accurate representation of primitive
Aryan.

23. In historical times we find Aryan split up into a
variety of languages, each with its own peculiarities
in sounds, in grammar, and in vocabulary. So different were these languages that the Greeks had no idea
of any similarity or relationship between their own
tongue and that of their Persian enemies; nor did the
Romans suspect that the Gauls and Germans they
fought spoke languages of the same stock as their own.
Whenever the Germanic languages are alluded to, it
is always in expressions like these, 'a Roman tongue
can hardly pronounce such names' or (after giving the
names of some Germanic tribes) 'the names sound
like a noisy war-trumpet, and the ferocity of these
barbarians adds horror even to the words themselves'.
Julian the Apostate compares the singing of Germanic
popular ballads to the croaking and shrill screeching
of birds.[1] Much of this, of course, must be put down
to the ordinary Greek and Roman contempt for
foreigners generally ; nor can it be wondered at that
they did not recognize in these languages congeners
of their own, for the similarities had been considerably
blurred by a great many important changes in sound
and in structure, so that it is only the patient research
of the nineteenth century that has enabled us to iden-
tify words in separate languages which are now so
dissimilar as not to strike the casual observer as in
any way related. What contributed, perhaps, more
than anything else to make Germanic words look
strange were two great phonetic changes affecting
large parts of the vocabulary, the *consonant-shift*[2] and
the *stress-shift*.

---

[1] Kluge, Paul's *Grundriss*, I, 354.

[2] In English books this change ('die erste Lautverschiebung')
is often, though not quite correctly, called Grimm's law. On

24. The consonant-shift must not be imagined as having taken place at one moment ; on the contrary it must have taken centuries, and modern research has begun to point out the various stages in this development. This is not the proper place to deal with detailed explanations of this important change, as we must hurry on to more modern times ; suffice it then to give a few examples to show how it affected the whole look of the language. Any *p* was changed to *f*—thus we have *father* corresponding to *pater* and similar forms in the cognate languages ; any *t* was made into *th* [þ], as in *three*—compare Latin *tres* ; any *k* became *h*—as *cornu = horn*.[1] And as any *b* or *d* or *g*, any *bh, dh, gh* was similarly shifted, you will understand that there were comparatively few words that were not altered past recognition ; still such there were, for instance, *mus*, now *mouse*, which contained none of the consonants susceptible of the shifting in question.

25. The second change affected the general character of the language even more thoroughly. Where previously the stress was sometimes on the first syllable of the word, sometimes on the second, or on the third, etc., without any seeming reason and without any regard to the intrinsic importance of that syllable, a complete revolution simplified matters so that the stress rules may be stated in a couple of lines : nearly all words were stressed on the first syllable ; the chief exceptions occurred only where the word was a verb beginning with one out of a definite number of prefixes, such as those we have in modern English *beget, forget, overthrow, abide*, etc. Verner has shown that this shifting of the place of the accent took place later than the Germanic consonant-shift, and we shall now inquire into the relative importance of the two.

Rask's and Grimm's merits in this discovery, see *Language*, p. 43 ff.

[1] Latin words are here chosen for convenience only as representing these old consonants with great fidelity ; but of course it must not be supposed that the English words named come from the Latin. *P, t, k* were not shifted after s.

26. The consonant-shift is important to the modern philologist, in so far as it is to him the clearest and least ambiguous criterion of the Germanic languages : a word with a shifted consonant is Germanic, and a word with an unshifted consonant in any of the Germanic languages must be a loan-word ; whereas the shifted stress is no such certain criterion, chiefly because many words had always had the stress on the first syllable. But if we ask about the intrinsic importance of the two changes, that is, if we try to look at matters from the point of view of the language itself, or rather the speakers, we shall see that the second change is really the more important one. It does not matter much whether a certain number of words begin with *p* or with *f*, but it does matter, or at any rate, it *may* matter, very much, whether the language has a rational system of accentuation or not ; and I have no hesitation in saying that the old stress-shift has left its indelible mark on the structure of the language and has influenced it more than any other phonetic change.[1] The significance of the stress shift will, perhaps, appear most clearly if we compare two sets of words in modern English. Something like the Aryan stress system is found in numerous words taken in recent times from the classical languages, thus *|family, fa|miliar, famili|arity* or *|photograph, pho|tographer, photo|-graphic*.[2] The shifted Germanic system is shown in such groups as *|love, |lover, |loving, |lovingly, |lovely, |loveliness, |loveless, |lovelessness,* or *|king, |kingdom, |kingship, |kingly, |kingless,* etc. As it is characteristic of all Aryan languages that suffixes play a much greater role than prefixes, word formation being generally by endings, it follows that where the Germanic stress system has come into force, the syllable that is most important has also the strongest stress, and that the relatively insignificant modifications of the chief

---

[1] Except perhaps the disappearance of so many weak *e*'s about 1400.

[2] I indicate stress by means of a short vertical stroke ' immediately *before* the beginning of the strong syllable.

idea which are indicated by formative syllables are
also accentually subordinate. This is, accordingly, a
perfectly logical system, corresponding to the principal
rule observed in sentence stress, viz. that the stressed
words are generally the most important ones. As,
moreover, want of stress tends everywhere to obscure
vowel-sounds, languages with movable accent are
exposed to the danger that related words, or different
forms of the same word, are made more different than
they would else have been, and their connexion is
more obscured than is strictly necessary ; compare, for
instance, the two sounds in the first syllable of *family*
[æ][1] and *familiar* [ə], or the different treatment of the
vowels in *photograph, photographer* and *photographic*
[ˈfoutograf, foˈtɔgrəfə, foutoˈgræfik]. The phonetic
clearness inherent in the consistent stress system is
certainly a linguistic advantage, and the obscuration
of the connexion between related words is generally
to be considered a drawback. The language of our
forefathers seems therefore to have gained considerably by replacing the movable stress by a fixed one.

27. The question naturally arises : why was the
accent shifted in this way? Two possible answers
present themselves. The change may have been either
a purely mechanical process, by which the first syllable
was stressed without any regard to signification, or
else it may have been a psychological process, by
which the root syllable became stressed because it
was the most important part of the word. As in the
vast majority of cases the root syllable is the first,
the question must be decided from those cases where
the two things are not identical. Kluge[2] infers from
the treatment of reduplicated forms of the perfect
corresponding to Latin *cecidi, peperci*, etc., that the
shifting was a purely mechanical process ; for it was
not the most important syllable that was stressed in

---

[1] A list of the phonetic symbols used in this book will be found on
the last page.

[2] Paul's *Grundriss*, I, 2, 389.

Gothic *haihait* 'called', *rairoþ* 'reflected', *lailot* 'let' (read *ai* as short *e*), while in the Old English forms of these words *heht, reord, leort* the vowel of the root syllable actually disappears. But it may be objected to this view that the reduplicated syllable was in some measure the bearer of the root signification, as it had enough left of the root to remind the hearer of it, and in pronouncing it the speaker had before him part at least of the significant elements. The first syllable of a reduplicated perfect must to him have been of a far greater importance than one of those prefixes which served only to modify to a small extent the principal idea expressed in the root syllable. The fact that the reduplicated syllable attracted the accent therefore speaks less strongly in favour of the mechanical explanation than does the want of stress on the verbal prefixes in the opposite direction, so that the case seems to me stronger for the psychological theory. In other words, we have here a case of *value-stressing*;[1] that part of the word which is of greatest value to the speaker and which therefore he especially wants the hearer to notice, is pronounced with the strongest stress.

28. We find the same principle of value-stressing everywhere, even in those languages whose traditional stress rests or may rest on other syllables than the root —this word is here used not in the sense of the etymologically original part of the word, but in the sense of what is to the actual instinct of the speaker intrinsically the most significant element—but in these languages it only plays the part of causing a deviation from the traditional stress now and then whereas in Germanic it became *habitual* to stress the root syllable, and this led to other consequences of some interest. In those languages where the stress syllable is not always the most significant one, the difference between stressed and unstressed syllables is generally less than in the Germanic languages ; there is a nicer and

---

[1] See my *Lehrbuch der Phonetik*, ch. 14, 3.

subtler play of accent, which we may observe in
French, perhaps, better than elsewhere. In *nous chan-
tons* the last syllable is stressed, but *chan-* is stronger
than *for-* in Eng. *we forget*, because its psychological
value is greater. Where a contrast is to be expressed
it will most often be associated with one of the tradi-
tionally unstressed syllables, and the result is that the
contrast is brought vividly before the mind with much
less force than is necessary in English ; in *nous chan-
tons, et nous ne dansons pas* you need not even make
chan and *dan* stronger, at any rate not much stronger
than the endings, while in English *we sing, but we don't
dance*, the syllables *sing* and *dance* must be spoken
with an enormous force, because they are in themselves strongly stressed even when no contrast is to be
pointed out. A still better example is French *c'est un
acteur et non pas un auteur* and English *he is an actor,
but not an author* ; the Frenchman produces the intended effect by a slight tap, so to speak, on the two
initial syllables of the contrasted words, while an
Englishman hammers or knocks the corresponding
syllables into the head of the hearer. The French
system is more elegant, more artistic ; the Germanic
system is heavier or more clumsy, perhaps, in such
cases as those just mentioned, but on the whole it
must be said to be more rational, more logical, as an
exact correspondence between the inner and the outer
world is established if the most significant element
receives the strongest phonetic expression. This
Germanic stress-principle has been instrumental in
bringing about important changes in other respects
than those considered here. But what has been said
here seems to me to indicate a certain connexion
between language and national character ; for has it
not always been considered characteristic of the Germanic peoples (English, Scandinavians, Germans) that
they say their say bluntly without much considering
the artistic effect, and that they emphasize what is
essential without always having due regard to nuances

or accessory notions? and does not the stress system we
have been considering present the very same aspect?

29. We do not know in what century the stress was
shifted,[1] but the shifting certainly took place centuries
before the immigration of the English into Great
Britain. To a similar remote period we must refer
several other great changes affecting equally all the
Germanic languages. One of the most important is the
simplification of the tense system in the verb, no
Germanic language having more than two tenses, a
present and a past. As many of the old endings
gradually wore off, they were not in themselves a
sufficiently clear indication of the difference of tense,
and the apophony or gradation (ablaut) of the root
vowel, which had at first been only an incidental consequence of differences of accentuation, was felt more
and more as the real indicator of tense. But neither
apophony nor the remaining endings were fit to make
patterns for the formation of tenses in new verbs ; consequently, we see very few additions to the old stock
of 'strong' verbs, and a new type of verbs, 'weak
verbs', is constantly gaining ground. Whatever may
have been the origin of the dental ending used in the
past tense of these verbs, it is very extensively used in
all Germanic languages and is, indeed, one of the
characteristic features of their inflexional system. It
has become the 'regular' mode of forming the preterit,
that is, the one resorted to whenever new verbs are
called into existence.

30. To this early period, while the English were still
living on the Continent with their Germanic brethren,
belong the first class of loan-words. No language is

---

[1] Nothing can be concluded from the existence at the time of
Tacitus of such series of alliterating names for members of the same
family as *Segestes Segimerus Segimundus*, etc. (Kluge, Paul's *Grundriss* [2]357, 388), for alliteration does not necessarily imply that the
syllable has the chief stress of the word ; cf. the French formulas
*messe et matines, Florient et Florette, Basans et Basilie, monts et
merveilles, qui vivra verra, à tort et à travers* (Nyrop, *Grammaire
historique*, 1, [3]453).

entirely pure ; we meet with no nation that has not adopted some loan-words, so we must suppose that the forefathers of the old Germanic tribes adopted words from a great many other nations with whom they came into contact ; and scholars have attempted to point out words borrowed very early from various sources. Some of these, however, are doubtful, and none of them are important enough to arrest our attention before we arrive at the period when Latin influence began to be felt in the Germanic world, that is, about the beginning of our Christian era. But before we look at these borrowings in detail, let us first consider for a moment the general lesson that may be derived from the study of words taken over from one language into another.

31. Loan-words have been called the milestones of philology, because in a great many instances they permit us to fix approximately the dates of linguistic changes. But they might with just as much right be termed some of the milestones of general history, because they show us the course of civilization and the wanderings of inventions and institutions, and in many cases give us valuable information as to the inner life of nations when dry annals tell us nothing but the dates of the deaths of kings and bishops. When in two languages we find no trace of the exchange of loan-words one way or the other, we are safe to infer that the two nations have had nothing to do with each other. But if they have been in contact, the number of the loan-words and still more the quality of the loan-words, if rightly interpreted, will inform us of their reciprocal relations, they will show us which of them has been the more fertile in ideas and on what domains of human activity each has been superior to the other. If all other sources of information were closed to us except such loan-words in our modern North-European languages as *piano, soprano, opera, libretto, tempo, adagio*, etc., we should still have no hesitation in drawing the conclusion that Italian music has played a great role all over Europe. Similar

instances might easily be multiplied, and in many ways
the study of language brings home to us the fact that
when a nation produces something that its neighbours
think worthy of imitation these will take over not only
the thing but also the name. This will be the general
rule, though exceptions may occur, especially when a
language possesses a native word that will lend itself
without any special effort to the new thing imported
from abroad. But if a native word is not ready to hand
it is easier to adopt the ready-made word used in the
other country; nay, this foreign word is very often imported even in cases where it would seem to offer no
great difficulty to coin an adequate expression by
means of native word-material. As, on the other hand,
there is generally nothing to induce one to use words
from foreign languages for things one has just as well
at home, loan-words are nearly always *technical* words
belonging to one special branch of knowledge or in-
dustry, and may be grouped so as to show what each
nation has learnt from each of the others. It will be
my object to go through the different strata of loans
in English with special regard to their significance in
relation to the history of civilization.

32. What, then, were the principal words that the
barbarians learnt from Rome in this period which may
be called the pagan or pre-Christian period?[1] One of
the earliest, no doubt, was *wine* (Lat. *vinum*), and a
few other words connected with the cultivation of the
vine and the drinking of wine such as Lat. *calicem*,
OE. *calic* (Germ. *kelch*), 'a cup'. It is worth noting, too,
that the chief type of Roman merchants that the Germanic people dealt with were the *caupones*, 'wine-
dealers, keepers of wine-shops or taverns'; for the
word German *kaufeň*, OE. *ceapian*, 'to buy', is derived
from it, as is also *cheap*, the old meaning of which was

---

[1] See especially Kluge, Paul's *Grundriss*, p. 327 ff.; Pogatscher,
Lautlehre der griech., lat. u. roman. Lehnworte im Altenglischen
(Strassb., 1888). I give the words in their modern English forms,
wherever possible.

'bargain, price'. (Cf. Cheapside.) Another word of commercial significance is *monger* (fishmonger, ironmonger, costermonger), OE. *mangere*, from an extinct verb *mangian*, derived from Lat. *mango*, 'retailer'. Lat. *moneta*, *pondo*, and *uncia* were also adopted as commercial terms : OE. *mynet*, 'coin, coinage', now *mint* ; OE. *pund*, now *pound* ; OE. *ynce*, now *inch* ; the sound-changes point to very early borrowing. Other words from the Latin connected with commerce and travel are : *mile*, *anchor*, *punt* (OE. *punt* from Lat. *ponto*) ; a great many names for vessels or receptacles of various kinds ; the following are still living : *cist* (chest), *omber* or *amber* (amber, from amphora), *disc* (dish), *cytel* (kettle), *mortere* (mortar), *earc* (ark), but many are extinct, e.g. *byden* (barrel), *bytt* (leathern flask), *cylle* (id.), *scutel* (dish), *orc* (pitcher), etc.[1] This makes us suspect a complete revolution in the art of cooking food, an impression which is strengthened by such Latin loan-words as *cook* (OE. *coc* from *coquus*), *kitchen* (OE. *cycene* from *coquina*) and *mill* (OE. *mylen* from *molina*), as well as names for a great many plants and fruits which had not previously been cultivated in the north of Europe, such as *pear* (OE. *cirs*, 'cherry'), *persoc*, 'peach' (the modern forms are later adoptions from the French), *plum* (OE. *plume* from *prunus*), *pea* (OE. *pise* from *pisum*), *cole* (*caul*, *kale*, Scotch *kail*, from Lat. *caulis*), OE. *næp*, found in the second syllable of mod. *turnip*, from *napus*, *beet*(root), *mint*, *pepper*, etc. As military words, though not wanting, were not taken over in such great numbers as one might expect, we have now gone through the principal categories of early loans from the Latin language, from which conclusions as to the state of civilization may be drawn. In comparing them with later loan-words from the same source we are struck by their concrete character. It was not Roman philosophy or the higher mental culture that impressed our Germanic fore-

---

[1] Pogatscher, p. 122. Cf. also Kluge, p. 331.

fathers ; they were not yet ripe for that influence, but
in their barbaric simplicity they needed and adopted
a great many purely practical and material things,
especially such as might sweeten everyday life. It is
hardly necessary to say that the words for such things
were learnt in a purely oral manner, as shown in many
cases by their forms ; and this, too, is a distinctive
feature of the oldest Latin loans as opposed to later
strata of loan-words. They were also short words,
mostly of one or two syllables, so that it would seem
that the Germanic tongues and minds could not yet
manage such big words as form the bulk of later loans.
These early words were easy to pronounce and to
remember, being of the same general type as most of
the indigenous words, and therefore they very soon
came to be regarded as part and parcel of the native
language, indispensable as the things themselves
which they symbolized.[1]

---

[1] Loan-words from later periods will take up much space in the
following chapters. There is now a very full treatment of the subject
in *A History of Foreign Words in English*, by Mary S. Serjeantson
(London, 1935). As the author's points of view differ very considerably from mine, being concerned chiefly with details and chronology,
whereas I try to bring out the broad lines and great principles, I
have found occasion to alter very little in my former exposition.

Chapter III

Old English

33. We now come to the first of those important historical events which have materially influenced the English language, namely, the settlement of Britain by Germanic tribes. The other events of paramount importance, which we shall have to deal with in succession, are the Scandinavian invasion, the Norman conquest, and the revival of learning. A future historian will certainly add the spreading of the English language in America, Australia, and South Africa. But none of these can compare in significance with the first conquest of England by the English, an event which was, perhaps, fraught with greater consequences for the future of the world in general than anything else in history. The more is the pity that we know so very little either of the people who came over or of the state of things they found in the country they invaded. We do not know exactly *when* the invasion began ; the date usually given is 449, but Bede, on whose authority this date rests, wrote about three hundred years later, and much may have been forgotten in so long a period. Many considerations seem to make it more advisable to give a much earlier date[1] ; however, as we must imagine that the invaders did not come all at once, but that the settlement took up a comparatively long period during which new hordes were continually arriving, the question of date is of no great consequence, and we are probably on the safe side if we say that after a long series of Germanic invasions the

[1] R. Thurneysen, *Wann sind die Germanen nach England gekommen?* in Eng. Studien, 22, 163.

greater part of the country was in their power in the latter half of the fifth century.

34. *Who* were the invaders, and where did they come from? This, too, has been a point of controversy.[1] According to Bede, the invaders belonged to the three tribes of Angles, Saxons, and Jutes ; and linguistic history corroborates his statement in so far as we have really three dialects, or groups of dialects : the Anglian dialects in the North with two subdivisions, Northumbrian and Mercian, the Saxon dialects in the greater part of the South, the most important of which was the dialect of Wessex (West-Saxon), and the Kentish dialect, Kent having been, according to tradition settled by the Jutes. These were closely connected linguistically with the Angles and Saxons, thus did not, like those inhabitants of Jutland whom we meet with in historical times, speak a Danish dialect. Though the Saxons were numerically superior to the Angles, the latter were influential enough to impose their name on the whole : the country is called England (OE. Englaland), the nation English (OE. Englisc, Engliscmon, cf. also Angelcynn, Angelþeod), and the language English (OE. Englisc, Englisc gereord). The continental language that shows the greatest similarity to English is Frisian, and it is

---

[1] The complicated and often contradictory evidence, from old chroniclers, archæology, place-names and personal names, has been ably dealt with by G. Schütte in *Our Forefathers* (Cambridge, 1933), II, 218–326, where also a full bibliography is found for each special question. See also A. Erdmann, *Über die Heimat und den Namen der Angeln*, Upsala, 1890.—H. Möller, Anzeiger für deutsches Altertum, XXII, 129 ff.—O. Bremer in Paul's *Grundriß* I, 2, 115 ff., where other references will be found.—Chambers, *Widsith*, 1912, pp. 237, 241.—J. Hoops, 'Angelsachsen' in *Reallexikon der germanischen Altertumskunde* (Strassburg, 1911).—A. Brandl, *Zur Geographie der altenglischen Dialekte* (Berlin, Akademie, 1915)—Luick, *Histor. Grammatik*, 1921, p. 10–11.—J. Hoops, *Englische Sprachkunde* (Stuttgart, 1923), p. 5 ff.—E. Wadstein, *On the Origin of the English* (Uppsala, 1927).—On the question of 'Standard Old English' (the language of Alfred or of Ælfric), see C. L. Wrenn, *Transact. of the Philological Soc.* 1933, p. 65 ff.

interesting to note that Frisian has some points in common with Kentish and some with Anglian, some even with the northernmost divisions of the Anglian dialect, points in which these OE. dialects differ from literary West-Saxon. Kentish resembles more particularly West Frisian, and Anglian East Frisian,[1] facts which justify us in looking upon the Frisians as the neighbours and relatives of the English before their emigration from the continent.

35. What language or what languages did the settlers find on their arrival in Britain? The original population was Keltic ; but what about the Roman conquest? The Romans had been masters of the country for centuries ; had they not succeeded in making the native population learn Latin as they had succeeded in Spain and Gaul? Some years ago Pogatscher[2] took up the view that they had succeeded, and that the Angles and Saxons found a Brito-Roman dialect in full vigour ; he endorsed Wright's view that if the Angles and Saxons had never come, we should have been now a people talking a Neo-Latin tongue, closely resembling French. But this view was very strongly attacked by Loth[3] and Pogatscher, in a subsequent article,[4] had to withdraw his previous theory, if not completely, yet to a great extent, so that he no longer maintains that Latin ever was the *national* language of Britain, though he does not go the length of saying with Loth that the Latin language disappeared from Britain when the Roman troops were withdrawn. The possibility is left that while people in the country spoke Keltic, the inhabitants of the towns spoke Latin, or that some of them did. However this may

---

[1] W. Heuser, *Altfriesisches Lesebuch*, 1903, pp. 1–5, and Indogermanische Forschungen, Anzeiger XIV, 29.

[2] *Zur Lautlehre der . . . Lehnworte im Altenglischen*, 1888.

[3] *Les mots latins dans les langues brittoniques.* Paris, 1892.

[4] *Angelsachsen und Romanen.* Engl. Studien, XIX, 329–352 (1894). See now R. E. Zachrisson, *Romans. Kelts and Saxons in Ancient Britain* (Uppsala, 1927).

be, the fact remains that the English found on their arrival a population speaking a different language from their own. Did that, then, affect their own language, and in what manner and to what extent?

36. In his *Student's History of England*, p. 31, Gardiner, who here follows Freeman, says : 'So far as British words have entered into the English language at all, they have been words such as *gown* or *curd*, which are likely to have been used by women, or words such as *cart* or *pony*, which are likely to have been used by agricultural labourers, and the evidence of language may therefore be adduced in favour of the view that many women and many agricultural labourers were spared by the conquerors.' Here, then, we seem to have a Keltic influence from which an important historical inference can be drawn. Unfortunately, however, not a single word of those adduced can prove anything of the kind. For *gown* is not an old Keltic word, but was taken over from French in the 14th century (medieval Latin *gunna*) ; *curd*, too, dates only from the 14th century, whereas if it had been introduced from Keltic in the old period we should certainly find it in older texts; 'it is not certain what relation, if any, the Keltic words hold to the English' (NED.). *Cart* is probably a native English word ; it is found in Keltic languages, but is there 'palpably a foreign word' (NED.) introduced from English ; and *pony*,[1] finally, is Lowland Scotch *powney* from Old French *poulenet*, 'a little colt', a diminutive of *poulain*, 'a colt'. Similarly, most of the other words of alleged Keltic origin are either Germanic or French words which the Kelts have borrowed from English, or else they have not been used in England more than a century or two ; in neither of these cases do they teach us anything with regard to the relations between the two nationalities fifteen hundred years ago.[2] The net result of modern inves-

---

[1] Skeat, *Notes on English Etymology*, 224.

[2] *Dry* 'magician', *cross*, and probably *curse* belong to a somewhat later stratum of words taken from Irish. See the able treatment of

tigation seems to be that (apart from numerous place-names) only about a dozen words did pass over into English from the British aborigines (among them are *ass, bannock, binn, brock*). How may we account for this very small number of loans? Are we to account for it, as some writers would, from the unscrupulous character of the conquest, the English having killed all those Britons who did not run away into the mountainous districts? The supposition of wholesale slaughter seems, however, to have been disproved by Zachrisson from the distribution of Keltic elements in place-names and the frequent occurrence of Keltic personal names among the Anglo-Saxons. The Britons were not exterminated, but absorbed by their Saxon conquerors. Their civilization and language vanished but the race remained. On the other hand, a thorough consideration of the general conditions under which borrowings from one language by another take place will give us a clue to the mystery.[1] And as the whole history of the English language may be described from one point of view as one chain of borrowings, it will be as well at the outset to give a little thought to this general question.

---

these questions in M. Förster, *Keltisches Wortgut im Englischen*, Halle, 1921. *Cradle*, OE. *cradol*, seems to be a diminutive of an old Germanic word meaning 'basket' (OHG. *chratto*). See also *bog* in NED. Windisch, in the article quoted below, note 1, thinks that the Germanic *tun* in English took over the meaning of Keltic *dunum* (Latin *arx*) on account of the numerous old Keltic names of places in *-dunum* ; but in OE. *tun* had more frequently the meaning of 'enclosure, yard' (cf. Dutch *tuin*), 'enclosed land round a dwelling', 'a single dwelling house or farm' (cf. Old Norse *tún* ; still in Devonshire and Scotland) ; it was only gradually that the word acquired its modern meaning of village or town, long after the influence of the Kelts must have disappeared.—*Slogan, pibroch, clan*, etc., are modern loans from Keltic.

[1] See especially Windisch, *Zur Theorie der Mischsprachen und Lehnwörter*. Berichte über die Verhandl. d. sächs. Gesellsch. d. Wissensch. XLIX, 1897, p. 101 ff.—G. Hempl, *Language-Rivalry and Speech-Differentiation in the Case of Race-Mixture*, Trans. of the Amer. Philol. Association XXIX, 1898, p. 30 ff.—A full treatment of the question of mixed languages and loan-words is found in my own book, *Language*, ch. XI.

37. The whole theory of Windisch about mixed
languages turns upon this formula : it is not the
foreign language a nation learns that it turns into a
mixed language, but its own native language becomes
mixed under the influence of the foreign language.
When we try to learn and talk a foreign language we
do not intermix it with words taken from our own
language ; our endeavour will always be to speak the
other language as purely as possible, and generally we
are painfully conscious of every native word that we use
in the middle of phrases framed in the other tongue.
But what we thus avoid in speaking a foreign language
we very often do in our own. One of Windisch's
illustrations is taken from Germany in the eighteenth
century. It was then the height of fashion to imitate
everything French, and Frederick the Great prided
himself on speaking and writing good French. In his
French writings one finds not a single German word,
but whenever he wrote German, French words and
phrases in the middle of German sentences abounded,
for French was considered more refined, more *dis-
tingué*. Similarly, in the last remains of Cornish, the
extinct Keltic language of Cornwall, numerous English
loan-words occur, but the English did not mix any
Cornish words with their own language, and the inhabitants of Cornwall themselves, whose native language
was Cornish, would naturally avoid Cornish words
when talking English, because in the first place English
was considered the superior tongue, the language of
culture and civilization, and second, the English
would not understand Cornish words. Similarly in the
Brittany of to-day, people will interlard their Breton
talk with French words, while their French is pure,
without any Breton words. We now see why so few
Keltic words were taken over into English.[1] There was
nothing to induce the ruling classes to learn the language of the inferior natives ; it could never be fashionable for them to show an acquaintance with that
despised tongue by using now and then a Keltic word.

_____

[1] And so few Gallic words into French.

On the other hand the Kelt would have to learn the
language of his masters, and learn it well ; he could not
think of addressing his superiors in his own unintelligible gibberish, and if the first generation did not learn
good English, the second or third would, while the
influence they themselves exercised on English would
be infinitesimal.   There can be no doubt that this
theory of Windisch's is in the main correct, though we
shall, perhaps, later on see instances where it holds
good only with some qualification. At any rate we
need look for no other explanation of the fewness of
Keltic words in English.

38. About 600 A.D. England was Christianized, and
the conversion had far-reaching linguistic consequences. We have no literary remains of the pre-
Christian period, but in the great epic of Beowulf we
see a strange mixture of pagan and Christian elements.
It took a long time thoroughly to assimilate the new
doctrine, and, in fact, much of the old heathendom
survives to this day in the shape of numerous super-
stitions.   On the other hand we must not suppose
that people were wholly unacquainted with Christianity before they were actually converted, and linguistic
evidence points to their knowing, and having had
names for, the most striking Christian phenomena
centuries before they became Christians themselves.
One of the earliest loan-words belonging to this sphere
is *church*, OE. *cirice*, *cyrice*, ultimately from Greek
kuriakón '(house) of the Lord' or rather the plural
kuriaká. It has been well remarked that 'it is by no
means necessary that there should have been a single
kiriká in Germany itself ; from 313 onwards, Christian
churches with their sacred vessels and ornaments were
well-known objects of pillage to the German invaders
of the Empire : if the first with which these made
acquaintance, wherever situated, were called *kuriaká*,
it would be quite sufficient to account for their
familiarity with the word'[1]. They knew this word so

---

[1] See the full and able article *church* in the N.E.D. We need not
suppose, as is often done, that the word passed through Gothic,

well that when they became Christians they did not adopt the word universally used in the Latin church and in the Romanic languages (*ecclesia*, *église*, *chiesa*, etc.), and the English even extended the signification of the word *church* from the building to the congregation, the whole body of Christians. *Minster*, OE. *mynster* from *monasterium*, belongs also to the earliest period. Other words of very early adoption were *devil* from *diabolus*, Greek *diábolos*, and *angel*, OE. *engel*[1] from *angelus*, Greek *ággelos*. But the great bulk of specifically Christian terms did not enter the language till after the conversion.

39. The number of new ideas and things introduced with Christianity was very considerable, and it is interesting to note how the English managed to express them in their language.[2] In the first place they adopted a great many foreign words together with the ideas. Such words are *apostle*, OE. *apostol*, *disciple*, OF. *discipul*, which has been more of an ecclesiastical word in English than in other languages, where it has the wider Latin sense of 'pupil' or 'scholar', while in English it is more or less limited to the twelve Disciples of Jesus or to similar applications. Further, the names of the whole scale of dignitaries of the church, from the *Pope*, OE. *papa*, downwards through *archbishop*, OE. *ercebiscop*, *bishop*, OE. *biscop*, to *priest*, OE. *preost*; so also *monk*, OE. *munuc*, *nun*, OE. *nunna*, with *provost*, OE. *prafost* (præpositus) and *profost* (propositus) *abbot*, OE. *abbod* (*d* from Romanic form) and the feminine OE. *abbudisse*. Here belong also such

---

where the word is not found in the literature that has come down to us.

[1] See below, § 86, on the relation between the OE. and the modern forms.

[2] See especially H. S. MacGillivray, *The Influence of Christianity on the Vocabulary of Old English* (Halle, 1902). I arrange his material from other points of view and must often pass the limits of his book, of which only one half has appeared. Cf. also A. Keiser, *The Influence of Christianity on the Vocabulary of OE. Poetry* (Univ. of Illinois, 1919).

obsolete words as *sacerd* 'priest', *canonic* 'canon, *decan* 'dean', *ancor* or *ancra* 'hermit' (Latin anachoreta). To these names of persons must be added not a few names of things, such as *shrine*, OE. *scrin* (scrinium), *cowl*, OE. *cugele* (cuculla), *pall*, OE. *pæll* or *pell* (pallium); *regol* or *reogol* '(monastic) rule', *capitul* 'chapter', *mæsse* 'mass', and *offrian*, in Old English used only in the sense of 'sacrificing, bringing an offering'; the modern usage in 'he offered his friend a seat and a cigar' is later and from the French.

40. It is worth noting that most of these loans were short words that tallied perfectly well with the native words and were easily inflected and treated in every respect like these; the composition of the longest of them *ercebiscop*, was felt quite naturally as a native one. Such long words as *discipul* or *capitul*, or as *exorcista* and *acolitus*, which are also found, never became popular words; and *anachoreta* only became popular when it had been shortened to the convenient *ancor*.

41. The chief interest in this chapter of linguistic history does not, however, to my mind concern those words that were adopted, but those that were not. It is not astonishing that the English should have learnt some Latin words connected with the new faith, but it is astonishing, especially in the light of what later generations did, that they should have utilized the resources of their own language to so great an extent as was actually the case. This was done in three ways : by forming new words from the foreign loans by means of native affixes, by modifying the sense of existing English words, and finally by framing new words from native stems.

At that period the English were not shy of affixing native endings to foreign words ; thus we have a great many words in *-had* (mod. *-hood*) : *preosthad* 'priesthood', *clerichad*, *sacerdhad*, *biscophad* 'episcopate', etc.; also such compounds as *biscopsetl* 'episcopal see', *biscopscir* 'diocese', and with the same ending *profostscir* 'provostship' and the interesting *scrifiscir*

'parish confessor's district' from *scrift* 'confession', a
derivative of *scrifan* (*shrive*) from Lat. *scribere* in the
sense 'impose penance, hear confession'. Note also
such words as *cristendom* 'Christendom, Christianity'
(also *cristnes*), and *cristnian* 'christen' or rather 'prepare a candidate for baptism'[1] and *biscopian* 'confirm'
with the noun *biscepung* 'confirmation'.

42. Existing native words were largely turned to
account to express Christian ideas, the sense only being
more or less modified. Foremost among these must be
mentioned the word *God*. Other words belonging to
the same class and surviving to this day are *sin*, OE.
synn, *tithe*, OE. *teoða*, the old ordinal for 'tenth';
easter, OE. *eastron*, was the name of an old pagan
spring festival, called after Austro, a goddess of
spring.[2] Most of the native words adapted to Christian
usage have since been superseded by terms taken from
Latin or French. Where we now say *saint* from the
French, the old word was *halig* (mod. holy), preserved
in *All-hallows-day* and *Allhallow-e'en*; the Latin *sanct*
was very rarely used. *Scaru*, from the verb *scieran*,
'shear, cut', has been supplanted by *tonsure*, *had* by
order, *hadian* by *consecrate* and *ordain*, *gesomnung* by
congregation, *þegnung* by *service*, *witega* by *prophet*,
prowere (from *prowian*, 'to suffer') by *martyr*, *prower-
had* or *prowung* by *martyrdom*, *niwcumen mann*
('newcome man') by *novice*, *hrycghrægel* (from *hrycg*,
'back', and *hrægel*, 'dress') by *dossal*, and *ealdor* by
prior. Compounds of the last-mentioned Old English
word were also applied to things connected with the
new religion, thus *teoðing-ealdor* 'dean' (chief of ten
monks). *Ealdormann*, the native term for a sort of
viceroy or lord-lieutenant, was used to denote the
Jewish High-Priests as well as the Pharisees. OE. *husl*,

---

[1] '*Christnian* signifies primarily the 'prima signatio' of the cate-
chumens as distinguished from the baptism proper.' MacGillivray,
p. 21. Cf. *fulwian* § 44.

[2] Connected with Sanscrit *usra* and Latin *aurora* and, therefore,
originally a dawn-goddess.

mod. *housel*, 'the Eucharist',[1] was an old pagan word
for sacrifice or offering ; an older form is seen in Gothic
hunsl. The OE. word for 'altar', *weofod*, is an interesting heathen survival, for it goes back to a compound *wigbeod*, 'idol-table', and it was probably only
because phonetic development had obscured its connexion with *wig*, 'idol' that it was allowed to remain
in use as a Christian technical term.

43. This second class is not always easily distinguished from the third, or those words that had not
previously existed but were now framed out of existing
native speech-material to express ideas foreign to the
pagan world. Word-composition and other formative
processes were resorted to, and in some instances the
new terms were simply fitted together from translations of the component parts of the Greek or Latin
word they were intended to render, as when Greek
euaggélion was rendered *god-spell* (good spell, afterwards with shortening of the first vowel *godspell*, which
was often taken to be the 'spell' or message of God),
mod. *gospel* ; thence *godspellere*, where now the foreign
word *evangelist* is used. *Heathen*, OE. *hæðen*, according to the generally accepted theory, is derived from
hæþ 'heath' in close imitation of Latin *paganus* from
pagus 'a country district'. Cf. also *þrynnes* or *þrines*
('three-ness') for *trinity*.

44. But in most cases we have no such literal rendering of a foreign term, but excellent words devised
exactly as if the framers of them had never heard of
any foreign expression for the same conception—as,
perhaps, indeed, in some instances they had not. Some
of these display not a little ingenuity. The Scribes and
Pharisees of the New Testament were called *boceras*
(from *boc* 'book') and *sunder-halgan* (from *sundor*
'apart, asunder, separate') ; in the north the latter
were also called *ælarwas* 'teachers of the Law' or *ældo*
'elders'. A patriarch was called *heahfæder* 'high-

---

[1] Still used in the nineteenth century, e.g. by Tennyson, as an
archaism.

father' or *ealdfæder* 'old-father'; the three Magi were
called *tungolwitegan* from *tungol* 'star', and *witega*
'wise man'. For 'chaplain' we have *handpreost* or
hiredpreost ('family-priest'); for 'acolyte' different
words expressive of his several functions: *huslþegn*
('Eucharist-servant'), *taporberend* ('taper-bearer') and
wæxberend ('wax-bearer'); instead of *ercebiscop* 'archbishop' we sometimes find *heahbiscop* and *ealdorbiscop*.
For 'hermit' *ansetla* and *westensetla* ('sole-settler',
'desert-settler') were used. 'Magic art' was called
scincræft ('phantom-art'); 'magician' *scincræftiga* or
scinlæca, scinnere, 'phantom' or 'superstition', *scin-
lac*. For the disciples of Christ we find, beside *discipul*
mentioned above, no less than ten different English
renderings (*cniht, folgere, gingra, hieremon, læringman,
leornere, leorning-cniht, leorning-man, underþeodda,
þegn*).[1] To 'baptize' was expressed by *dyppan* 'dip'
(cf. German *taufen*, Dan. *døbe*) or more often by
fulwian (from *ful-wihan* 'to consecrate completely');
'baptism' by *fulwiht* or, the last syllable being
phonetically obscured, *fulluht*, and John the Baptist
was called *Johannes se fulluhtere*.

45. The power and boldness of these numerous
native formations can, perhaps, be best appreciated if
we go through the principal compounds of *God* : *godbot*
'atonement made to the church', *godcund* 'divine,
religious, sacred', *godcundnes* 'divinity, sacred office',
godferht 'pious', *godgield* 'idol', *godgimm* 'divine gem',
godhad 'divine nature', *godmægen* 'divinity', *godscyld*
'impiety', *godscyldig* 'impious', *godsibb* 'sponsor', *god-
sibbræden* 'sponsorial obligations', *godspell* (cf., however, §43), *godspelbodung* 'gospel-preaching', *godspellere* 'evangelist', *godspellian* 'preach the gospel',
godspellisc 'evangelical', *godspeltraht* 'gospel-com-
mentary', *godspræce* 'oracle', *godsunu* 'godson',
godþrymm 'divine majesty', *godwræc* 'impious', *god-
wræcnes* 'impiety'. Such a list as this, with the
modern translations, shows the gulf between the old

---

[1] MacGillivray, p. 44.

system of nomenclature, where everything was native and, therefore, easily understood by even the most uneducated, and the modern system, where with few exceptions classical roots serve to express even simple ideas ; observe that although *gospel* has been retained, the easy secondary words derived from it have given way to learned formations. Nor was it only religious terms that were devised in this way ; for Christianity brought with it also some acquaintance with the higher intellectual achievements in other domains, and we find such scientific terms as *lœce-crœft* 'leech-craft' for medicine, *tungol-œ* 'star-law' for astronomy, *efnniht* for equinox, *sunn-stede* and *sunn-gihte* for solstice, *sunnfolgend* (sunfollower) for heliotrope, *tid* 'tide' and *gemet* 'measure' for tense and mood in grammar, *foresetnes* for preposition, etc., in short a number of scientific expressions of native origin, such as is equalled among the Germanic languages in Icelandic only.[1]

46. If now we ask, why did not the Anglo-Saxons adopt more of the ready-made Latin or Greek words, it is easy to see that the conditions here are quite different from those mentioned above when we asked a similar question with regard to Keltic. There we had a real race-mixture, where people speaking two different languages were living in actual contact in the same country. Here we have no Latin-speaking nation or community in actual intercourse with the English ; and though we must suppose that there was a certain mouth-to-mouth influence from missionaries which might familiarize part of the English nation with some of the specifically Christian words, these were certainly at first introduced in far greater number through the medium of writing, exactly as is the case with Latin and Greek importations in recent times. Why, then, do we see such a difference between the practice of that remote period and our own time? One of the

---

[1] On later Old English loans from Latin see especially O. Funke, *Die gelehrten lateinischen Lehn- und Fremdwörter in der altengl. Lit.* (Halle, 1914).

reasons seems obviously to be that people then did
not know so much Latin as they learnt later, so that
these learned words, if introduced, would not have
been understood. We have it on King Alfred's authority that in the time immediately preceding his own
reign 'there were very few on this side of the Humber
who could understand their [Latin] rituals in English,
or translate a letter from Latin into English, and I
believe that there were not many beyond the Humber.
There were so few of them that I cannot remember a
single one south of the Thames when I came to the
throne . . . and there was also a great multitude of
God's servants, but they had very little knowledge of
the books, for they could not understand anything of
them, because they were not written in their language.'[1] And even in the previous period which Alfred
regrets, when 'the sacred orders were zealous in teaching and learning', and when, as we know from Bede
and other sources,[2] Latin and Greek studies were
pursued successfully in England, we may be sure that
the percentage of those who would have understood
the learned words, had they been adopted into English,
was not large. There was, therefore, good reason for
devising as many popular words as possible. However, the manner in which our question was put was
not, perhaps, quite fair, for we seemed to presuppose
that it would be natural for a nation to adopt as many
foreign terms as its linguistic digestion would admit,
and that it would be matter for surprise if a language
had fewer foreign elements than Modern English.
But on the contrary, it is rather the natural thing for
a language to utilize its own resources before drawing
on other languages. The Anglo-Saxon principle of
adopting only such words as were easily assimilated
with the native vocabulary, for the most part names

---

[1] King Alfred's West-Saxon Version of Gregory's Pastoral Care,
Preface (Sweet's translation).

[2] See T. N. Toller, *Outlines of the History of the English Language*,
Cambridge, 1900, p. 68 ff.

of concrete things, and of turning to the greatest
possible account native words and roots, especially for
abstract notions—that principle may be taken as a
symptom of a healthful condition of a language and a
nation : witness Greek, where we have the most
flourishing and vigorous growth of abstract and other
scientifically serviceable terms on a native basis that
the world has ever seen, and where the highest
development of intellectual and artistic activity went
hand in hand with the most extensive creation of
indigenous words and an extremely limited importation of words from abroad. It is not, then, the Old
English system of utilizing the vernacular stock of
words, but the modern system of neglecting the native
and borrowing from a foreign vocabulary that has to
be accounted for as something out of the natural state
of things. A particular case in point will illustrate this
better than long explanations.

47. To express the idea of a small book that is
always ready at hand, the Greeks had devised the word
egkheirídion from *en* 'in', *kheír* 'hand' and the suffix
-idion denoting smallness; the Romans similarly employed their adjective *manualis* 'pertaining to *manus*,
the hand' with *liber* 'book' understood. What could
be more natural then, than for the Anglo-Saxons to
frame according to the genius of their own language
the compound *handboc* ? This naturally would be
especially applied to the one kind of handy books
that the clergy were in particular need of, the book
containing the occasional and minor public offices of
the Roman church. Similar compounds were used,
and are used, as a matter of course, in the other cognate languages—German *handbuch*, Danish *håndbog*,
etc. But in the Middle English period, *handboc* was
disused, the French (Latin) *manual* taking its place,
and in the sixteenth century the Greek word (*enchiri-
dion*) too was introduced into the English language.
And so accustomed had the nation grown to preferring
strange and exotic words that when in the nineteenth

century *handbook* made its reappearance, it was treated as an unwelcome intruder. The oldest example of the new use in the NED. is from 1814, when an anonymous book was published with the title *A Handbook for modelling wax flowers'*. In 1833 Nicolas in the preface to a historical work wrote, 'What the Germans would term and which, if our language admitted of the expression, would have been the fittest title for it, *The Handbook of History'*—but he dared not use that title himself. Three years later Murray the publisher ventured to call his guide-book *A Hand-Book for Travellers on the Continent*, but reviewers as late as 1843 apologized for copying this coined word. In 1838 Rogers speaks of the word as a tasteless innovation, and Trench in his *English Past and Present* (1854 ; 3rd ed., 1856, p. 71) says, 'we might have been satisfied with "manual" and not put together that very ugly and very unnecessary word "handbook", which is scarcely, I should suppose, ten or fifteen years old'. Of late years, the word seems to have found more favour, but I cannot help thinking that state of language a very unnatural one where such a very simple, intelligible and expressive word has to fight its way instead of being at once admitted to the very best society.

48. The Old English language, then, was rich in possibilities, and its speakers were fortunate enough to possess a language that might with very little exertion on their part be made to express everything that human speech can be called upon to express. There can be no doubt that if the language had been left to itself, it would easily have remedied the defects that it certainly had, for its resources were abundantly sufficient to provide natural and expressive terms even for such a new world of concrete things and abstract ideas as Christianity meant to the Anglo-Saxons. It is true that we often find Old English prose clumsy and unwieldy, but that is more the fault of the literature than of the language itself. A good prose style is everywhere a late acquirement, and the work of whole generations of good authors is needed to bring about the easy flow of written prose. Neither, perhaps, were the subjects treated of in the extant Old English prose literature those most suitable for the development of the highest literary qualities. But if we look at such a closely connected language as Old Norse, we find in that language a rapid progress to a narrative prose style which is even now justly admired in its numerous sagas ; and I do not see so great a difference between the two languages as would justify a scepticism with regard to the perfectibility of Old English in the same direction. And, indeed, we have positive proof in a few passages that the language had no mean power as a literary medium ; I am thinking of Alfred's report of the two great Scandinavian explorers, Ohthere and Wulfstan, who visited him, of a few passages in the Saxon Chronicle, and especially of some pages of the homilies of Wulfstan, where we find an impassioned prose of real merit.

49. If Old English prose is undeveloped, we have a very rich and characteristic poetic literature, ranging from powerful pictures of battles and of fights with mythical monsters to religious poems, idyllic descriptions of an ideal country and sad ones of moods of melancholy. It is not here the place to dwell upon the literary merit of these poems, as we are only concerned with the language. But to anyone who has taken the trouble—and it is a trouble—to familiarize himself with that poetry, there is a singular charm in the language it is clothed in, so strangely different from modern poetic style. The movement is slow and leisurely ; the measure of the verse does not invite us to hurry on rapidly, but to linger deliberately on each line and pause before we go on to the next. Nor are the poet's thoughts too light-footed ; he likes to tell us the same thing two or three times. Where a single *he* would suffice he prefers to give a couple of such descriptions as 'the brave prince, the bright hero, noble in war, eager and spirited' etc., descriptions

which add no new trait to the mental picture, but
which, nevertheless, impress us artistically and work
upon our emotions, very much like repetitions and
variations in music. These effects are chiefly produced
by heaping synonym on synonym, and the wealth of
synonymous terms found in Old English poetry is
really astonishing, especially in certain domains,
which had for centuries been the stock subjects of
poetry. For 'hero' or 'prince' we find in Beowulf
alone at least thirty-six words (*æðeling, æscwiga,
aglæca, beadorinc, beaggyfa, bealdor, beorn, brego, brytta,
byrnwiga, ceorl, cniht, cyning, dryhten, ealdor, eorl,
eðelweard, fengel, frea, freca, fruma, hæleð, hlaford,
hyse, leod, mecg, nið, oretta, ræswa, rinc, secg, þegn,
þengel, þeoden, wer, wiga*). For 'battle' or 'fight' we
have in Beowulf at least twelve synonyms (*beadu,
guð, heaðo, hild, lindplega, nið, orleg, ræs, sacu, geslyht,
gewinn, wig*). Beowulf has seventeen expressions for
the 'sea' (*brim, flod, garsecg, hæf, heaðu? holm, holm-
wylm, hronrad, lagu, mere, merestræt, sæ, seglrad,
stream, wæd, wæg, yþ*), to which should be added
thirteen more from other poems (*flodweg, flodwielm,
flot, flotweg, holmweg, hronmere, mereflod, merestream,
sæflod, sæholm, sæstream, sæweg, yþmere*). For 'ship' or
'boat' we have in Beowulf eleven words (*bat, brenting,
ceol, fær, flota, naca, sæbat, sægenga, sæwudu, scip, sund-
wudu*), and in other poems at least sixteen more
words (*brimhengest, brimþisa, brimwudu, cnearr, flod-
wudu, flotscip, holmærn, merebat, merehengest, mere-
þyssa, sæflota, sæhengest, sæmearh, yþbord, yþhengest,
yþhof, yþlid, yþlida*).

50. How are we to account for this wealth of synonyms? We may subtract, if we like, such compound
words as are only variations of the same comparison,
as when a ship is called a sea-horse, and then different
words for sea (*sæ, mere, yþ*) are combined with the
words *hengest* 'stallion' and *mearh* 'mare'; but even
if this class is not counted, the number of synonyms is
great enough to call for an explanation. A language

has always many terms for those things that interest
the speakers in their daily doings ; thus Sweet says:
'If we open an Arabic dictionary at random, we may
expect to find something about a camel : 'a young
camel', 'an old camel', 'a strong camel', 'to feed a
camel on the fifth day', 'to feel a camel's hump to
ascertain its fatness', all these being not only simple
words, but root-words'.[1] And when we read that the
Araucanians (in Chile) distinguished nicely in their
languages between a great many shades of hunger, our
compassion is excited, as Gabelentz remarks.[2] In the
case of the Anglo-Saxons, however, the conclusion we
are justified in drawing from their possessing such a
great number of words connected with the sea is not,
perhaps, that they were a seafaring nation, but rather,
as these words are chiefly poetical and not used in
prose, that the nation *had been* seafaring, but had given
up that life while reminiscences of it were still lingering
in their imagination.

51. In many cases we are now unable to see any
difference in signification between two or more words,
but in the majority of these instances we may assume
that even if, perhaps, the Anglo-Saxons in historical
times felt no difference, their ancestors did not use
them indiscriminately. It is characteristic of primitive
peoples that their languages are highly specialized, so
that where we are contented with one generic word
they have several specific terms. The aborigines of
Tasmania had a name for each variety of gum-tree and
wattle-tree, etc., but they had no equivalent for the
expression 'a tree'. The Mohicans have words for
cutting various objects, but none to convey *cutting*
simply. The Zulus have such words as 'red cow',
'white cow', 'brown cow', etc., but none for 'cow'
generally. In Cherokee, instead of one word for 'washing' we find different words, according to what is
washed, 'I wash myself,—my head,—the head of

---

[1] Sweet. *The Practical Study of Language*, 1899, p. 163.

[2] Gabelentz, *Sprachwissenschaft*, 1891, *p.* 463.

somebody else,—my face,—the face of somebody else,
—my hands or feet,—my clothes,—dishes,—a child,
etc.[1]

52. Very little has been done hitherto to investigate
the exact shades of meaning in Old English words,[2]
but I have little doubt that when we now render a
number of words indiscriminately by 'sword', they
meant originally distinct kinds of swords, and so in
other cases as well. With regard to washing, we find
something corresponding, though in a lesser degree, to
the exuberance of Cherokee, for we have two words,
wacsan (*wascan*) and *þwean*, and if we go through all
the examples given in Bosworth and Toller's Dictionary, we find that the latter word is always applied to
the washing of persons (hands, feet, etc.), never to
inanimate objects, while *wascan* is used especially of
the washing of clothes, but also of sheep, of 'the in-
wards' (of the victim, Leviticus I, 9 and 13).[3] Observe
also that *wascan* was originally used in the present
tense only (as Kluge infers from -*sk*-)—a clear instance
of that restriction in the use of words which is so
common in the old stages of the language, but which
so often appears unnatural to us.

53. The old poetic language on the whole showed a
great many divergences from everyday prose in the
choice of words, in the word-forms, and also in the
construction of the sentences. King Alfred in his prose
always uses the form *het* as the preterit of *hatan*, but
when he breaks out occasionally into a few lines of
poetry he says *heht* instead. This should not surprise

---

[1] Jespersen, *Language*, London, 1922, p. 430 ff.

[2] A notable contribution towards this study is L. Schücking,
Untersuchungen zur Bedeutungslehre der angels. Dichtersprache,
Heidelberg, 1915.

[3] In a late text (R. Ben. 59, 7), we find the contrast *agðer ge fata
þwean, ge wæterclaðas wascan*, which does not agree exactly with the
distinction made above. Curiously enough, in Old Norse, *vaska*
is in the Sagas used only of washing the head with some kind of
soap. In Danish, as well as in English, *vaske*, *wash*, is now the only
word in actual use.

us, for we find the same thing everywhere, and the difference between the dictions of poetry and of prose is perhaps greater in old or more primitive languages than in those most highly developed. In English, certainly, the distance between poetical and prose language was much greater in this first period than it has ever been since. The language of poetry seems to have been to a certain extent identical all over England, a kind of more or less artificial dialect, absorbing forms and words from the different parts of the country where poetry was composed at all, in much the same way as Homer's language had originated in Greece. This hypothesis seems to me to offer a better explanation of the facts than the current theory, according to which the bulk of Old English poetry was written at first in Northumbrian dialect and later translated into West-Saxon with some of the old Anglian forms kept inadvertently—and translated to such an extent that no trace of the originals should have been preserved. The very few and short pieces extant in old Northumbrian dialect are easily accounted for, even if we accept the theory of a poetical *koinē* or standard language prevailing in the time when Old English poetry flourished. But the whole question should be taken up by a more competent hand than mine.

54. The external form of Old English poetry was in the main the same as that of Old Norse, Old Saxon, and Old High German poetry ; besides definite rules of stress and quantity, which were more regular than might at first appear, but which were not so strict as those of classical poetry, the chief words of each line were tied together by alliteration, that is, they began with the same sound, or, in the case of *sp, st, sc*, with the same sound group. The effect is peculiar, and may be appreciated in such a passage as this (I italicize the alliterative letters):

> *Str*æt wæs *st*anfah, *st*ig wisode
> *g*umum ætg*æ*dere. *G*uðbyrne scan

*h*eard *h*ondlocen,   *h*ringiren scir
*s*ong in *s*earwum,   þa hie to *s*ele furðum
in hyra *g*ry*r*e*g*eatwum   *g*angan cwomon.
*S*etton *s*æmeðe   *s*ide scyldas,
*r*ondas *r*eg*n*hearde   wiþ þæs *r*ecedes weal;
*b*ugon þa to *b*ence,—*b*yrnan hringdon,
*g*uþ*s*earo *g*umena ;   *g*aras stodon,
*s*æmanna *s*earo   *s*amod ætgædere,
*œ*scholt *u*fan græg ;   wæs se *i*renbreat
*w*æpnum ge*w*urðad. þa þær *w*lonc hæleþ
oretmecgas   æfter *œ*ðelum frægn :
'Hwanon *f*erigeaþ ge   *f*ætte scyldas,
*g*ræge syrcan,   ond *g*rimhelmas,
*h*eresceafta *h*eap ?   Ic eom *H*roðgares
*a*r ond *o*mbiht.   Ne seah ic *e*lþeodige
þus *m*anige *m*en   *m*odiglicran.
*W*en ic þæt ge for *w*lenco,   nalles for *w*ræcsiðum,
ac for *h*igeþrymmum   *H*roðgar sohton.'[1]

55. Very rarely, combined with alliteration, we find a sort of rime or assonance. In the prose of the last period of Old English the same artistic means were often resorted to to heighten the effect, and we find in Wulfstan's homilies such passages as the following, where all tricks of phonetic harmony are brought into play : 'in mordre and on mane, in susle and on sare, in

[1] Beowulf, 320 ff.; in W. E. Leonard's rendering :

The street was laid with bright
       stones ;   the road led on the band ;
The battle-byrnies shimmered,   the hard, the linked-by-hand
The iron-rings, the gleaming,   amid their armor sang,
Whilst thither, in dread war-gear,   to hall they marched alang ;
The ocean-weary warriors   set down their bucklers wide,
Their shields, so hard and hardy,   against that House's side ;
They stacked points up, these
       seamen,   their ash-wood, gray-tipped
           spears;

And bent to bench, as clankéd   their byrnies, battle-gears—
An iron-troop well-weaponed!   Then proud a Dane forthwith
Did of these men-at-arms there   enquire the kin and kith :
'Ye bear these plated bucklers   hither from what realms ;
These piléd shafts of onset,   gray sarks, and visored helms?
The Henchman and the Herald   of Hrothgar, lo, am I!
Never so many strangers   I've seen of mood more high.
I ween that it is for prowess,   and not for exile far,
That 't is indeed for glory,   that ye have sought Hrothgar'.

wean and on wyrmslitum, betweonan deadum and
deoflum, in bryne and on biternesse, in bealewe and on
bradum ligge, in yrmþum, and on earfeðum, on swylt-
cwale and sarum sorgum, in fyrenum bryne and on
fulnesse, in toða gristbitum and in tintegrum' or again
'þær is êce ece and þær is sorgung and sargung, and a
singal heof ; þær is benda bite and dynta dyne, þær is
wyrma slite and ealra wædla gripe, þær is wanung and
granung, þær is yrmða gehwylc and ealra deofla
geþring'.[1]

56. Nor has this love of alliterative word-combina-
tions ever left the language ; we find it very often in
modern poetry, where however it is always subordinate
to end-rime, and we find it in such stock phrases as :
'it can neither *m*ake nor *m*ar me', '*b*usy as *b*ees'
(Chaucer, E 2422), '*p*art and *p*arcel', '*f*aint and *f*eeble',
'*d*ucks and *d*rakes' (sometimes : 'play dick-duck-
drake); Stevenson, Merry Men, 277), 'what ain't *m*issed
ain't *m*ourned' (Pinero, Magistrate, 5), 'as *b*old as
*b*rass', '*f*ree and *f*ranke' (Caxton, Reynard 41),
'*b*arnes are *b*lessings' (Shakesp. All's I, 3, 28), 'as
*c*ool as a *c*ucumber', 'as *s*till as (a) *s*tone' (Chaucer, E
121, 'as any stoon', E 171, 'he stode stone style',
Malory 145), 'over *s*tile and *s*tone' (Chaucer, B 1988),
'from *t*op to *t*oe' ('from the top to toe', Shakesp.
R 3, III, 1, 155), '*m*ight and *m*ain', '*f*uss and *f*ume',
'*m*anners *m*akyth *m*an', '*c*are *k*illed a *c*at', '*r*ack
and *r*uin', '*n*ature and *n*urture' (Shakesp. Tp. IV,
1, 189 ; English Men of Science, their Nature and

---

[1] 'In murder and in crime, in torment and grief, in pangs and
in snakebites, between dead men and devils, in flames and in tor-
ture, in harm and in extensive fire, in misery and labour, in agony
and serious sorrows, in blazing flames and in filth, in tooth-gnashing
and in torments', and 'There is eternal ache and sorrow and lamen-
tation, and never-ending grief ; there is gnawing of chains and noise
of blows ; there snakes will bite and all miseries attack ; there are
groanings and moanings, troubles of every kind and a crowding
together of all devils.' Wulfstan, Homilies, ed. by Napier, p. 187,
209. It is worthy of note that these poetical flights occur in descriptions of hell.

Nurture, the title of a book by Galton), etc., etc., even to Thackeray's 'faint fashionable fiddle-faddle and feeble court slipslop'. Alliteration sometimes modifies the meaning of a word, as when we apply *chick* to human offspring in 'no chick or child', or when we say 'a *labour* of *love*', without giving to *labour* the shade of meaning which it generally has as different from *work*. The word *foe*, too, which is generally used in poetry or archaic prose only, is often used in ordinary prose for the sake of alliteration in connexion with *friend* ('Was it an irruption of a friend or a foe?' Meredith, *Egoist*, 439 ; 'The Danes of Ireland had changed from foes to friends', Green, *Short Hist.* 107). Indeed alliteration comes so natural to English people, that Tennyson says that 'when I spout my lines first, they come out so alliteratively that I have sometimes no end of trouble to get rid of the alliteration'.[1] I take up the thread of my narrative after this short digression.

---

[1] *Life*, by his son, Tauchn. ed. II, 285; cf. R. L. Stevenson, *The Art of Writing*, p. 31, and what the Danish poet and metricist, E. v. d. Recke, says to the same effect, *Principerne for den danske verskunst*, 1881, p. 112 ; see also the amusing note by De Quincey, *Opium Eater*, p. 96 (Macmillan's Library of Engl. Classics): 'Some people are irritated, or even fancy themselves insulted, by overt acts of alliteration, as many people are by puns. On their account let me say, that although there are here [in the passage to which the note is appended] eight separate f's in less than half a sentence, this is to be held as pure accident. In fact, at one time there were nine f's in the original cast of the sentence, until I, in pity of the affronted people, substituted *female agent* for *female friend*.' The reader need not be reminded of the excessive use of alliteration in Euphuism and of Shakespeare's satire in *Love's Labour's Lost* and *Midsummer Night's Dream*.

Chapter IV

The Scandinavians

57. The Old English language, as we have seen, was
essentially self-sufficing ; its foreign elements were few
and did not modify the character of the language as a
whole. But we shall now consider three very important factors in the development of the language, three
superstructures, as it were, that came to be erected on
the Anglo-Saxon foundation, each of them modifying
the character of the language, and each preparing the
ground for its successor. A Scandinavian element,
a French element, and a Latin element now enter
largely into the texture of the English language, and
as each element is characteristically different from the
others, we shall treat them separately. First, then,
the Scandinavian element.[1]

---

[1] The chief works on these loan-words, most of them treating
nearly exclusively phonetic questions, are: Erik Björkman, *Scandinavian Loan-Words in Middle English* (Halle, I, 1900, II, 1902), an
excellent book ; Erik Brate, *Nordische Lehnwörter im Orrmulum*
(Beiträge zur Gesch. d. deutschen Sprache X, Halle, 1884) ; Arnold
Wall, *A Contribution towards the Study of the Scandinavian Element
in the English Dialects* (Anglia XX, Halle, 1898) ; G. T. Flom,
Scandinavian Influence on Southern Lowland Scotch (New York,
1900). The dialectal material of the two last-mentioned treatises
is necessarily to a great extent of a doubtful character. See also
Kluge in Paul's *Grundriss d. germ. Philol.*, 2nd ed., p. 931 ff. (Strassburg, 1899), Skeat, *Principles of English Etymology*, p. 453 ff.
(Oxford, 1887), P. Thorson, *Anglo-Norse Studies* (Amsterdam, 1936),
and some other works mentioned below. I have excluded doubtful
material ; but a few of the words I give as Scandinavian have been
considered as native by other writers. In most cases I have been
convinced by the reasons given by Björkman.

58. The English had resided for about four centuries in the country called after them, and during that time they had had no enemies from abroad. The only wars they had been engaged in were internal struggles between kingdoms belonging to, but not yet feeling themselves as one and the same nation. The Danes were to them not deadly enemies but a brave nation from over the sea, that they felt to be of a kindred race with themselves. The peaceful relations between the two nations may have been more intimate than is now generally supposed. An attempt has been made to show that an interesting but hitherto mysterious Old English poem which is generally ascribed to the eighth century is a translation of a lost Scandinavian poem dealing with an incident in what was later to become the Volsunga Saga.[1] If this were not rather doubtful it would establish a literary intercourse between England and Scandinavia previous to the Viking ages, and therefore accord with the fact that the old Danish legends about King Hrothgar and his beautiful hall Heorot were preserved in England, even more faithfully than by the Danes themselves. Had the poet of *Beowulf* been able to foresee all that his countrymen were destined to suffer at the hands of the Danes, he would have chosen another subject for his great epic, and we should have missed the earliest noble outcome of the sympathy so often displayed by Englishmen for the fortunes of Denmark. But as it is, in *Beowulf* no coming events cast their shadow before,[2] and the English nation seems to have been taken entirely by surprise when about 790 the long

---

[1] W. W. Lawrence, *The First Riddle of Cynewulf*; W. H. Schofield, *Signy's Lament*. (Publications of the Modern Language Association of America, vol. XVII, Baltimore, 1902.)

[2] This was written before Schücking (*Beiträge*, 43, 347) had called in question the date usually assigned to *Beowulf* (ab. 700). Schücking thinks it was written ab. 900 at a Scandinavian court in England. See against this R. W. Chambers, *Beowulf*, 2nd ed. (Cambridge, 1932), pp. 322, 397, 487. On different strata in *Beowulf*, see especially W. A. Berendsohn, *Zur Vorgeschichte des Beowulf* (Copenhagen, 1935).

series of inroads began, in which 'Danes' and 'heath-
ens' became synonyms for murderers and plunderers.
At first the strangers came in small troops and
disappeared as soon as they had filled their boats with
gold and other valuables ; but from the middle of the
ninth century, 'the character of the attack wholly
changed. The petty squadrons which had till now
harassed the coast of Britain made way for larger
hosts than had as yet fallen on any country in the west;
while raid and foray were replaced by the regular
campaign of armies who marched to conquer, and
whose aim was to settle on the land they won'.[1]
Battles were fought with various success, but on the
whole the Scandinavians proved the stronger race and
made good their footing in their new country. In the
peace of Wedmore (878), King Alfred, the noblest and
staunchest defender of his native soil, was fain to leave
them more than half of what we now call England ; all
Northumbria, all East Anglia, and one half of Central
England made out the district called the Danelaw.

59. Still, the relations between the two races were
not altogether hostile. King Alfred not only effected
the repulse of the Danes ; he also gave us the first
geographical description of the countries that the fierce
invaders came from, in the passage already referred to
(§ 48). Under the year 959, one of the chroniclers says
of the Northumbrian king that he was widely revered
on account of his piety, but in one respect he was
blamed : 'he loved foreign vices too much and gave
heathen (i.e., Danish) customs a firm footing in this
country, alluring mischievous foreigners to come to
this land'. And in the only extant private letter in
Old English[2] the unknown correspondent tells his
brother Edward that 'it is a shame for all of you to
give up the English customs of your fathers and to
prefer the customs of heathen men, who grudge you

---

[1] J. R. Green, *A Short History of the English People*, Illustr. ed.,
p. 87.

[2] Edited by Kluge, Engl. Studien VIII, 62.

your very life ; you show thereby that you despise
your race and your forefathers with these bad habits,
when you dress shamefully in Danish wise with bared
neck and blinded eyes' (with hair falling over the
eyes?). We see, then, that the English were ready to
learn from, as well as to fight with, the Danes. It
is a small but significant fact that in the glorious
patriotic war-poem written shortly after the battle
of Maldon (993) which it celebrates, we find for the
first time one of the most important Scandinavian
loan-words, *to call* ; this shows how early the linguistic
influence of the Danes began to be felt.

60. A great number of Scandinavian families settled
in England never to return, especially in Norfolk,
Suffolk and Lincolnshire, but also in Yorkshire,
Northumberland, Cumberland, Westmorland, etc.
Numerous names of places, ending in *-by, -thorp* (*-torp*),
-beck, -dale, -thwaite, etc., bear witness to the pre-
ponderance of the invaders in great parts of England,
as do also many names of persons found in English
from about 1000 A.D.[1] But these foreigners were not
felt by the natives to be foreigners in the same
manner as the English themselves had been looked
upon as foreigners by the Kelts. As Green has it,
'when the wild burst of the storm was over, land,
people, government, reappeared unchanged. England
still remained England ; the conquerors sank quietly
into the mass of those around them ; and Woden
yielded without a struggle to Christ. The secret of this
difference between the two invasions was that the
battle was no longer between men of different races.
It was no longer a fight between Briton and German,
between Englishman and Welshman. The life of these

---

[1] Björkman, *Nordische Personennamen in England* (Halle, 1910),
H. Lindkvist, *Middle-English Place-Names of Scandinavian Origin*
(Uppsala, 1912), E. Ekwall, *Scandinavians and Celts in the North-
West of England* (Lund, 1918), and in *Introduction to the Survey of
Engl. Place-Names*, I (Cambridge, 1924). According to Ekwall, the
Scandinavians in the North-West did not come direct from Norway,
but through Ireland.

northern folk was in the main the life of the earlier
Englishmen. Their customs, their religion, their social
order were the same ; they were in fact kinsmen
bringing back to an England that had forgotten its
origins the barbaric England of its pirate forefathers.
Nowhere over Europe was the fight so fierce, because
nowhere else were the combatants men of one blood
and one speech. But just for this reason the fusion
of the northmen with their foes was nowhere so peaceful and so complete.'[1] It should be remembered, too,
that it was a Dane, King Knut, who achieved what
every English ruler had failed to achieve, the union
of the whole of England into one peaceful realm.

61. King Knut was a Dane, and in the Saxon
Chronicle the invaders were always called Danes, but
from other sources we know that there were Norwegians too among the settlers. Attempts have been
made to decide by linguistic tests which of the two
nations had the greater influence in England,[2] a question beset with considerable difficulties and which
need not detain us here. Suffice it to say that some
words, such as ME. *boun*, Mod. *bound* 'ready' (to go
to), *busk, boon, addle*, point rather to a Norwegian
origin, while others such as *-by* in place names, *drown*,
ME. *sum* 'as', agree better with Danish forms. In
the great majority of cases, however, the Danish and
Norwegian forms were at that time either completely
or nearly identical, so that no decision as to the special
homeland of the English loans is warranted. In the
present work I therefore leave the question open,
quoting Danish or ON. (Old Norse, practically = Old

---

[1] J. R. Green, *A Short History of the English People*, Illustr. ed.,
p. 87.

[2] Brate thought the loan-words exclusively Danish ; Kluge, Wall,
and Björkman consider some of them Danish, others Norwegian,
though in details they arrive at different results. See Björkman,
Zur dialektischen Provenienz der nordischen Lehnwörter im Englischen,
Språkvetensk. sällskapets förhandlingar, 1898–1901, Uppsala, and
his *Scand. Loan-Words*, p. 281 ff. Cf. also Ekwall as quoted on p. 58,
and J. Hoops, *Englische Sprachkunde* (Stuttgart, 1923), p. 26 f.

Icelandic) forms according as it is most convenient in
each case, meaning simply Scandinavian.[1]

62. In order rightly to estimate the Scandinavian
influence it is very important to remember how great
the similarity was between Old English and Old Norse.
To those who know only modern English and modern
Danish, this resemblance is greatly obscured, first on
account of the dissimilarities that are unavoidable
when two nations live for nearly one thousand years
with very little intercommunication, and when there
is, accordingly, nothing to counterbalance the natural
tendency towards differentiation, and secondly on
account of a powerful foreign influence to which each
nation has in the meantime been subjected, English
from French, and Danish from Low German. But
even now we can see the essential conformity between
the two languages, which in those times was so much
greater as each stood so much nearer to the common
source. An enormous number of words were then
identical in the two languages, so that we should now
have been utterly unable to tell which language they
had come from if we had had no English literature
before the invasion ; nouns such as *man, wife, father,
folk, mother, house, thing, life, sorrow, winter, summer,*
verbs like *will, can, meet, come, bring, hear, see, think,
smile, ride, stand, sit, set, spin,* adjectives and adverbs
like *full, wise, well, better, best, mine* and *thine, over* and
under, etc. etc. The consequence was that an Englishman would have no great difficulty in understanding
a viking—nay, we have positive evidence that Norse
people looked upon the English language as one with
their own. On the other hand, Wulfstan speaks of the
invaders as 'people who do not know your language'
(ed. Napier, p. 295), and in many cases indeed the

---

[1] Björkman's final words are : 'These facts would seem to point to
the conclusion that a considerable number of Danes were found
everywhere in the Scandinavian settlements, while the existence in
great numbers of Norwegians was confined to certain definite
districts.'

words were already so dissimilar that they were easily
distinguished, for instance, when they contained an
original *ai*, which in OE. had become long *a* (OE.
swan = ON. *sveinn*), or *au*, which in OE. had become
ea (OE. *leas* = ON. *lauss, louss*), or *sk*, which in English became *sh* (OE. *scyrte*, now *shirt* = ON. *skyrta*).

63. But there are, of course, many words to which
no such reliable criteria apply, and the difficulty in
deciding the origin of words is further complicated by
the fact that the English would often modify a word,
when adopting it, according to some more or less
vague feeling of the English sound that corresponded
generally to this or that Scandinavian sound. Just as
the name of the English king Æðelred Eadgares sunu
is mentioned in the Norse saga of Gunnlaugr Orm-
stunga as Aðalráðr Játgeirsson, in the same manner
shift is an Anglicized form of Norse *skipta*[1]; ON.
brúðlaup 'wedding' was modified into *brydlop* (cf. OE.
bryd 'bride'; a consistent Anglicizing would be
brydhleap); *tíðende* is unchanged in Orrms *tiþennde*,
but was generally changed into *tiding(s)*, cf. OE. *tid*
and the common English ending -*ing*; ON. *þjónusta*
'service' appears as *þeonest, þenest*, and *þegnest*;
ON. words with the negative prefix *ú* are made into
English *un-*, e.g. *untime* 'unseasonableness', *unbain*
(ON. *úbeinn*) 'not ready', *unrad* or *unræd* 'bad counsel'[2]; cf. also *wæpnagetæc* below, and others.

64. Sometimes the Scandinavians gave a fresh lease
of life to obsolescent or obsolete native words. The
preposition *till*, for instance, is found only once or
twice in OE. texts belonging to the pre-Scandinavian
period, but after that time it begins to be exceedingly
common in the North, from whence it spreads southward; it was used as in Danish with regard to both
time and space and it is still so used in Scotch. Similarly *dale* (OE. *dæl*) 'appears to have been reinforced

---

[1] In ME. forms with *sk* are also found; Björkman, p. 126.

[2] Though the Scand. form is also found in a few instances : *oulist*
'listless,' *oumautin* 'swoon'.

from Norse (*dal*), for it is in the North that the word
is a living geographical name' (NED.), and *barn*,
Scotch *bairn* (OE. *bearn*) would probably have disappeared in the North, as it did in the South, if it had
not been strengthened by the Scandinavian word.
The verb *blend*, too, seems to owe its vitality (as well
as its vowel) to Old Norse, for *blandan* was very rare
in Old English.

65. We also see in England a phenomenon which, I
think, is paralleled nowhere else to such an extent,
namely, the existence side by side for a long time,
sometimes for centuries, of two slightly differing forms
for the same word, one the original English form and
the other Scandinavian. In the following the first
form is the native one, the form after the dash the
imported one.

66. In some cases both forms survive in standard
speech, though, as a rule, they have developed slightly
different meanings : *whole* (formerly *hool*)—*hale* ; both
were united in the old phrase 'hail and hool' | *no*—
nay ; the latter is now used only to add an amplifying
remark ('it is enough, nay too much'), but formerly it
was used to answer a question, though it was not so
strong a negative as *no* ('Is it true? Nay.' 'Is it not
true? No') | *rear*—*raise* | *from*—*fro*, now used only in
'to and fro' | *shirt*—*skirt* | *shot*—*scot* | *shriek*—*screak*,
screech | *true*—*trigg*, 'faithful, neat, tidy' | *edge*—*egg*
vb. ('to egg on', 'to incite'). OE. *leas* survives only in
the suffix *-less* (nameless, etc.), while the Scand. *loose*
has entirely supplanted it as an independent word.

67. In other cases, the Scandinavian form survives
in dialects only, while the other belongs to the literary
language: *dew*—*dag*, 'dew, thin rain'; vb. 'to drizzle' |
leap—*loup* | *neat*—*nowt*, 'cattle' | *church*—*kirk* |
churn—*kirn* | *chest*—*kist* | *mouth*—*mun* | *yard*—*garth*,
'a small piece of enclosed ground'. All these dialectal
forms belong to Scotland or the North of England.

68. As a rule, however, one of the forms has in
course of time been completely crowded out by the

other. The surviving form is often the native form, as in the following instances : *goat—gayte* | *heathen— heythen, haithen* | *loath—laith* | *grey—gra, gro* | *few— a, fo* | *ash(es)—ask* | *fish—fisk* | *naked—naken* | *yarn —garn* | *bench—bennk* | *star—sterne* | *worse— werre.* Similarly the Scand. *thethen, hethen, hwethen* are generally supposed to have been discarded in favour of the native forms, OE. *þanon, heonan, hwanon,* to which was added an adverbial *s* : *thence, hence, whence* ; but in reality these modern forms may just as well be due to the Scandinavian ones ; for the loss of *th,* cf. *since* from *sithence* (*sithens,* OE. *siþþan* + *s*).

69. This then leads us on to those instances in which the intruder succeeded in ousting the legitimate heir. Caxton, in a well-known passage, gives us a graphic description of the struggle between the native *ey* and the Scandinavian *egg* :

And certaynly our langage now used varyeth ferre from that whiche was used and spoken whan I was borne. For we englysshe men ben borne under the domynacyon of the mone, whiche is never stedfaste, but ever waverynge, wexynge one season, and waneth & dyscreaseth another season. And that comyn englysshe that is spoken in one shyre varyeth from a nother. In so moche that in my dayes happened that certayn marchauntes were in a shippe in tamyse, for to have sayled over the see into zelande. And for lacke of wynde, thei taryed atte forlond, and wente to lande for to refreshe them. And one of theym named sheffelde,[1] a mercer, cam in-to an hows and axed for mete ; and specyally he axyd after eggys. And the goode wyf answerde, that she coude speke no frenshe. And the marchaunt was angry, for he also coude speke no frenshe, but wolde have hadde egges, and she understode hym not. And thenne at laste a nother sayd that he wolde have eyren. Then the good wyf sayd that she understod

---

[1] Probably a north-country man.

hym wel. Loo, what sholde a man in thyse dayes
now wryte, egges or eyren. Certaynly it is harde to
playse every man, by cause of dyversite & chaunge
of langage.[1]

Very soon after this was written, the Old English
forms *ey*, *eyren* finally went out of use.

70. Among other word-pairs similarly fated may be
mentioned : OE. *a*, ME. *o*, 'ever' — *ay* (both were
found together in the frequent phrase 'for ay and oo'
| *tho* (cf. *those*) — *they* | *theigh*, *thah*, *theh* and other
forms — *though* | *swon* — *swain* (boatswain, etc.) |
ibirde — *birth* | *eie* — *awe* | *punresdæi* — *Thursday* | *in*
(on) *pe lifte* — *on lofte*, now *aloft* | *swuster* — *sister* |
chetel — *kettle* ; and finally not a few words with
English *y* over against Scand. *g* : *yete* — *get* | *yeme*,
'care, heed' — *gom(e)*, dialectal *gaum*, 'sense, wit,
tact' | *yelde* — *guild*, 'fraternity, association' | *yive* or
yeve — *give* | *yift* — *gift*. In this last-mentioned word
gift, not only is the initial sound due to Scandinavian,
but also the modern meaning, for the Old English
word meant 'the price paid by a suitor in consideration of receiving a woman to wife' and in the plural
'marriage, wedding'. No subtler linguistic influence
can be imagined than this, where a word has been
modified both with regard to pronunciation and meaning, and curiously enough has by that process been
brought nearer to the verb from which it was originally
derived (*give*).

71. In some words the old native form has survived,
but has adopted the signification attached in Scandinavian to the corresponding word ; thus *dream* in OE.
meant 'joy', but in ME. the modern meaning of
'dream' was taken over from ON., *draumr*, Dan.,
dröm ; analogous cases are *bread* (OE. *bread*, 'frag-
ment'), *bloom* (OE. *bloma*, 'mass of metal'?). In one
word, this same process of sense-shifting has historical
significance ; the OE. *eorl* meant vaguely a 'nobleman'

---

[1] Caxton's *Eneydos*, pp. 2–3. (E.E.T.S. Extra Series, 57). Cf. R.
Hittmair, *Aus Caxtons Vorreden* (Leipzig, 1934), p. 110.

or more loosely 'a brave warrior' or 'man' generally ;
but under Knut it took over the meaning of the Norse
jarl, 'an under-king' or governor of one of the great
divisions of the realm, thus paving the way for the
present signification of *earl* as one of the grades in
the (French) scale of rank. OE. *freond* meant only
'friend', whereas ON. *frœndi*, Dan. *frœnde* means
'kinsman', but in Orrm and other ME. texts the
word sometimes has the Scand. meaning[1] and so it
has to this day in Scotch and American dialects (see
many instances in J. Wright's Dialect Dictionary,
e.g. 'We are near friends, but we don't speak') ; the
Scotch proverb, 'Friends agree best at a distance'
corresponds to the Danish 'Frænde er frænde værst'.
OE. *dwellan* or *dwelian* meant only 'to lead astray,
lead into error, thwart' or intr. 'to go astray'[2] ; the
intransitive meanings, 'to tarry, abide, remain in a
place', which corresponds with the Scandinavian
meanings, are not found till the beginning of the 13th
century. OE. *ploh* is found only with the meaning
of 'a measure of land' (still in Scotch *pleuch*), but in
ME. it came to mean the implement *plough* (OE. *sulh*)
as in ON. *plógr*. OE. *holm* meant 'ocean', but the
modern word owes its signification of 'islet, flat
ground by a river' to Scandinavian *holmr*.

72. These were cases of native words conforming to
foreign speech habits ; in other instances the Scandinavians were able to place words at the disposal of the
English which agreed so well with other native words
as to be readily associated with them, nay which were
felt to be fitter expressions for the ideas than the Old
English words and therefore survived. *Death* (deaþ)
and *dead* are OE. words, but the corresponding verbs
were *steorfan* and *sweltan* ; now it is obvious that

---

[1] Saxon Chron., 1135, which is given in the NED. as an instance
of this meaning, appears to me to be doubtful.

[2] *Dwelode*, in Ælfric, *Homilies*, 1, 384, is wrongly translated by
Thorpe 'continued,' so that Kluge is wrong in giving this passage
as the earliest instance of the modern meaning ; it means 'wandered,
went astray.'

Danish *deya* (now dø) was more easily associated with
the noun and the adjective than the old verbs, and
accordingly it was soon adopted (*deyen*, now *die*), while
sweltan was discarded and the other verb acquired the
more special signification of *starving*. *Sæte* (Mod.E.
seat) was adopted because it was at once associated
with the verbs *to sit* and *to set*. The most important
importation of this kind was that of the pronominal
forms *they*, *them* and *their*, which entered readily into
the system of English pronouns beginning with the
same sound (*the*, *that*, *this*) and were felt to be more
distinct than the old native forms which they supplanted. Indeed these were liable to constant confusion with some forms of the singular number (*he*,
him, *her*) after the vowels had become obscured, so
that *he* and *hie*, *him* and *heom*, *her* (*hire*) and *heora*
could no longer be kept easily apart. We thus find
the obscured form, which was written *a* (or *'a*), in use
for 'he' till the beginning of the 16th century (compare
the dialectal use, for instance, in Tennyson's 'But
Parson a cooms an' a goäs'), and in use for 'she' and
for 'they' till the end of the 14th century. Such a state
of things would naturally cause a great number of
ambiguities ; but although the *th*-forms must consequently be reckoned a great advantage to the
language, it took a long time before the old forms
were finally displaced, nay, the dative *hem* still
survives in the form *'em* ('take 'em'), which is now
by people ignorant of the history of the language
taken to be a shortened *them* ; *her* 'their' is the only
form for the possessive of the plural found in Chaucer
(who says *they* in the nominative) and there are two
or three instances in Shakespeare. One more Scandinavian pronoun is *same*, which was speedily
associated with the native adverb *same* (*swa*, *same*,
'similarly'). Other words similarly connected with the
native stock are *want* (adj. and vb.), which reminded
the English of their own *wan* 'wanting', *wana* 'want'
and *wanian* 'wane, lessen', and *ill*, which must have

appeared like a stunted form of *evil*, especially to a
Scotchman who had made his own *devil* into *deil* and
even into *ein*.

73. If now we try to find out by means of the loan-
word test (see above, § 31) what were the spheres of
human knowledge or activity in which the Scandinavians were able to teach the English, the first thing
that strikes us is that the very earliest stratum of
loan-words,[1] words which by the way were soon to
disappear again from the language,[2] relate to war and
more particularly to the navy : *orrest* 'battle', *fylcian*
'to collect, marshal', *liþ* 'fleet', *barda, cnear, scegþ*
different sorts of warships, *ha* 'rowlock'. This agrees
perfectly well with what the Saxon Chronicle relates
about the English being inferior to the heathen in
ship-building, until King Alfred undertook to con-
struct a new kind of warship.[3]

74. Next, we find a great many Scandinavian law-
terms ; they have been examined by Professor Steenstrup in his well-known work on 'Danelag'.[4] He has
there been able, in an astonishing number of cases, to
show conclusively that the vikings modified the legal
ideas of the Anglo-Saxons, and that numerous new
law-terms sprang up at the time of the Scandinavian
settlements which had previously been utterly unknown. Most of them were simply the Danish or Norse
words, others were Anglicizings, as when ON. *vap-
natak* was made into *wæpnagetæc* (later *wapentake*) or
when ON. *heimsokn* appears as *hamsocn* 'house-break-
ing or the fine for that offence', or *saklauss* as *sacleas*
'innocent'. The most important of these juridical
imports is the word *law* itself, known in England from

---

[1] See Björkman, p. 5.

[2] They were naturally supplanted by French words; see below.

[3] ON. *bāt* (boat) is generally supposed to be borrowed from OE.
bāt, but according to E. Wadstein, *Friserna och forntida handels-
vägar* (Göteborg, 1920), both were borrowed from Frisian. The
latest treatment of this phonetically difficult word is by J. Sverdrup
(*Maalogminne*,1922),who thinks that it is a native Scandinavian word.

[4] Copenhagen, 1882 (= Normannerne IV).

the 10th century in the form *lagu,* which must have
been the exact Scandinavian form, as it is the direct
forerunner of the ON. form *lǫg,* ODan. *logh.*[1] *By-law*
is now felt to be a compound of the preposition *by* and
law, but originally *by* was the Danish *by* 'town,
village' (found in Derby, Whitby, etc.), and the Danish genitive-ending is preserved in the other English
form *byr-law.* Other words belonging to this class are
niðing 'criminal, wretch', *thriding* 'third part', preserved in the mutilated form *riding,*[2] *carlman* 'man'
as opposed to woman, *bonda* or *bunda* 'peasant',
lysing 'freedman', *þræll,* Mod. *thrall, mall* 'suit,
agreement', *wiþermal* 'counterplea, defence', *seht*
'agreement', *stefnan* 'summon', *crafian* now *crave,*
landcop or anglicized *landceap* and *lahcop* or *lahceap*
(for the signification see Steenstrup, p. 192 ff.) ; *ran*
'robbery' ; *infangenþeof* later *infangthief* 'jurisdiction
over a thief apprehended within the manor'. It will
be seen that with the exception of *law, bylaw, thrall*
and *crave*—the least juridical of them all—these
Danish law-terms have disappeared from the language
as a simple consequence of the Norman conquerors
taking into their own hands the courts of justice and
legal affairs generally. Steenstrup's research, which is
largely based on linguistic facts, may be thus sum-
marized. The Scandinavian settlers reorganized the
administration of the realm and based it on a uniform
and equable division of the country ; taxes were
imposed and collected after the Scandinavian pattern ; instead of the lenient criminal law of former
times, a virile and powerful law was introduced which
was better capable of intimidating fierce and violent
natures. More stress was laid on personal honour, as

---

[1] The OE. word was *œ* or *œw,* which meant 'marriage' as well and
was restricted to that sense in late OE., until it was displaced by
the French word.

[2] *North-thriding* being heard as *North-riding* ; in the case of the
two other ridings of Yorkshire, *East-thriding* and *West-thriding,* the
th-sound was assimilated to the preceding *t,* the result in all three
cases being the same misdivision of the word ('metanalysis').

when a sharp line was drawn between stealthy or clan-
destine crimes and open crimes attributable to
obstinacy or vindictiveness. Commerce, too, was
regulated so as to secure trade.

75. Apart from these legal words it would be very
difficult to point out any single group of words belonging to one and the same sphere from which a superiority of any description might be concluded. *Window* is
borrowed from *vindauga* ('wind-eye'); but we dare
not infer that the northern settlers taught the English
anything in architecture, for the word stands quite
alone; besides, OE. had another word for 'window',
which is also based on the eye-shape of the windows
in the old wooden houses : *eagþyrel* 'eye-hole' (cf.
nosþyrel 'nostril').[1] Nor does the borrowing of *steak*,
ME. *steyke* from ON. *steik*, prove any superior cooking on the part of the vikings. But it is possible that
the Scandinavian *knives* (ME. *knif* from Scand. *knif*)
were better than or at any rate different from those of
other nations, for the word was introduced into French
(*canif*) as well as into English.

76. If, then, we go through the lists of loan-words,
looking out for words from which conclusions as to
the state of culture of the two nations might be drawn,
we shall be doomed to disappointment, for they all
seem to denote objects and actions of the most commonplace description and certainly do not represent
any new set of ideas hitherto unknown to the people
adopting them. We find such everyday nouns as
*husband, fellow, sky, skull, skin, wing, haven, root, skill,
anger, gate*,[2] etc. Among the adjectives adopted from

---

[1] Most European languages use the Lat. *fenestra* (G. *fenster*,
Dutch *venster*, Welsh *ffenester*), which was also imported from
French into English as *fenester*, in use from 1290 to 1548. Slavic
languages have *okno*, derived from *oko* 'eye.' On the eye-shape of
old windows, see R. Meringer, Indogerm. Forschungen, XVI, 1904,
p. 125).

[2] *Gate* 'way, road, street,' frequent in some northern towns in the
names of streets, frequent also in ME. adverbial phrases *algate*

Scand. we find *meek, low, scant, loose, odd*,[1] *wrong, ill,
ugly, rotten.* The impression produced perhaps by this
list that only unpleasant adjectives came into English
from Scandinavia, is easily shown to be wrong, for
happy and *seemly* too are derived from Danish roots,
not to speak of *stor*, which was common in Middle
English for 'great', and dialectal adjectives like *glegg*
'clear-sighted, clever', *heppen*, 'neat, tidy', *gain*
'direct, handy' (Sc. and North E. the gainest way,
ON. hinn gegnsta veg, Dan., den genneste vej). The
only thing common to the adjectives, then, is seen to
be their extreme commonplaceness, and the same
impression is confirmed by the verbs, as for instance,
*thrive, die, cast, hit, take, call, want, scare, scrape,
scream, scrub, scowl, skulk, bask, drown, ransack, gape,
guess* (doubtful), etc. To these must be added numerous words preserved only in dialects (north country
and Scotch) such as *lathe* 'barn' Dan. *lade, hoast*
'cough' Dan. *hoste, flit* 'move' Dan. *flytte, gar* 'make,
do' Dan. *göre, lait* 'search for' Dan. *lede, red up* 'to
tidy' Dan. *rydde op, keek in* 'peep in', *ket* 'carrion,
horseflesh, tainted flesh, rubbish', originally 'flesh,
meat' as Dan. *kød*, etc., all of them words belonging
to the same familiar sphere, and having nothing about
them that might be called technical or indicative of
a higher culture. The same is true of that large class
of words which have been mentioned above (§ 65–72),
where the Scandinavians did not properly bring the
word itself, but modified either the form or the signification of a native word ; among them we have seen
such everyday words as *get, give, sister, loose, birth,
awe, bread, dream*, etc.[2] It is precisely the most
indispensable elements of the language that have

---

anothergate(s) (corrupted into *anotherguess*), etc. In the sense 'manner of going' it is now spelt *gait*.

[1] Cf. North-Jutland dialect (Vendsyssel) *oj* 'odd (number)'.

[2] It is noticeable, too, that the native word *heaven* has been more
and more restricted to the figurative and religious acceptation,
while *sky* is used of the visible firmament, a meaning it has in
Jutlandish dialects : the ordinary Danish meaning is 'cloud.'

undergone the strongest Scandinavian influence, and
this is raised into certainty when we discover that a
certain number of those grammatical words, the small
coin of language, which Chinese grammarians term
'empty words', and which are nowhere else transferred
from one language to another, have been taken over
from Danish into English : pronouns like *they, them,
their, the same* and probably *both* ; a modal verb like
Scotch *maun, mun* (ON. *munu,* Dan. *mon, monne*) ;
comparatives like *minne* 'lesser', *min* 'less', *helder*
'rather' ; pronominal adverbs like *hethen, thethen,
whethen* 'hence, thence, whence', *samen* 'together' ;
conjunctions like *though, oc* 'and', *sum,* which for a long
time seemed likely to displace the native *swa* (*so*) after
a comparison, until it was itself displaced by *eallswa
> as* ; prepositions like *fro* and *till* (see above, § 64).[1]

77. It is obvious that all these non-technical words
can show us nothing about mental or industrial
superiority ; they do not bear witness to the currents
of civilization ; what was denoted by them cannot
have been new to the English ; we have here no new
ideas, only new names. Does that mean, then, that
the loan-word test which we are able to apply elsewhere fails in this one case, and that linguistic facts
can tell us nothing about the reciprocal relations of
the two races? No ; on the contrary, the suggestive-
ness of these loans leaves nothing to be desired, they
are historically significant enough. If the English
loan-words in this period extend to spheres where
other languages do not borrow, if the Scandinavian
and the English languages were woven more intimately together, the reason must be a more intimate
fusion of the two nations than is seen anywhere else.
They fought like brothers and afterwards settled down
peacefully, like brothers, side by side. The numbers of
the Danish and Norwegian settlers must have been

---

[1] Another preposition, *umbe,* was probably to a large extent due
to Scandinavian, the native form being *ymbe, embe* ; but perhaps in
some texts *u* in *umbe* may represent the vowel [y].

considerable, else they would have disappeared without leaving such traces in the language.

78. It might at the first blush seem reasonable to think that what was going on among Scandinavian settlers in England was parallel to what we see going on now in the United States. But there is really no great similarity between the two cases. The language of Scandinavian and other settlers in America is often a curious mixture, but it is very important to notice that it is Danish or Norwegian, sprinkled with English words : 'han har fencet sin farm og venter en god krop' he has fenced his farm and expects a good crop ; 'lad os krosse streeten' let us cross the street ; 'tag det træ' take that tray ; 'hun suede ham i courten for 25,000 daler', etc. But this is *toto cœlo* different from the English language of the Middle Ages. And if we do not take into account those districts where Scandinavians constitute the immense majority of the population and keep up their old speech as pure as circumstances will permit, the children or at any rate the children's children of the immigrants speak English, and very pure English too, without any Danish admixture. The English language of America has no loan-words worth mentioning from the languages of the thousands and thousands of Germans, Scandinavians, French, Poles and others that have settled there. Nor are the reasons far to seek.[1] The immigrants come in small groups and find their predecessors half, or more than half, Americanized ; those belonging to the same country cannot, accordingly, maintain their nationality collectively ; they come in order to gain a livelihood, generally in subordinate positions where it is important to each of them separately to be as little different as possible from his new surroundings, in garb, in manners, and in language. The faults each individual commits in

---

[1] See G. Hempl's paper on *Language-Rivalry* quoted above, p. 35. Hempl's very short mention of the Scandinavians in England is, perhaps, the least satisfactory portion of his paper ; none of his classes apply to our case.

talking English, therefore, can have no consequences of lasting importance, and at any rate his children are in most respects situated like the children of the natives and learn the same language in essentially the same manner. In old times, of course, many a Dane in England would speak his mother-tongue with a large admixture of English, but that has no significance in linguistic history, for in course of time the descendants of the immigrants would no longer learn Scandinavian as their mother-tongue, but English. But that which is important is the fact of the English themselves intermingling their own native speech with Scandinavian elements. Now the manner in which this is done shows us that the culture or civilization of the Scandinavian settlers cannot have been of a higher order than that of the English, for then we should have seen in the loan-words special groups of technical terms indicative of this superiority. Neither can their state of culture have been much inferior to that of the English, for in that case they would have adopted the language of the natives without appreciably influencing it. This is what happened with the Goths in Spain, with the Franks in France and with the Danes in Normandy, in all of which cases the Germanic tongues were absorbed into the Romanic languages.[1] It is true that the Scandinavians were, for a short time at least, the rulers of England, and we have found in the juridical loan-words linguistic

[1] It is instructive to contrast the old speech-mixture in England with what has been going on for the last two centuries in the Shetland Islands. Here the old Norwegian dialect ('Norn') has perished as a consequence of the natives considering it more genteel to speak English (Scotch). All common words of their speech now are English, but they have retained a certain number of Norn words, all of them technical, denoting different species of fish, fishing implements, small parts of the boat or of the house and its primitive furniture, those signs in clouds, etc., from which the weather was forecast at sea, technicalities of sheep rearing, nicknames for things which appear to them ludicrous or ridiculous, etc.—all of them significant of the language of a subjugated and poor population. (J. Jakobsen, *Det norrøne sprog på Shetland*, Copenhagen, 1897).

corroboration of this fact ; but the great majority
of the settlers did not belong to the ruling class.
Their social standing must have been, on the whole,
slightly superior to the average of the English, but the
difference cannot have been great, for the bulk of
Scandinavian words are of a purely democratic
character. This is clearly brought out by a comparison
with the French words introduced in the following centuries, for here language confirms what history tells us,
that the French represent the rich, the ruling, the
refined, the aristocratic element in the English nation.
How different is the impression made by the Scandinavian loan-words. They are homely expressions for
things and actions of everyday importance ; their
character is utterly democratic. The difference is also
shown by so many of the French words having never
penetrated into the speech of the people, so that they
have been known and used only by the 'upper ten',
while the Scandinavian ones are used by high and low
alike ; their shortness too agrees with the monosyllabic
character of the native stock of words, consequently
they are far less felt as foreign elements than many
French words ; in fact, in many statistical calculations
of the proportion of native to imported words in
English, Scandinavian words have been more or less
inadvertently included in the native elements. Just as
it is impossible to speak or write in English about
higher intellectual or emotional subjects or about
fashionable mundane matters without drawing largely
upon the French (and Latin) elements, in the same
manner Scandinavian words will crop up together with
the Anglo-Saxon ones in any conversation on the
thousand nothings of daily life or on the five or six
things of paramount importance to high and low alike.
An Englishman cannot *thrive* or be *ill* or *die* without
Scandinavian words ; they are to the language what
bread and *eggs* are to the daily fare. To this element
of his language an Englishman might apply what
Wordsworth says of the daisy :

Thou unassuming common-place
Of Nature, with that homely face
And yet with something of a grace
Which Love makes for thee!

79. The form in which the words were borrowed
occasions very few remarks. Those nouns which in
Scand. had the nominative ending -*r*, did not keep it,
the kernel only of the word (= accus.) being taken
over. In one instance the Norse genitive-ending
appears in English ; the Norse phrase *á náttar þeli* 'in
the middle of the night' (*þel* means 'power, strength')
was Anglicized into *on nighter tale* (Cursor Mundi), or
bi nighter tale (Havelock, Chaucer, etc.). The -*t* in
neuters of adjectives, that distinctive Scandinavian
trait, is found in *scant*,[1] *want* and (*a*)*thwart*. Most
Norse verbs have the weak inflexion in English, as
might be expected (e.g., *die*, which in Old Scand. was
a strong verb), but there are some noteworthy exceptions, *take*, *rive*, *thrive*, that are strongly inflected as
in Scand. There is at least one interesting word with
the Scand. passive voice in -*sk* (from the reflexive
pronoun *sik*) : *busk*[2] (and *bask*[3] ?) but in English they
are treated like active forms. The shortness of the *sk*-
forms may have led to their being taken over as
inseparable wholes, for ON. *ǫðlask* and *þrivask* lost
the reflexive ending in English *addle* 'acquire, earn'
and *thrive*.[4]

As the Scandinavians and the English could understand one another without much difficulty it was
natural that many niceties of grammar should be sac-
rificed, the intelligibility of either tongue coming to
depend mainly on its mere vocabulary.[5] So when we

[1] Properly *skammt*, neuter of *skammr* 'short' ; the derived verb
skemta, Dan. *skemte* 'joke' is found in ME. *skemten*.

[2] ON. *búa-sk* 'prepare onself.'

[3] ON. *baða-sk* 'bathe oneself' (doubtful).

[4] On the form of Scandinavian words, see also Ekwall, *Anglia
Beiblatt*, 21, 47.

[5] Jespersen, *Chapters on English*, p. 37. Compare the explanation
of the similar simplification of Dutch in South Africa given by H.
Meyer, *Die Sprache der Buren* (Göttingen, 1901), p. 16.—E. Classen.

find that the wearing away and levelling of grammatical forms in the regions in which the Danes chiefly settled was a couple of centuries in advance of the same process in the more southern parts of the country, the conclusion does not seem unwarrantable that this acceleration of the tempo of linguistic simplification is due to the settlers, who did not care to learn English correctly in every minute particular and who certainly needed no such accuracy in order to make themselves understood.

80. With regard to syntax our want of adequate early texts in Scandinavia as well as in North England makes it impossible for us to state anything very definite ; but the nature of those loans which we are able to verify, warrants the conclusion that the intimate fusion of the two languages must certainly have influenced syntactical relations, and when we find in later times numerous striking correspondences between English and Danish, it seems probable that some at least of them date from the Viking settlements. It is true, for instance, that relative clauses without any pronoun are found in very rare cases in Old English ; but they do not become common till the Middle English period, when they abound ; the use of these clauses is subject to the same restrictions in both languages, so that in ninety out of a hundred instances where an Englishman leaves out the relative pronoun, a Dane would be able to do likewise, and vice versa. The rules for the omission or retention of the conjunction *that* are nearly identical. The use of *will* and *shall* in Middle English corresponds pretty nearly with Scandinavian ; if in Old English an auxiliary was used to express futurity, it was generally *sceal*, just as in modern Dutch (*zal*) ; *wile* was rare. In Modern English the older rules have been greatly modified, but in many cases where English commen-

---

Mod. Language Review, 14, 94, thinks that the prevalence of the plural ending -*s* over -*n* is due to the Danes, who had no pl. in -*n* and whose -*r* was similar to *s*.

tators on Shakespeare note divergences from modern
usage, a Dane would have used the same verb as
Shakespeare. Furness, in his note to the sentence,
'Besides it should appear' (Merch. III, 2, 289 = 275
Globe ed.), writes : 'It is not easy to define this
"should" . . . . The Elizabethan use of *should* is to
me always difficult to analyse. Compare Stephano's
question about Caliban : Where the devil should he
learn our language?' Now, a Dane would say 'det
skulde synes', and 'Hvor fanden skulde han lære vort
sprog?' Abbott (Shakesp. Grammar, §319) says
'There is a difficulty in the expression "perchance I
will"; but, from its constant recurrence, it would
seem to be a regular idiom'; a Dane, in the three
quotations given, would say *vil*. And similarly in other
instances. 'He could have done it' agrees with 'han
kunde have gjort det' as against 'er hätte es tun
können' (and French 'il aurait pu le faire'), and the
Scotch idiom 'He wad na wrang'd the vera Deil'
(Burns), 'ye wad thought Sir Arthur had a pleasure
in it' (Scott), where Caxton and the Elizabethans
could also omit *have*, has an exact parallel in Danish
'vilde gjort', etc.[1] Other points in syntax might
perhaps be ascribed to Scandinavian influence, such
as the universal position of the genitive case before its
noun (where Old English like German placed it very
often after it) ; but in these delicate matters it is not
safe to assert too much, as in fact many similarities
may have been independently developed in both
languages.[2]

---

[1] Jespersen, *Mod. Engl. Grammar*, IV, 10, 9.

[2] On cultural and literary relations between Scandinavia and
England see H. G. Leach, *Angevin Britain and Scandinavia* (Har-
vard University Press, 1921). But when it is said (p. 20) that a
Danish farmer from West Jutland has no trouble in keeping up a
friendly conversation with a Yorkshireman, credence is given to
a popular belief without any basis in facts. F. M. Stenton's paper,
The Danes in England (British Academy, 1927) deals in a very able
way with the cultural side of the Danish settlements.

Chapter V

The French

81. If with regard to the Scandinavian invasion
historical documents were so scarce that the linguistic
evidence drawn from the number and character of the
loan-words was a very important supplement to our
historical knowledge of the circumstances, the same
cannot be said of the Norman Conquest. The Normans, much more than the Danes, were felt as an alien
race ; their occupation of the country attracted much
more notice and lasted much longer ; they became the
ruling class and as such were much more spoken of in
contemporary literature and in historical records than
the comparatively obscure Scandinavian element; and
finally, they represented a higher culture than the
natives and had a literature of their own, in which
numerous direct statements and indirect hints tell us
about their doings and their relations with the native
population. No wonder, therefore, that historians
should have given much more attention to this fuller
material and to all the interesting problems connected
with the Norman conquest than to the race-mixture
attending the Scandinavian immigrations. This is
true in respect not only of political and social history,
but also of the language, in which the Norman-French
element is so conspicuous, and so easily accessible to
the student that it has been discussed very often and
from various points of view. And yet there is still
much work for future investigators to do. In accordance with the general plan of my work, I shall in this
chapter deal chiefly with what has been of permanent
importance to the future of the English language, and
endeavour to characterize the influence exercised by

French as contrasted with that exercised by other languages with which English has come into contact.

82. The Normans became masters of England, and they remained masters for a sufficiently long time to leave a deep impress on the language. The conquerors were numerous and powerful, but the linguistic influence would have been far less if they had not continued for centuries in actual contact and constant intercourse with the French of France, of whom many were induced by later kings to settle in England. We need only go through a list of French loan-words in English to be firmly convinced of the fact that the immigrants formed the upper classes of the English society after the conquest, so many of the words are distinctly aristocratic. It is true that they left the old words *king* and *queen* intact, but apart from these nearly all words relating to government and to the highest administration are French ; see, for instance, *crown, state, government* and to *govern, reign, realm* (OFr. realme, Mod. Fr. royaume), *sovereign, country, power, minister, chancellor, council* (and *counsel*), *authority, parliament, exchequer. People* and *nation,* too, were political words ; the corresponding OE. *þeod* soon went out of ordinary use. Feudalism was imported from France, and with it were introduced a number of words, such as *fief, feudal, vassal, liege,* and the names of the various steps in the scale of rank : *prince, peer, duke* with *duchess, marquis, viscount, baron.* It is, perhaps, surprising that *lord* and *lady* should have remained in esteem, and that *earl* should have been retained, *count* being chiefly used in speaking of foreigners, but the earl's wife was designated by the French word *countess,* and *court* is French, as well as the adjectives relating to court life, such as *courteous, noble, fine* and *refined. Honour* and *glory* belong to the French, and so does *heraldry,* while nearly all English expressions relating to that difficult science (*argent, gules, verdant,* etc.) are of French origin, some of them curiously distorted.

83. The upper classes, as a matter of course, took into their hands the management of military matters ; and although in some cases it was a long time before the old native terms were finally displaced (*here* and *fird*, for instance, were used till the fifteenth century when *army* began to be common), we have a host of French military words, many of them of very early introduction. Such are *war* (ME. werre, Old North Fr. werre, Central French guerre) and *peace, battle, arms, armour, buckler, hauberk, mail* (chain-mail ; OFr. maille 'mesh of a net'), *lance, dart, cutlass, banner, ensign, assault, siege*, etc. Further, *officer, chieftain* (*captain* and *colonel* are later), *lieutenant, sergeant, soldier, troops, dragoon, vessel, navy* and *admiral* (orig. *amiral* in English as in French, ultimately an Arabic word). Some words which are now used very extensively outside the military sphere were without any doubt at first purely military, such as *challenge, enemy, danger, escape* (scape), *espy* (spy), *aid, prison, hardy, gallant, march, force, company, guard*, etc.

84. Another natural consequence of the power of the Norman upper classes is that most of the terms pertaining to the law are of French origin, such as *justice, just, judge* ; *jury, court* (we have seen the word already in another sense), *suit, sue, plaintiff* and *defendant*, a *plea, plead*, to *summon, cause, assize, session, attorney, fee, accuse, crime, guile, felony, traitor, damage, dower, heritage, property, real estate, tenure, penalty, demesne, injury, privilege*. Some of these are now hardly to be called technical juridical words, and there are others which belong still more to the ordinary vocabulary of everyday life, but which were undoubtedly at first introduced by lawyers at the time when procedure was conducted entirely in French[1] ;

---

[1] From 1362 English was established as the official language spoken in the courts of justice, yet the curious mongrel language known as 'Law French' continued in use there for centuries ; Cromwell tried to break its power, but it was not finally abolished till an act of Parliament of 1731. On the position of the French

for instance, *case, marry, marriage, oust, prove, false*
(perhaps also *fault*), *heir*, probably also *male* and
female, while *defend* and *prison* are common to the
juridical and the military worlds. *Petty* (Fr. petit, was,
I suspect, introduced by the jurists in such combinations as *petty jury, petty larceny, petty constable, petty
sessions, petty averages, petty treason* (still often spelt
petit treason), etc., before it was used commonly. The
French *puis né* in its legal sense remains *puisne* in
English (in law it means 'younger or inferior in rank',
but originally 'later born'), while in ordinary language
it has adopted the spelling *puny*, as if the *-y* had been
the usual adjective ending.

85. Besides, there are a good many words that have
never become common property, but have been known
to jurists only, such as *mainour* (to be taken with the
mainour, to be caught in the very act of stealing, from
Fr. manœuvre), *jeofail* ('an oversight', the acknow-
ledgment of an error in pleading, from je faille), *cestui
que trust, cestui (a) que vie* and other phrases equally
shrouded in mystery to the man in the street. *Larceny*
has been almost exclusively the property of lawyers,
so that it has not ousted *theft* from general use ; such
words as *thief* and *steal* were of course too popular to
be displanted by French juridical terms, though
burglar is probably of French origin. It is also worth
observing how many of the phrases in which the
adjective is invariably placed after its noun are law
terms, taken over bodily from the French, e.g. *heir
male, issue male, fee simple, proof demonstrative, malice
prepense* (or, Englished, *malice aforethought*),[1] *letters
patent* (formerly also with the adjective inflected,
letters patents, Shakesp. R 2, II, 1, 202), *attorney general*
(and other combinations of *general*, all of which are
official, though some of them are not juridical).

86. As ecclesiastical matters were also chiefly under

language in England, see J. Vising, *Anglo-Norman Language and
Literature* (London, 1923).

[1] Cf. also *lords spiritual* and *lords temporal* ; the *body politic*.

the control of the higher classes, we find a great many
French words connected with the church, such as
religion, service, trinity, saviour, virgin, angel (OFr.
angele, now Fr. ange ; the OE. word engel was taken
direct from Latin, see § 38), *saint, relic, abbey, cloister,
friar* (ME. frere as in French), *clergy, parish, baptism,
sacrifice, orison, homily, altar, miracle, preach, pray,
prayer, sermon, psalter* (ME. sauter), *feast* ('religious
anniversary'). Words like *rule, lesson, save, tempt,
blame, order, nature,* which now belong to the common
language and have very extensive ranges of signification, were probably at first purely ecclesiastical
words. As the clergy were, moreover, teachers of
morality as well as of religion they introduced the whole
gamut of words pertaining to moral ideas from *virtue* to
vice : *duty, conscience, grace, charity, cruel, chaste, covet,
desire, lechery, fool* (one of the oldest meanings is
'sensual'), *jealous, pity, discipline, mercy,* and others.

87. To these words, taken from different domains,
may be added other words of more general meaning,
which are highly significant as to the relations between
the Normans and the English, such as *sir* and *madam,
master* and *mistress* with their contrast *servant* (and the
verb to *serve*), further, *command* and *obey, order, rich*
and *poor* with the nouns *riches* and *poverty* ; *money,
interest, cash, rent,* etc.

88. It is a remark that was first made by John
Wallis[1] and that has been very often repeated,
especially since Sir Walter Scott made it popular in
Ivanhoe, that while the names of several animals in
their lifetime are English (*ox, cow, calf, sheep, swine,
boar, deer*), they appear on the table with French
names (*beef, veal, mutton, pork, bacon, brawn, venison*).
This is generally explained from the masters leaving
the care of the living animals to the lower classes, while
they did not leave much of the meat to be eaten by
them. But it may with just as much right be con-
tended that the use of the French words here is due to

---

[1] *Grammatica linguae Anglicanae,* 1653.

the superiority of the French *cuisine*, which is shown
by a great many other words as well, such as *sauce,
boil, fry, roast, toast, pasty, pastry, soup, sausage, jelly,
dainty*; while the humbler *breakfast* is English, the
more sumptuous meals, *dinner* and *supper*, as well as
feasts generally, are French.

89. We see on the whole that the masters knew how
to enjoy life and secure the best things to themselves ;
note also such words as *joy* and *pleasure, delight, ease*
and *comfort* ; *flowers* and *fruits* may be mentioned in
the same category. And if we go through the different
objects or pastimes that make life enjoyable to people
having plenty of leisure (this word, too, is French) we
shall find an exceedingly large number of French
words. The *chase*[1] of course was one of the favourite
pastimes, and though the native *hunt* was never displaced, yet we find many French terms relating to the
chase, such as *brace* and *couple, leash, falcon, quarry,
warren, scent, track*. The general term *sport*, too, is of
course a French word ; it is a shortened form of *desport*
(*disport*). *Cards* and *dice* are French words, and so are
a great many words relating to different games (*part-
ner, suit, trump*), some of the most interesting being
the numerals used by card and dice players : *ace, deuce,
tray, cater, cinque, size* ; cf. Chaucer's 'Sevene is my
chaunce, and thyn is cynk and treye' (C 653).

90. The French led the fashion in the Middle Ages,
just as they do to some extent even now, so we expect
to find a great many French words relating to dress ;
in fact, in going through Chaucer's Prologue to the
Canterbury Tales, where in introducing his gallery of
figures he seldom omits to mention their dress, one will
see that in nearly all cases where etymologists have
been able to trace the special names of particular garments to their sources these are French. And of course,
such general terms as *apparel, dress, costume,* and
garment are derived from the same language.

---

[1] This is the Central French form of the word that was taken over
in a North French dialect form as *catch* (Latin *captiare*).

91. The French were the teachers of the English in most things relating to art ; not only such words as *art, beauty, colour, image, design, figure, ornament, to paint,* but also the greater number of the more special words of technical significance are French ; from architecture may be mentioned, by way of specimens : *arch, tower, pillar, vault, porch, column, aisle, choir, reredos, transept, chapel, cloister* (the last of which belong here as well as to our § 86), not to mention *palace, castle, manor, mansion,* etc. If we go through the names of the various kinds of artisans, etc., we cannot fail to be struck with the difference between the more homely or more elementary occupations which have stuck to their old native names (such as *baker, miller, smith, weaver, saddler, shoemaker, wheelwright, fisherman, shepherd,* and others), on the one hand, and on the other those which brought their practitioners into more immediate contact with the upper classes, or in which fashion perhaps played a greater part ; these latter have French names, for instance, *tailor, butcher, mason, painter, carpenter* and *joiner* (note also such words as *furniture, table, chair,* while the native name is reserved for the humbler *stool,* etc.).

92. I am afraid I have tired the reader a little with all these long lists of words. My purpose was to give abundant linguistic evidence for the fact that the French were the rich, the powerful, and the refined classes. It was quite natural that the lower classes should soon begin to imitate such of the expressions of the rich as they could catch the meaning of. They would adopt interjections and exclamations like *alas, certes, sure, adieu* ; and perhaps *verray* (later *very*) was at first introduced as an exclamation. Whole phrases were adopted : in the Ancrene Riwle (about 1225) we find (p. 268), *Deuleset* (Dieu le sait) in two manuscripts, while a third has *Crist hit wat* ; and three hundred years later we find 'As good is a becke (= a wink), as is a *dewe vow garde*' (Bale, *Three Lawes* 1, 1470). As John of Salisbury (Johannes Sarisberiensis) says

expressly in the twelfth century,[1] it was the fashion to
interlard one's speech with French words ; they were
thought modish, and that will account for the fact that
many non-technical words too were taken over, such
as *air, age* (juridical?), *arrive* (military?), *beast, change,
cheer, cover, cry, debt* (juridical?), *feeble, large, letter,
manner, matter, nurse* and *nourish, place, point, price,
reason, turn, use*, and a great many other everyday
words of very extensive employment.

93. If, then, the English adopted so many French
words because it was the fashion in every respect to
imitate their 'betters', we are allowed to connect this
adoption of *non-technical* words with that trait of their
character which in its exaggerated form has in modern
times been termed snobbism or toadyism, and which
has made certain sections of the English people more
interested in the births, deaths and especially mar-
riages of dukes and marquises than in anything else
outside their own small personal sphere.

94. But when we trace this feature of snobbishness
back to the first few centuries after the Norman conquest, we must not forget that there were great differences, so that some people would affect many French
words and others would stick as far as possible to the
native stock of words. We see this difference in the
literary works that have come down to us. In Layamon's *Brut*, written very early in the thirteenth century and amounting in all to more than 56,000 short
lines, the number of words of Anglo-French origin is
only about 150.[2] The *Orrmulum*, which was written
perhaps twenty years later, contains more than 20,000
lines, yet even Kluge, who criticizes the view that this
very tedious work contains no French words, has not
been able to find in it more than twenty-odd words of
French origin.[3] But in the contemporary prose work

---

[1] Quoted by D. Behrens, Paul's *Grundriss*, I[2], 963.

[2] Skeat, *Principles of English Etymology*, II (1891), p. 8 ; Morris,
Historical Outl. of Engl. Accidence (1885), p. 338.

[3] Kluge, *Das französische Element im Orrmulum*, Englische
Studien, XXII, p. 179.

Ancrene Riwle,[1] we find on 200 pages about 500 French words. A couple of centuries later, it would be a much harder task to count the French words in any author, as so many words had already become part and parcel of the English language ; but even then one author used many more than another. Chaucer undoubtedly employs a far greater number of French words than most other writers of his time. Nor would it be fair to ascribe all these borrowings to what I have mentioned as snobbism ; the greater a writer's familiarity with French culture and literature, the greater would be his temptation to introduce French words for everything above the commonplaces of daily life.

95. The following table shows the strength of the influx of French words at different periods ; it comprises one thousand words (the first hundred French words in the New English Dictionary for each of the first nine letters and the first 50 for *j* and *l*) and gives the half-century to which the earliest quotation in that Dictionary belongs.[2] After + I add the corresponding numbers found by A. Koszal[3] for those volumes of NED. which had not appeared when I worked up my statistics. It should be remembered that many or even most of these words, at any rate the more popular ones, had probably been in use some time before these

---

[1] This, and not *Ancren Riwle*, is the correct title. All genitive plurals in the work end in *-ene*. Miss A. Paues has been kind enough at my suggestion to look up the manuscripts and confirmed my suspicion that the form *Ancren* is due to a mistake by the editor, James Morton.

[2] I have followed the authority of the same Dictionary also in regard to the question of the origin of the words, reckoning thus as French some words which I should perhaps, myself have called Latin. Derivative words that have certainly or probably arisen in English (e.g. *daintily*, *damageable*) have been excluded, as also those perfectly unimportant words for which the NED. gives less than five quotations. Most of them cannot really be said to have ever belonged to the English language. Cf. also R. Mettig, *Die franz. Elemente im Alt- und Mittelengl.*, Engl. St., 41, 176 ff.

[3] *Bulletin de la Faculté des Lettres de Strasbourg* (Jan., 1937). The letters Q, U, and W did not yield a full hundred.

quotations. Even if, however, the average age of French words is say fifty years greater than here indicated, the table retains its value for the comparative chronology of the language :

		carried forward :	581 +526
Before 1050	2 + 0	1451—1500	76 + 68
1051—1100	2 + 1	1501—1550	84 + 80
1101—1150	1 + 2	1551—1600	91 + 89
1151—1200	15 + 11	1601—1650	69 + 63
1201—1250	64 + 39	1651—1700	34 + 48
1251—1300	127 +122	1701—1750	24 + 32
1301—1350	120 +118	1751—1800	16 + 33
1351—1400	180 +164	1801—1850	23 + 35
1401—1450	70 + 69	1851—1900	2 + 14
	581 +526		1000 +988

The list shows conclusively that the linguistic influence did not begin immediately after the conquest, and that it was strongest in the years 1251–1400, to which nearly half of the borrowings belong. Further, it will be seen that the common assumption that the age of Dryden was particularly apt to introduce new words from French is very far from being correct.

96. In a well-known passage, Robert of Gloucester (ab. 1300) speaks about the relation of the two languages in England : 'Thus,' he says, 'England came into Normandy's hand ; and the Normans at that time (*þo* ; it is important not to overlook this word) could speak only their own language, and spoke French just as they did at home, and had their children taught in the same manner, so that people of rank in this country who came of their blood all stick to the same language that they received of them, for if a man knows no French people will think little of him. But the lower classes still[1] stick to English and to their own language. I imagine there are in all the world no countries that

---

[1] *yute* '*yet*' ; sometimes curiously mistranslated, hold to their own *good* speech.

do not keep their own language except England alone. But it is well known that it is the best thing to know both languages, for the more a man knows the more is he worth.' This passage raises the question : How did common people manage to learn so many foreign words?—and how far did they assimilate them?

97. In a few cases the process of assimilation was facilitated by the fact that a French word happened to resemble an old native one ; this was sometimes the natural consequence of French having in some previous period borrowed the corresponding word from some Germanic dialect. Thus no one can tell exactly how much modern *rich* owes to OE. *rice* 'powerful, rich', and how much to French *riche* ; the noun (Fr. and ME.) *richesse* (now *riches*) supplanted the early ME. *richedom*. The old native verb *choose* was supplemented with the noun *choice*, from Fr. *choix*. OE. *hergian* and OFr. *herier, harier*, run together in Mod.E. *harry* ; OE. *hege* and Fr. *haie* run together in *hay* 'hedge, fence'. It is difficult to separate two *main*'s, one of which is OE. *mægen* 'strength, might' and the other OFr. *maine* (Latin *magnus* ; the root of both words is ultimately the same), cf. *main sea* and *main force*. The modern *gain* (noun and verb) was borrowed in the 15th century from French (*gain, gaain* ; *gagner, gaaignier*, cf. It. *guadagnare*, a Germanic loan), but it curiously coincided with an earlier noun *gain* (also spelt *gein, geyn, gayne*, etc., oldest form *gaʒhenn*), which meant 'advantage, use, avail, benefit, remedy' and a verb *gain* (*gayne, geʒʒnenn*) 'to be suitable or useful, avail, serve', both from Old Norse. When French *isle* (now *île*) was adopted, it could not fail to remind the English of their old *iegland, iland* and eventually it corrupted the spelling of the latter into *island*. *Neveu* (now spelled *nephew*) recalled OE. *nefa, meneye* (*menye*, Fr. *maisnie* 'retinue, troop') recalled *many* (OE. *menigeo*), and *lake*, the old *lacu* 'stream, river.'[1]

---

[1] This is still the meaning of *lake* in some dialects.

There is some confusion between Eng. *rest* (repose)
and OFr. *rest* (remainder). In grammar, too, there
were a few correspondences, as when nouns had
the voiceless and the corresponding verbs the voiced
consonants ; French *us—user*, now *use* sb. pronounced
[ju·s], vb. [ju·z] just as Eng. *house*, sb. [haus], vb.
[hauz] ; French *grief—griever*, Eng. *grief—grieve*, just
as *half—halve*. Note also the formation of nouns in
-*er* (*baker*, etc.), which is hardly distinguishable from
French formations in words like *carpenter* (Fr. -*ier*),
interpreter (ME. *interpretour*, Fr. -*eur*), etc. But on the
whole such more or less accidental similarities between
the two languages were few in number and could not
materially assist the English population in learning
the new words that were flooding their language.

98. A greater assistance may perhaps have been
derived from a habit which may have been common
in conversational speech, and which was at any rate
not uncommon in writing, that of using a French word
side by side with its native synonym, the latter serving
more or less openly as an interpretation of the former
for the benefit of those who were not yet familiar with
the more refined expression. Thus in the *Ancrene
Riwle* (ab. 1225) : *cherité*, þet is *luve* (p. 8) | in *des-
peraunce*, þet is in *unhope* & in *unbileave* forte beon
iboruwen (p. 8) | Understondeð þet two *manere temp-
taciuns*—two *kunne vondunges*—beoð (p. 180) | *pa-
cience*, þet is *polemodnesse* (ibid.) | *lecherie*, þet is
golnesse (p. 198) | *ignoraunce*, þet is *unwisdom* & *un-
witenesse* (p. 278). I quote from Behrens's collection
of similar collocations[1] the following instances that
prove conclusively that the native word was then
better known than the imported one : *bigamie* is un-
kinde [unnatural] þing, on engleis tale *twiewifing*
(Genesis & Exod. 449) | *twelfe iferan*, þe Freinsce heo
cleopeden *dusze pers* (Layamon, I, 1, 69) | þat craft : *to*

---

[1] *Franz. Studien*, V., 2, p. 8. Cf. also 'of whiche *tribe*, that is to
seye, *kynrede* Jesu Crist was born' (Maundeville, 67). R. Hittmair,
Aus Caxtons Vorreden, p. 21 f.

lokie in pan lufte, þe craft his ihote [is called] *astronomie* in oþer kunnes speche [in a speech of a different kind] (ib. II, 2, 598). It is well worth observing that in all these cases the French words are perfectly familiar to a modern reader, while he will probably require an explanation of the native words that served then to interpret the others. In Chaucer we find similar double expressions, but they are now introduced for a totally different purpose ; the reader is evidently supposed to be equally familiar with both, and the writer uses them to heighten or strengthen the effect of the style[1] ; for instance : He coude songes *make* and wel *endyte* (A 95) = Therto he coude *endyte* and *make* a thing (A 325) | *faire* and *fetisly* (A 124 and 273) | *swinken* with his handes and *laboure* (A 186) | Of studie took he most *cure* and most *hede* (A 303) | *Poynaunt* and *sharp* (A 352) | At sessiouns ther was he *lord* and *sire* (A 355).[2] In Caxton this has become quite a mannerism, see, e.g.: I shal so *awreke* and *avenge* this trespace (Reynard 56, cf. p. 116, *advenge* and *wreke* it) | in *honour* and *worship* (ib. p. 56) | *olde* and *auncyent* doctours (p. 62) | *feblest* and *wekest* (p. 64) | I toke a *glasse* or a *mirrour* (p. 83) | Now ye shal here of the *mirrour* ; the *glas* . . . (p. 84) | *good* ne *proffyt* (p. 86) | *fowle* and *dishonestly* (p. 94) | *prouffyt* and *fordele* (p. 103). It will be observed that with the exception of the last word, the language has preserved in all cases both the synonyms that Caxton uses side by side, so that we may consider this part of the English vocabulary as settled towards the end of the fifteenth century.

[1] Cf. F. Karpf, *Studien zur Syntax* . . . *Chaucers*, 1930, p. 103 ff. This use of two expressions for the same idea is extremely common in the middle ages and the beginning of the modern period, and it is not confined to those cases where one was a native and the other an imported word ; see Kellner, *Engl. Studien*, XX, p. 11 ff. (1895) ; Greenough and Kittredge, *Words and their Ways*, p. 113 ff.; so also in Danish, see Vilh. Andersen in *Dania*, p. 80 ff. (1890), and *Danske Studier*, 1893, p. 7 ff.

[2] Cf. also, Curteis he was, lowly, and servisable (A 99) ; Curteys he was, and lowly, of servyse A 250).

99. Many of the French words, such as *cry, claim, state, poor, change,* and, indeed, most of the words enumerated above (§ 82–92), and, one might say, nearly all the words taken over before 1350 and not a few of those of later importation, have become part and parcel of the English language, so that they appear to us all just as English as the pre-Conquest stock of native words. But, a great many others have never become so popular. There are a great many gradations between words of everyday use and such as are not at all understood by the common people, and to the latter class may sometimes belong words which literary people would think familiar to everybody. Hyde Clark relates an anecdote of a clergyman who blamed a brother preacher for using the word *felicity,* 'I do not think all your hearers understood it ; I should say *happiness.*' 'I can hardly think,' said the other, 'that any one does not know what *felicity* means, and we will ask this ploughman near us. Come hither, my man ! you may have been at church and heard the sermon ; you heard me speak of *felicity* ; do you know what it means?' 'Ees, sir !' 'Well, what does *felicity* mean?' 'Summut in the inside of a pig, but I can't say altogether what.'[1] Note also the way in which Touchstone addresses the rustic in *As You Like It* (V., 1, 52), 'Therefore, you Clowne, abandon,—which is in the vulgar leave,—the societie—which in the boorish is companie,—of this female,—which in the common is woman ; which together is, abandon the society of this Female, or, Clowne, thou perishest ; or, to thy better understanding, dyest.'

100. From what precedes we are now in a position to understand some at least of the differences that have developed in course of time between two synonyms when both have survived, one of them native, the other French. The former is always nearer the nation's heart than the latter, it has the strongest

---

[1] *A Grammar of the English Tongue,* 4th ed., London, 1879, p.61.

associations with everything primitive, fundamental, popular, while the French word is often more formal, more polite, more refined and has a less strong hold on the emotional side of life. A *cottage* is finer than a *hut*, and fine people often live in a cottage, at any rate in summer. The word *bill* was too vulgar and familiar to be applied to a hawk, which had only a *beak* (the French term, whereas *bill* is the A.S. *bile*). 'Ye shall say, this hauke has a large *beke*, or a short *beke* and call it not *bille*' (Book of St. Alban's, fol. a 6, back).[1] To *dress* means to adorn, deck, etc., and thus generally presupposes a finer garment than the old word to *clothe*, the wider signification of which it seems, however, to be more and more appropriating to itself. *Amity* means 'friendly relations, especially of a public character between states or individuals', and thus lacks the warmth of *friendship*. The difference between *help* and *aid* is thus indicated in the Funk-Wagnalls Dictionary : '*Help* expresses greater dependence and deeper need than *aid*. In extremity we say "God *help* me!" rather than "God *aid* me!" In time of danger we cry "*help! help!*" rather than "*aid! aid!*" To *aid* is to second another's own exertions. We can speak of *helping* the helpless, but not of *aiding* them. *Help* includes *aid*, but *aid* may fall short of the meaning of *help*.' All this amounts to the same thing as saying that *help* is the natural expression, belonging to the indispensable stock of words, and therefore possessing more copious and profounder associations than the more literary and accordingly colder word *aid* ; cf. also *assist*. *Folk* has to a great extent been superseded by *people*, chiefly on account of the political and social employment of the word ; Shakespeare rarely uses *folk* (four times) and *folks* (ten times), and the word is evidently a low-class word with him ; it is rare in the Authorized Version, and Milton never uses it ; but in recent usage *folk* has been gaining ground, partly, perhaps, from antiqua-

---

[1] Skeat, *The Works of G. Chaucer*, vol. III, p. 261.

rian and dialectal causes. *Hearty* and *cordial* made
their appearance in the language at the same time (the
oldest quotations 1380 and 1386, NED.), but their
force is not the same, for 'a hearty welcome' is warmer
than 'a cordial welcome', and *hearty* has many applications that *cordial* has not (heartfelt, sincere;
vigorous : a hearty slap on the back ; abundant : a
hearty meal), etc. *Saint* smacks of the official recognition by the Catholic Church, while *holy* refers much
more to the mind. *Matin(s)* is used only with reference
to church service, while *morning* is the ordinary word.
Compare also *darling* with *favourite*, *deep* with *profound*, *lonely* with *solitary*, *indeed* with *in fact*, *to give*
or *to hand* with *to present* or *to deliver*, *love* with
charity, etc.

101. In some cases the chief difference between the
native word and the French synonym is that the
former is more colloquial and the latter more literary,
e.g. *begin—commence*, *hide—conceal*, *feed—nourish*,
hinder—prevent, *look for—search for*, *inner* and *outer—
interior* and *exterior*, and many others. In a few cases,
however, the native word is more literary. *Valley* is
the everyday word, and *dale* has only lately been introduced into the standard language from the dialects of
the hilly northern counties. *Action* has practically
supplanted *deed* in ordinary language, so that the
latter can be reserved for more dignified speech.

102. In spite of the intimate contact between
French and English it sometimes happens that French
words which have been introduced into other Germanic languages and belong to their everyday
vocabulary are not found in English or are there much
more felt to be foreign intruders than in German or
Danish. This is true for instance of *friseur, manchette,
réplique*, of *gêne* and the verb *gêner* (the NED. has no
instances of it, but a few are found in the Stanford
Dict.). *Serviette* is rarer than *napkin*. *Atelier* is not
common ; it occurs in Thackeray's *The Newcomes*,
p. 242, where immediately afterwards the familiar

word *studio* is used : did English artists go more to
Italy and less to Paris to learn their craft than their
Scandinavian and German confrères? To the same
class belong the following words, which, when found
in English books, are generally indicated to be foreign
by italic letters : *naïve*, *bizarre*, and *motif*—the last
word an interesting recent doublet of *motive*.

103. As the grammatical systems of the two languages
were very different, a few remarks must be made here
about the form in which French words were adopted.
Substantives and adjectives were nearly always taken
over in the accusative case, which differed in most
words from the nominative in having no *s*. The latter
ending is, however, found in a few words, such as
fitz (Fitzherbert, etc.; in French, too, the nominative
fils has ousted the old acc. *fil* ; *fitz* is an Anglo-Norman
spelling), *fierce* (OFr. nom. *fiers*, acc. *fier*), *Piers* and
James.[1] In the plural, Old French had a nominative
without any ending and an accusative in *-s*, and
English popular instinct naturally associated the
latter form with the native plural ending in *-es*.[2]
In course of time those words which had for a long
time, in English as in French, formed their plural
without any ending (e.g. *cas*) were made to conform
with the general rule (sg. *case*, pl. *cases*).[3] French

---

[1] But from the accusative *Jame* (e.g. Ancrene, R. 10), Chaucer
has *by seint Jame* (riming with *name*, D 1443); hence *Jem*, *Jim*.
A similar vacillation is found in the name *Steven*, *Stephen*, where
now the *s*-less form has prevailed, but where formerly the Fr. nom.
was also found (seynt stevyns, Malory, 104). Where the French
inflexion was irregular, owing to Latin stress shifting, etc., the
accusative was adopted, in *emperor* (*-our*, OFr. nom. *emperere*),
companion (OFr. nom. *compain*), *neveu*, *nephew* (OFr. nom. *nies*) and
others, but the nom. is kept in *sire* (OFr. acc. *seignor*), *mayor* (OFr.
maire, acc. *majeur*).

[2] The prevalence of the *-s* plural in English cannot possibly be
due to French influence, see *Progress in Language*, p. 169 = *Chapters
on English*, p. 33.

[3] Note *invoice*, *trace* (part of a horse's harness), and *quince*, where
the French plural ending now forms part of the English singular;
cf. Fr. *envoi*, *trait*, *coign*.

adjectives had the *s* added to them just like French
nouns, and we find a few adjectives with the plural *s*,
as in *the goddes celestials* (Chaucer) ; *letters patents*
survived as a fixed group till the time of Shakespeare
(§ 85). But the general rule was to treat French
adjectives exactly like English ones.

104. As to the verbs, the rule is that the stem of the
French present plural served as basis for the English
form ; thus (*je survis*), *nous survivons, vous survivez,
ils survivent* became *survive* (*je résous*), *résolvons*, etc.,
became *resolve*, OFr. (*je desjeun*), *nous disnons*, etc.,
became *dine* ; thus is explained the frequent ending
-ish, in *punish, finish*, etc. English *bound* (to leap),
accordingly, cannot be the French *bondir*, which would
have yielded *bondish*, but is an English formation from
the noun *bound*, which is the French *bond*. I think
that *levy* is similarly formed on the noun *levy*, which
is Fr. *levée* ; but in *sally* the *y* represents the *i* which
made the Fr. *ll mouillé*. Where the French infinitive
was imported it was generally in a substantival
function, as in *dinner, remainder, attainder, rejoinder*,
cf. the verbs *dine, remain, attain, rejoin* ; so also the
law terms *merger, user* and *misnomer*. Still we have a
few verbs in which the ending *-er* can hardly be anything else but the French infinitive ending : *render*
(which is thereby kept distinct from *rend*), *surrender*,
tender (where the doublet *tend* also exists), and perhaps *broider* (*embroider*). There is a curious parallel
to the Norse *bask* and *busk* (79) in *saunter*, where the
French reflective pronoun has become fixed as an
inseparable element of the word, from *s'auntrer*,
another form for *s'aventurer*, 'to adventure oneself'.

105. French words have, as a matter of course,
participated in all the sound changes that have taken
place in English since their adoption. Thus words
with the long [i] sound have had it diphthongized into
[ai], e.g. *fine, price, lion*. The long [u], written *ou*,
has similarly become [au], e.g. OFr. *espouse* (Mod. Fr.
épouse), ME. *spouse*, pronounced [spu·ze], now pron.

[spauz], Fr. *tour*, Mod. E. *tower*. Compare also the treatment of the vowels in *grace, change, beast* (OFr. *beste*), *ease* (Fr. *aise*), etc. Such changes of loan-words are seen everywhere : they are brought about gradually and insensibly. But there is another change which has often been supposed to have come about in a different manner. A great many words are now stressed on the first syllable which in French were stressed on the final syllable, and this is often ascribed to the inability of the English to imitate the French accentuation. All English words, it is said, had the stress on the first syllable, and this habit was unconsciously extended to foreign words on their first adoption into the language. We see this manner of treating foreign words in Icelandic at the present day. But the explanation does not hold good in our case. English had a few words with unstressed first syllable (*be-, for-*, etc., see above, § 25), and as a matter of fact French words in English were for centuries accented in the French manner, as shown conclusively by Middle English poetry. It was only gradually that more and more words had their accent shifted on to its present place. The causes of this shifting were the same as are elsewhere at work in the same direction.[1] In many words the first syllable was felt as psychologically the most important one, as in *punish, finish, matter, manner, royal, army* and other words ending with meaningless or formative syllables. The initial syllable very often received the accent of contrast. In modern speech we stress the otherwise unstressed syllables to bring out a contrast clearly, as in 'not *op*pose but *sup*pose' or 'If on the one hand speech gives *ex*pression to ideas, on the other hand it receives *im*pressions from them' (Romanes, *Mental Evolution in Man*, p. 238), and in the same manner we must imagine that in the days when *real, formal, object, subject* and a hundred similar words were normally

---

[1] See the detailed exposition in my *Modern English Grammar* (Heidelberg, Carl Winter), I, 1909, ch. V.

stressed on the last syllable, they were so often contrasted with each other that the modern accentuation became gradually the habitual one. This will explain the accent of *January*, *February*, *cavalry*, *infantry*, *primary*, *orient*, and other words. An equally powerful principle is rhythm, which tends to avoid two consecutive strong syllables ; compare modern *go down*ǀ*stairs*, but *the* ǀ*downstairs room, she is fif*ǀ*teen*, but ǀ*fifteen* ǀ*years*. Chaucer stresses many words in the French manner, except when they precede a stressed syllable, in which case the accent is shifted, thus *co*ǀ*syn* (cousin), but ǀ*cosyn myn* ; *in felici*ǀ*te par*ǀ*fit*, but *a* ǀ*verray* ǀ*parfit* ǀ*gentil* ǀ*knight* ; *se*ǀ*cre* (secret), but in ǀ*secre wyse*, etc. An instructive illustration is found in such a line as this (*Cant. Tales*, D. 1486) :

In ǀ*divers* ǀ*art and in di*ǀ*vers fi*ǀ*gures*.

These principles—value-stressing, contrast, rhythm —will explain all or most of the instances in which English has shifted the French stress ; but it is evident that it took a very long time before the new forms of the words which arose at first only occasionally through their influence were powerful enough finally to supplant the older forms.[1]

106. Not long after the intrusion of the first French words we begin to see the first traces of a phenomenon which was to attain very great proportions and which must now be termed one of the most prominent features of the language, namely hybridism. Strictly speaking, we have a hybrid (a composite word formed of elements from different languages) as soon as an English inflexional ending is added to a French word, as in the genitive *the Duke's children* or the superlative *noblest*, etc., and from such instances we rise by insensible gradations to others, in which the fusion is more surprising. From the very first we find verbal

---

[1] In many recent borrowings the accent is not shifted, cf. *machine*. *intrigue*, where the retention of the French *i*-sound is another sign that the words are of comparatively modern introduction.

nouns in *-ing* or *-ung* formed from French verbs
(indeed, they are found at a time when they could not
be formed from every native verb, § 197), e.g.
prechinge ; *riwlunge* (Ancrene Riwle) ; *scornunge* and
servinge (Layamon) ; *spusinge* (Owl and N.). Other
instances of English endings added to French words
are *faintness* (from the end of the fourteenth century),
closeness (half a century later), *secretness* (Chaucer
secreenesse, B 773), *simpleness* (Shakespeare and
others), *materialness* (Ruskin), *abnormalness* (Benson),
etc. Further, a great many adjectives in *-ly* (courtly,
princely, etc.) and, of course, innumerable adverbs
with the same ending (faintly, easily, nobly[1]) ; adjectives
in *-ful* (beautiful, dutiful, powerful, artful) and *-less* (art-
less, colourless) ; nouns in *-ship* (courtship, companionship) and *-dom* (dukedom, martyrdom) and so forth.

107. While hybrid words of this kind are found in
comparatively great numbers in most languages,
hybrids of the other kind, i.e. composed of a native
stem and a foreign ending, are in most languages much
rarer than in English. Before such hybrids could be
formed, there must have been already in the language
so great a number of foreign words with the same
ending that the formation would be felt to be perfectly
transparent. Here are to be mentioned the numerous
hybrids in *-ess* (shepherdess, goddess ; Wycliffe has
dwelleresse ; in a recent volume I have found 'seeress
and prophetess'), in *-ment* (endearment and enlighten-
ment are found from the 17th century, but bewilder-
ment not before the 19th ; wonderment, frequent in
Thackeray ; oddment, R. Kipling, hutment), in *-age*
mileage, acreage, leakage, shrinkage, wrappage, break-
age, cleavage, roughage, shortage, etc.) ; in *-ance*
(hindrance, used in the fifteenth century in the mean-

---

[1] Also *naïvely*, used by Pope, Ruskin, Leslie Stephen, and many
others. But some have an unwarranted aversion to the word. In
the *New Statesman* (Dec. 19, 1914) I find : 'In Hardy's elegy on
Swinburne there occurs the horrid hybrid, "naïvely"—a neologism
exactly calculated, one would suppose, to make the classic author
of Atalanta turn in his grave' (L. Strachey).

ing 'injury'; in the signification now usual it is found
as early as 1526, and perhaps we may infer from its
occurring neither in the Bible, nor in Shakespeare,
Milton and Pope, that it was felt to be a bastard,
though Locke, Cowper, Wordsworth, Shelley and
Tennyson admit it; forbearance, originally a legal
term; furtherance); in -*ous* (murderous; thunderous;
slumberous is used by Keats and Carlyle); in -*ry*
(fishery, bakery, etc.; gossipry, Mrs. Browning;
Irishry; forgettery, jocularly formed after memory);
in -*ty* (oddity, womanity, nonceword after humanity);
in -*fy* (fishify, Shakespeare; snuggify, Ch. Lamb;
Torify, Ch. Darwin; scarify, Fielding; tipsify, Thackeray; funkify, speechify[1]) with the corresponding
nouns in -*fication*: uglification, Shelley.[2]

108. One of the most fertile English derivative endings is -*able*, which has been used in a great number of
words besides those French ones which were taken
over ready made (such as *agreeable, variable, tolerable*).
In comparatively few cases it is added to substantives
(*serviceable, companionable, marriageable, peaceable,
seasonable*). Its proper sphere of usefulness is in forming adjectives from verbs, rarely in an active sense
(*suitable* = that suits, *unshrinkable*), but generally in
a passive sense (*bearable* = that can or may be borne).
Thus we have now *drinkable, eatable, steerable* (bal-
loons), *weavable, unutterable, answerable, punishable,
unmistakable*, etc., and hundreds of others, so that
everybody has a feeling that he is free to form a new
adjective of this kind as soon as there is any necessity
for, or convenience in, using it, just as he feels no
hesitation in adding -*ing* to any verb, new or old. And
of course, no one ever objects to these adjectives (or
the corresponding nouns in -*ability*) because they are
hybrids or bastards, any more than one would object
to forms like *acting* or *remembering* on the same score.

---

[1] Cf. also 'Daphne—before she was happily treeified', Lowell,
Fable for Critics.

[2] See below on hybrids with Latin and Greek endings (§ 123).

109. These adjectives have now become so indispensable that the want is even felt of forming them from composite verbal expressions, such as *get at*. But though *get-at-able* and *come-at-able* are pretty frequently heard in conversation, most people shrink from writing or printing them. Sterne has *come-at-ability*, Congreve *uncome-atable*, Smiles *get-atability*, and George Eliot in a letter, *knock-upable*. Tennyson, too, writes in a jocular letter, 'thinking of you as no longer the *comeatable, runupableto, smokeablewith* J. S. of old'. Note here the place of the preposition in the last two adjectives, and compare 'enough to make the house *unliveable in* for a month' (*The Idler*, May 1892, 366), 'the husband being fairly good-natured and *livable-with*' (Bernard Shaw, *Ibsenism*, 41), and 'she is *unspeakable to*' (Benson, *Dodo the Second*, 121). It is obvious that these adjectives are too clumsy to be ever extensively used in serious writing. But there is another way out of the difficulty which is really much more conformable to the genius of the language, namely, to leave out the preposition in all those cases where there can be no doubt of the preposition understood. *Unaccountable* (= that cannot be accounted *for*) has long been accepted by everybody; I have found it, for instance, in Congreve, Addison, Swift, Goldsmith, De Quincey, Miss Austen, Dickens and Hawthorne. *Indispensable* has been—well, indispensable, for two centuries and a half. *Laughable* is used by Shakespeare, Dryden, Carlyle, Thackeray, etc. *Dependable, disposable, objectionable,* and *available* are in general use.[1] All this being granted, it is difficult to see why *reliable* should have been one of the most abused words. It is certainly formed in accordance with the fundamental laws of the lan-

---

[1] Jane Austen writes, 'There will be work for five summers before the place is *liveable*' (Mansf. Park, 216) = the above-mentioned *liveable-in*. Cf. below *gazee* and others in -*ee* (§ 111). The principle of formation is the same as in *waiter*, 'he who waits *on* people', *caller*, 'he who calls *on* some one'.

guage ; it is short and unambiguous, and what more should be needed? Those who measure a word by its age will be glad to hear that Miss Mabel Peacock has found it in a letter, bearing the date of 1624, from the pen of the Rev. Richard Mountagu, who eventually became a bishop. And those who do not like using a word unless it has been accepted by great writers will find a formidable array of the best names in Fitz-edward Hall's list[1] of authors who have used the word.[2] It is curious to note that the word which is always extolled at the expense of *reliable* as an older and nobler word, namely *trustworthy*, is really much younger ; it has not been traced further back than the beginning of the nineteenth century ; besides, any impartial judge will find its sound less agreeable to the ear on account of the consonant group—*stw*—and the heavy second syllable. But then the synonym *trusty* avoids that fault.

110. Fitzedward Hall in speaking about the recent word *aggressive*[3] says, 'It is not at all certain whether the French *agressif* suggested *aggressive*, or was suggested by it. They may have appeared independently of each other'. The same remark applies to a great many other formations on a French or Latin basis ; even if the several components of a word are Romanic, it by no means follows that the word was first used by a Frenchman. On the contrary, the greater facility and the greater boldness in forming new words and turns of expression which characterizes English generally in contradistinction to French, would in many

---

[1] On English adjectives in *-able*, with special reference to *reliable*, (London, 1877). Fitzedward Hall reverted to the subject on several other occasions.

[2] Coleridge, Sir Robert Peel, John Stuart Mill, Wilberforce, Dickens, Charles Reade, Walter Bagehot, Anthony Trollope, Newman, Gladstone, S. Baring-Gould, Sir Leslie Stephen, H. Maudsley, Saintsbury, Henry Sweet, Thomas Arnold. I leave out, rather arbitrarily I fear, more than a score of the names given by Fitzedward Hall.

[3] *Modern English*, 314.

cases speak in favour of the assumption that an innovation is due to an English mind. This I take to be true with regard to *dalliance*, which is so frequent in ME. (*dalyaunce*, etc.), while it has not been recorded in French at all. The wide chasm between the most typical English meaning of *sensible* (a sensible man, a sensible proposal) and those meanings which it shares with French *sensible* and Lat. *sensibilis*, probably shows that in the former meaning the word was an independent English formation. *Duration* as used by Chaucer may be a French word ; it then went out of the language, and when it reappeared after the time of Shakespeare it may just as well have been re-formed in England as borrowed ; *duratio* does not seem to have existed in Latin. *Intensitas* is not a Latin word, and *intensity* is older than *intensité*.

111. In not a few cases, the English soil has proved more fertilizing than the French soil from which words were transplanted. In French, for instance, *mutin* has fewer derivatives than in English, where we have *mutine* sb., *mutine* vb. (Shakespeare), *mutinous*, *mutinously*, *mutinousness*, *mutiny* sb., *mutiny* vb., *mutineer* sb., *mutineer* vb., *mutinize*, of which it is true that *mutine* and *mutinize* are now extinct. We see the same thing in such a recent borrowing as *clique*, which stands alone in French while in English two centuries have provided us with *cliquedom*, *cliqueless*, *cliquery*, *cliquomania*, *cliquomaniac*, *clique* vb., *cliquish*, *cliquishness*, *cliquism*, *cliquy* or *cliquey*. From *due* we have *duty*, to which no French correspondent word has been found in France itself, although *dueté*, *duity*, *deweté* are found in Anglo-French writers ; in English *duty* is found from the 13th century, and we have moreover *duteous*, *dutiable*, *dutied*, *dutiful*, *dutifully*, *dutifulness*, *dutiless*, none of which appear to be older than the 16th century. *Aim*, the noun as well as the verb, is now among the most useful and indispensable words in the English vocabulary and it has some derivatives, such as *aimer*, *aimful*, and *aimless*, but in French the

two verbs from which it originates, *esmer* < Lat.
æstimare, and *aasmer*, < Lat. adæstimare, have totally
disappeared. Note also the differentiations of the
words *strange* and *estrange*, *state* and *estate*;[1] of *entry*
(< Fr. *entrée*[2]) and *entrance*, while in French *entrance*
has been given up ; and the less perfect one of *guaran-
ty* (action) and *guarantee* (person), not to speak of
warrant and *warranty*. The extent to which foreign
speech-material has been turned to account is really
astonishing, as is seen, perhaps, most clearly in the
extensive use of the derivative ending *-ee*. This was
originally the French participial ending *-é* used in a
very few cases such as *apelé*, E. *appelee* as opposed to
apelor, E. *appellor*, *nominee*, *presentee*, etc., and then
gradually extended in legal use to words in which
such a formation would be prohibited in French by
formal as well as syntactical reasons : *vendee* is the
man to whom something is sold (l'homme à qui on a
vend*u* quelque chose), cf. also *referee*, *lessee*, *trustee*,
etc. Now these formations are no longer restricted
to juridical language, and in general literature there
is some disposition to turn this ending to account as
a convenient manner of forming passive nouns ;
Goldsmith and Richardson have *lovee*, Sterne speaks
of 'the mortgager and mortgagee . . . the jester
and jestee'; further the *gazee* (De Quincey) = the one
gazed *at*, *staree* (Edgeworth), *cursee* and *laughee*
(Carlyle), *flirtee*, *floggee*, *wishee*, *bargainee*, *beatee*, *ex-
aminee*, *callee* (our callee = the man we call on),
etc. Such a word as *trusteeship* is eminently characteristic of the composite character of the language :
Scandinavian *trust* + a French ending used in a
manner unparalleled in French + an old English
ending.

112. French influence has not been restricted to one
particular period (see § 95), and it is interesting to

---

[1] Compare also the juridical *estray* and the ordinary *stray*.

[2] This word has recently been re-adopted : *entrée*, 'made-dish
served between the chief courses'.

compare the forms of old loan-words with those of
recent ones, in which we can recognize traces of the
changes the French language has undergone since
medieval times. Where a *ch* in an originally French
word is pronounced as in *change, chaunt,* etc. (with the
sound-group tʃ), the loan is an old one ; where it is
sounded as in *champagne* (with simple ʃ), we have a
recent loan. *Chief* is thus shown to belong to the first
period, while its doublet *chef* (= chef de cuisine) is
much more modern. It is curious that two pet-names
should now be spelled in the same way *Charlie*,
although they are distinct in pronunciation : the masculine is derived from the old loan *Charles* and has,
therefore, the sound [tʃ], the feminine is from the
recent loan *Charlotte* with [ʃ]. Similarly *g* as in *age*,
siege, judge, pronounced [dʒ], is indicative of old loans,
while the pronunciation [ʒ] is only found in modern
adoptions, such as *rouge*. Initially, however, [ʒ] is
not found in English without a preposed [d] ; thus
gentle, genteel and *jaunty* represent three layers of
borrowing from the same word, but they have all of
them the same initial sound. Other instances of the
same French word appearing in more than one shape
according to its age in English are *saloon* and *salon*,
suit and *suite*, *liquor* and *liqueur, rout* 'big party,
retreat' and *route* (the diphthong in the former word
is an English development of the long [u] § 105),
quart, pronounced [kwɔ·t], and *quart*, pronounced
[ka·t], 'a sequence of four cards in piquet', cf. also
quarte or *carte* in fencing.

113. In some cases, we witness a curious reshaping
of an early French loan-word, by which it is made more
like the form into which the French has meanwhile
developed. This, of course, can only be explained by
the uninterrupted contact between the two nations.
Chaucer had *viage* just as Old French, but now the
word is *voyage* ; *leal* has given way to *loyal*,[1] *marchis* to
marquis ; the noun *flaute* and the verb *floyten* are now

---

[1] Both forms are used together in Dickens, *Our Mutual Friend*, 49.

made into *flute* like Mod. Fr. *flûte*.[1] Similarly the
signification of ME. *douten* like that of OFr. *douter*
was 'to fear' (cf. *redoubt*), but now in both languages
this signification has disappeared. *Danger* was at first
adopted in the Old French sense of 'dominion, power',
but the present meaning was developed in France
before it came to England. The many parallelisms
in the employment of *cheer* and Fr. *chère* could not
very well have arisen independently in both languages
at once. This continued contact constitutes a well-
marked contrast between the French and the Scandinavian influence, which seems to have been broken off
somewhat abruptly after the Norman conquest.

---

[1] Cf. below the Latinizing of many French words (§ 116).

Chapter VI

Latin and Greek

114. Although Latin has been read and written in England from the Old English period till our own days, so that there has been an uninterrupted possibility of Latin influence on the English language, yet we may with comparative ease separate the latest stratum of loans from the two strata already considered (in § 32, 39). It embodies especially abstract or scientific words, adopted exclusively through the medium of writing and never attaining to the same degree of popularity as words belonging to the older strata. The words adopted are not all of Latin origin, there are perhaps more Greek than Latin elements in them, if we count the words in a big dictionary. Still the more important words are Latin and most of the Greek words have entered into English through Latin, or have, at any rate, been Latinized in spelling and endings before being used in English, so that we have no occasion here to deal separately with the two stocks. The great historical event, without which this influence would never have assumed such gigantic dimensions, was the revival of learning. Through Italy and France the Renaissance came to be felt in England as early as the fourteenth century, and since then the invasion of classical terms has never stopped, although the multitude of new words introduced was greater, perhaps, in the fourteenth, the sixteenth and the nineteenth than in the intervening centuries. The same influence is conspicuous in all European languages, but in English it has been stronger than in any other language, French perhaps excepted. This fact cannot, I think, be principally due to any greater zeal for classical learning on the part of the English than of other nations. The reason seems rather to be that the natural power of resistance possessed by a

Germanic tongue against these alien intruders had been already broken in the case of the English language by the wholesale importation of French words. They paved the way for the Latin words which resembled them in so many respects, and they had already created in English minds that predilection for foreign words which made them shrink from consciously coining new words out of native material. If French words were more *distingués* than English ones. Latin words were still more so, for did not the French themselves go to Latin to enrich their own vocabulary ? The first thing noticeable about this class of Latin importation is, therefore, that it cannot be definitely separated from the French loans.

115. A great many words may with equal right be ascribed to French and to Latin, since their English form would be the same in both cases and the first users would probably know both languages.[1] This is especially the case with those words which in French are not popular survivals of spoken Latin words, but later borrowings from literary Latin, *mots savants*, as Brachet termed them in contradistinction to *mots populaires*. As examples of words that may have been taken from either language, I shall mention only *grave*, *gravity*, *consolation*, *solid*, *infidel*, *infernal*, *position*.

116. A curious consequence of the Latin influence during and after the Renaissance was that quite a number of French words were remodelled into closer resemblance with their Latin originals. Chaucer uses *descrive* (riming with *on lyve* 'alive', H. 121 ; still in Scotch), but in the 16th century the form *describe* makes its appearance. *Perfet* and *parfet* (Fr. *perfait*, *parfait*) were the normal English forms for centuries. Milton writes *perfeted* (*Areop.*, 10); but the *c* was introduced from the Latin, at first in spelling only, but afterwards in pronunciation as well.[2] Similarly *verdit*

---

[1] Cf. Luick, *Histor. Grammatik*, p. 70 f.

[2] Bacon writes (*New Atlantis*, 15) : all nations have *enterknowledge* one of another. In recent similar words, *inter-* is always used.

has given way to *verdict*. Where Chaucer had *peynture*
as in French (peinture), *picture* is now the established
form. The Latin prefix *ad* is now seen in *advice* and
adventure, while Middle English had *avis* (*avys*) and
aventure. The latter form is still retained in the phrase
at aventure, where, however, *a* has been apprehended
as the indefinite article (at a venture), and another
remnant of the old form is disguised in *saunter* (Fr.
s'aventurer 'to adventure oneself'). *Avril* (avrille) has
been Latinized into *April*; and a modern reader does
not easily recognize his *February* in ME. *feouerele* or
feouerrere[1] (u = v, cf. *février*). In *debt* and *doubt*, which
used to be *dette* and *doute* as in French, the spelling
only has been affected ; compare also *victuals* for
vittles (Fr. *vitailles*, cf. *battle* from *bataille*). Similarly
bankerota (cf. Italian), *banqueroute*, *bankrout* (Shakesp.)
had to give way to *bankrupt*; the oldest example of the
p-form in the NED. dates from **1533**. The form
langage was used for centuries, before it became
language by a curious crossing of French and Latin
forms. *Egal* was for more than two centuries the
commoner form ; *equal*, now the only recognized form,
was apparently a more learned form and was used for
instance in Chaucer's *Astrolabe*, while in his poems he
writes *egal*; Shakespeare generally has *equal*, but *egal*
is found a few times in some of the old editions of his
plays. Tennyson tries to re-introduce *egality* by the
side of *equality*, not as an ordinary word, however, but
as applied to France specially ('That cursed France
with her egalities !' *Aylmer's Field*). French and Latin
forms coexist, more or less differentiated, in *complaisance* and *complacence* (*complacency*), *genie* (rare)
and *genius*, *base* and *basis* (Greek). *Certainty* (Fr.) and
certitude (Lat.) are often used indiscriminately, but
there is now a tendency to restrict the latter to merely
subjective certainty, as in Cardinal Newman's 'my
argument is : that *certitude* was a habit of mind, that
certainty was a quality of propositions ; that prob-

---

[1] Juliana, p. 78, 79.

abilities which did not reach to logical *certainty*, might suffice for a mental *certitude*', etc.[1] Note also the curious difference made between *critic* with stress on the first syllable, adjective[2] and agent noun (from Lat. or Greek direct? or through French?) and *critique* with stress on the second syllable, action noun (late borrowing from Fr.) ; Pope uses *critick'd* as a participle (stress on the first), while a verb *critique* with stress on the last syllable is found in recent use ; *criticize*, which since Milton has been the usual verb, is a pseudo-Greek formation.

117. Intricate relations between French and Latin are sometimes shown in derivatives: *colour* is from French, as is evident from the vowel in the first syllable [ʌ]; but in *discoloration* the second syllable is sometimes made [kɔl] as from Latin, and sometimes [kʌl] as from French. Compare also *example* from French, *exemplary* from Latin. *Machine* with *machinist* and *machinery* are from the French, witness the pronunciation [mə'ʃi·n]; but *machinate* and *machination* are taken direct from Latin and accordingly pronounced [mækineit, mæki'neiʃən] ; so these two groups which ought by nature to belong together are kept apart, and no one knows whether the obsolete *machinal* should go with one or the other group, some dictionaries pronouncing [mə'ʃi·nəl] and other ['mækinəl]—a suggestive symptom of the highly artificial state of the language !

118. It would be idle to attempt to indicate the number of Latin and Greek words in the English language, as each new treatise on a scientific subject adds to their number. But it is interesting to see what proportion of the Latin vocabulary has passed into English. Professors J. B. Greenough and G. L. Kittredge have counted the words beginning with A in Harper's Latin Dictionary, excluding proper names, doublets, parts of verbs, and adverbs in *-e* and *-ter*. 'Of the three thousand words there catalogued, one

---

[1] *Apologia pro Vita Sua* (London, 1900), p. 20.
[2] With the by-form *critical*.

hundred and fifty-four (or about one in twenty)
have been adopted bodily into our language in some
Latin form, and a little over five hundred have some
English representative taken, or supposed to be taken,
through the French. Thus we have in the English
vocabulary about one in four or five of all the words
found in the Latin lexicon under A. There is no reason
to suppose that this proportion would not hold good
approximately for the whole alphabet.'[1]

119. It must not be imagined that all the Latin
words as used in English conform exactly with the
rules of Latin pronunciation or with the exact classical
meanings. 'My instructor,' says Fitzedward Hall,[2]
'took me to task for saying ᐟ*doctrinal.* "Where an
English word is from Latin or Greek, you should
always remember the stress in the original, and the
quantity of the vowels there." I replied: "If others, in
their solicitude to proᐟpāgat refinement, choose to be
irᐟritated or ᐟexcīted, because of what they take to
be my genuᐟīne igᐟnōrance in oraᐟtory, they should at
least be sure that their discomposure is not gratuᐟītous.'
Among words used in English with a different signification from the classical one, may be mentioned
enormous (Latin *enormis* 'irregular', later also 'very
big', in English formerly also *enorm* and *enormious*),
item (Latin *item* 'also', used to introduce each article
in a list, except the first), *ponder* (Lat. *ponderare* 'to
weigh, examine, judge', transitive), *premises* ('ad-
juncts of a building', originally things set forth or
mentioned in the beginning), *climax* (Greek *klímax*
'a ladder or gradation'; in the popular sense of
culminating point it is found in Emerson, Dean
Stanley, John Morley, Miss Mitford, and other
writers of repute), *bathos* (Greek *báthos* 'depth'; in
the sense of 'ludicrous descent from the elevated to the
commonplace' it is due to Pope ; the adjective *bathetic*,

---

[1] *Words and their Ways*, 1902, p. 106.

[2] Fitzedward Hall, *Two Trifles.* Printed for the Author, 1895.
I have changed his symbol for stress, indicating here as elsewhere
the beginning of the strong syllable by a prefixed little stroke.

formed on the analogy of *pathetic*, was first used by
Coleridge). It should be remembered, however, that
when once a certain pronunciation or signification has
been firmly established in a language, the word fulfils
its purpose in spite of ever so many might-have-beens,
and that, at any rate, correctness in one language
should not be measured by the yard of another
language. *Transpire* is perfectly legitimate in the
sense 'to emit, or to be emitted through the pores of
the skin' and in the derived sense 'to become known,
to become public gradually' although there is no Latin
verb *transpirare* in either of these senses ; if, therefore,
the occasional use of the verb in the sense of 'happen'
(pretty frequent in newspapers, but also e.g. in Charlotte Brontë) is objectionable, it is not on account of
any deviation from Latin usage, but because it has
arisen through a vulgar misunderstanding of the
English signification of an English word. Stuart Mill
exaggerates the danger of such innovations when he
writes : 'Vulgarisms, which creep in nobody knows
how, are daily depriving the English language of
valuable modes of expressing thought. To take a
present instance : the verb *transpire* . . . Of late a
practice has commenced of employing this word, for
the sake of finery, as a mere synonym of *to happen* :
"the events which have *transpired* in the Crimea",
meaning the incidents of the war. This vile specimen
of bad English is already seen in the despatches of
noblemen and viceroys : and the time is apparently
not far distant when nobody will understand the
word if used in its proper sense . . . The use of "aggravating" for "provoking", in my boyhood a vulgarism of
the nursery, has crept into almost all newspapers,
and into many books ; and when writers on criminal
law speak of aggravating and extenuating circumstances, their meaning, it is probable, is already
misunderstood.'[1] Let me add two small notes to Mill's
remarks. First, that *aggravate* in the sense of 'exas-

---

[1] Stuart Mill, *A System of Logic*, People's edition, 1886, p. 451.

perate, provoke' is exemplified in the NED. from
Cotgrave (1611), T. Herbert (1634), Richardson (1748)
—thus some time before Mill heard it in his nursery—
and Thackeray (1848). And secondly, that the verb
which Mill uses to explain it, *provoke*, is here used in a
specifically English sense which is nearly as far removed
from the classical signification as that of *aggravate* is.
But we shall presently see that the English have taken
even greater liberties with the classical languages.

120. When the influx of classical words began, it
had its *raison d'être* in the new world of old but forgotten ideas, then first revealed to medieval Europe.
Instead of their narrow circle of everyday monoton-
ousness, people began to suspect new vistas, in art as
well as in science, and classical literature became a
fruitful source of information and inspiration. No
wonder, then, that scores and hundreds of words
should be adopted together with the ideas they stood
for, and should seem to the adopters indispensable
means of enriching a language which to them appeared
poor and infertile as compared with the rich store-
houses of Latin and Greek. But as times wore on, the
ideas derived from classical authors were no longer
sufficient for the civilized world, and, just as it will happen with children outgrowing their garments, the modern mind outgrew classicism, without anybody noticing
exactly when or how. New ideas and new habits of life
developed and demanded linguistic expression, and
now the curious thing happened that classical studies
had so leavened the minds of the educated classes that
even when they passed the bounds of the ancient world
they drew upon the Latin and Greek vocabulary in
preference to their own native stock of words.

121. This is seen very extensively in the nomenclature of modern science, in which hundreds of
chemical, botanical, biological and other terms have
been framed from Latin and Greek roots, most of them
compound words and some extremely long compounds.
It is certainly superfluous here to give instances of

such formations, as a glance at any page of a comprehensive dictionary will supply a sufficient number of them, and as one needs only a smattering of science to be acquainted with technical words from Latin and Greek that would have struck Demosthenes and Cicero as bold, many of them even as indefensible or incomprehensible innovations. It is not, perhaps, so well known that quite a number of words that belong to the vocabulary of ordinary life and that are generally supposed to have the best-ascertained classical pedigree, have really been coined in recent times more or less exactly on classical analogies. Some of them have arisen independently in several European countries. Such modern coinages are, for instance, *eventual* with *eventuality, immoral, fragmental* and *fragmentary, primal, annexation, fixation and affixation, climatic.* There are scores of modern formations in *-ism*,[1] e.g. *absenteeism, alienism, classicism, colloquialism, favouritism, individualism, mannerism, realism,* not to speak of those made from proper names, such as *Swinburnism, Zolaism,* etc. Among the innumerable words of recent formation in *-ist* may be mentioned *dentist, florist, jurist, oculist, copyist* (formerly *copist* as in some continental languages), *determinist, economist, ventriloquist, individualist, plagiarist, positivist, socialist, terrorist, nihilist, tourist.* For *calculist* the only author quoted in the NED. is Carlyle. *Scientist* has often been branded as an 'ignoble Americanism' or 'a cheap and vulgar product of trans-Atlantic slang', but Fitzedward Hall has pointed out that it was fabricated and advocated in 1840, together with *physicist,* by Dr. Whewell. Whoever objects to such words as *scientist* on the plea that they are not correct Latin formations, would have to blot out of his vocabulary such well-established words as *suicide, telegram, botany, sociology, tractarian, vegetarian, facsimile* and *orthopedic* ; but then, happily, people are not consistent.

---

[1] See Fitzedward Hall, *Modern English,* p. 311. His lists have also been utilized in the rest of this paragraph.

122. Authors sometimes coin quasi-classic words without finding anybody to pass them on, as when Milton writes 'our *inquisiturient* Bishops' (*Areop.*, 13). Coleridge speaks of '*logodœdaly* or verbal legerdemain'. Thackeray of a lady's '*viduous* mansion' (*Newc.*, 794), Dickens of '*vocular* exclamations' (*Oliver Twist*); Tennyson writes in a letter (*Life*, I, 254) 'you range no higher in my *andrometer*'; Bulwer-Lytton says 'a cat the most *viparious* [meaning evidently 'tenacious of life'] is limited to nine lives'; and Mrs. Humphrey Ward, 'his air of old-fashioned *punctilium*'.[1] I have here on purpose mixed correct and incorrect forms, jocular and serious words, because my point was to illustrate the love found in most English writers of everything Latin or Greek, however unusual or fanciful. Sometimes jocular 'classicisms' survive and are adopted into everybody's language, such as *omnium gatherum* (whence Thackeray's bold heading of a chapter 'Snobbium Gatherum'), *circumbendibus* (Goldsmith, Coleridge) and *tandem*, which originated in a university pun on the two senses of English 'at length'.

123. Hybrids, in which one of the component parts was French and the other native English, have been mentioned above (§ 106 f.). Here we shall give some examples of the corresponding phenomenon with Latin and Greek elements, some of which may, however, have been imported through French. The ending *-ation* is found in *starvation, backwardation,* and others; note also the American *thunderation* ('It was an accident, sir.' 'Accident the thunderation,' Opie Read, *Toothpick Tales*, Chicago, 1892, p. 35). *Johnsoniana, Miltoniana*, etc., are quite modern; the ending *ana* alone is now also used as a detached noun. In *-ist* we have *walkist*, which is sometimes used to denote a *professional* walker, and is therefore distinguished by the more learned ending. Compare also *turfite* and the

---

[1] Dictionaries recognize *punctilio*, a curious transformation of the Spanish *puntillo*; there is a late Latin *punctillum*, but not with the meaning of 'punctiliousness'.

numerous words in *-ite* derived from proper names :
Irvingite, Ruskinite, etc. The same ending is frequently
used in mineralogy and chemistry, one of the latest
additions to these formations being *fumelessite* =
smokeless gunpowder. Hybrids in *-ism* (cf. § 121)
abound ; *heathenism* has been used by Bacon, Milton,
Addison, Freeman and others ; *witticism* was first used
by Dryden, who asks pardon for this new word ; *block-
headism* is found in Ruskin ; further *funnyism, free-
lovism,* etc.; the curious *wegotism* may be classed with
the jocular *drinkitite* on the analogy of *appetite.*
Girlicide, after suicide, is another jocular formation
(Smedley, *Frank Fairlegh* I, 190, not in NED.). To the
same sphere belong Byron's *weatherology* and some
words in *-ocracy,* such as *landocracy, shopocracy, bar-
risterocracy, squattocracy,* Carlyle's *strumpetocracy,* and
Meredith's *snipocracy* (*Evan Harrington,* 174, from
snip as a nickname for a tailor). On the other hand
squirearchy (with *squirearchical*) seems to have quite
established itself in serious language. Among verbal
formations must be mentioned those in *-ize* : he
womanized his language (Meredith, *Egoist,* 32), *London-
izing* (ibid., 80), *soberize,* etc. Adjectives are formed in
-ative : *talkative, babblative, scribblative,* and *sooth-
ative,* of which only the first is recognized ; in *-aceous* :
gossipaceous (Darwin, *Life and Letters,* I, 375) ; in
-arious : *burglarious* (Stevenson, *Dynamiter,* 130), and
-iacal : *dandiacal* (Carlyle, *Sartor,* 188). Even if many
of these words are 'nonce-words', it cannot be denied
that the process is genuinely English and perfectly
legitimate—within reasonable limits at any rate.

124. Some Latin and Greek prepositions have in
recent times been extensively used to form new words.
Ex-, as in *ex-king, ex-head-master,* etc.,[1] seems first to
have been used in French, but it is now common to
most or all Germanic languages as well ; in English
this formation did not become popular till the end of
the 18th century. *Anti* : the anti-taxation movement ;

---

[1] 'A pair of ex-white satin shoes' (Thackeray).

an antiforeign party ; 'Mr. Anti-slavery Clarkson' (De Quincey, *Opium-Eater*, 197) ; 'chairs unpleasant to sit in—anticaller chairs they might be named' (H. Spencer, *Facts and Comments*, 85). *Co-* : 'a friend of mine, co-godfather to Dickens's child with me' (Tennyson, *Life*, II, 114) ; 'Wallace, the co-formulator of the Darwinian theory' (Clodd, *Pioneers of Evolution*, 68). *De-*, especially with verbs in -*ize* : de-anglicize, de-democratize, deprovincialize, denationalize ; less frequently as in de-tenant, de-miracle (Tennyson). *Inter-* : intermingle, intermix, intermarriage, interbreed, intercommunicate, interdependence, etc. *International* was coined by Bentham in 1780 : it marks linguistically the first beginning of the era when relations between nations came to be considered like relations between citizens, capable of peaceful arrangement according to right rather than according to might. A great many other similar adjectives have since been formed : *intercollegiate, interracial, interparliamentary*, etc. Where no adjective existed, the substantive is used unchanged, but the combination is virtually an adjective : *interstate* affairs ; an *interisland* steamer ; 'international, inter-club, inter-team, inter-college or inter-school contests' (quoted in NED.) ; 'in short inter-whiff sentences' (Kinglake, *Eothen*, 125). *Pre-* : the pre-Darwinian explanations ; prenuptial friendships (Pinero, *Second Mrs. Tanqueray*, p. 6, what are called on p. 8 'ante-nuptial acquaintances') ; 'in the pre-railroad, pre-telegraphic period' (G. Eliot) ; the pre-railway city ; the pre-board school ; a bunch of pre-Johannesburg Transvaals ; the pre-mechanical civilized state (all these are quotations from H. G. Wells) ; in your pre-smoking days (Barrie) ; pre-war prices. *Pro-* : the pro-Boers ; pro-foreign proclivities ; a pro-Belgian, or rather pro-King Leopold speaker. As any number of such derivatives or compounds can be formed with the greatest facility, the utility and convenience of these certainly not classical expedients cannot be reasonably denied,

though it may be questioned whether it would not
have been better to utilize English prepositions for
the same purposes, as is done with *after-* (an after-
dinner speech) and sometimes with *before-* ('the before
Alfred remains of our language', Sweet ; 'smoking his
before-breakfast pipe', Conan Doyle).[1] A few words
must be added on *re-*, which is used in a similar manner in any number of free compounds, such as *rebirth,*
and especially verbs : re-organize, re-sterilize, re-
submit, re-pocket, re-leather, re-case, etc. Here *re-*
is always strongly stressed and pronounced with a
long vowel [i·], and by that means these recent
words are in the spoken language easily distinguished
from the older set of *re*-words, where *re* is either
weakly stressed or else, when strongly stressed, pronounced with short [e]. We have therefore such pairs
as *recollect* = to remember, and *re-collect* = to collect
again; he *recovered* the lost umbrella and had it *re-covered*;
reform and *re-form* (reformation and re-formation), *re-
create* and *re-create, remark* and *re-mark, resign* and *resign, resound* and *re-sound, resort* and *re-sort.* In the
written language the distinction is not always observed.

125. Latin has influenced English not only in vocabulary, but also in style and syntax. The absolute
participle (as in 'everything considered', or 'this being
the case') was introduced at a very early period in
imitation of the Latin construction.[2] It is comparatively rare in Old English, where it occurs chiefly in
close translations from Latin. In the first period of
Middle English it is equally rare, but in the second
period it becomes a little more frequent. Chaucer
seems to have used it chiefly in imitation of the Italian
construction, but this Italian influence died out with
him, and French influence did very little to increase
the frequency of the construction. In the beginning of
the Modern English period the absolute participle,

[1] Cf. my *Mod. E. Grammar*, II, p. 343.

[2] Morgan Callaway, *The Absolute Participle in Anglo-Saxon*
Baltimore, 1889). Charles Hunter Ross, *The Absolute Participle
in Middle and Modern English* (Baltimore, 1893).

though occurring more often than formerly, 'had not become thoroughly naturalized. It limited itself to certain favorite authors where the classical element largely predominated, and was used but sparingly by authors whose style was essentially English' (Ross, p. 38). But after 1660, when English prose style developed a new phase, which was saturated with classical elements, the construction rapidly gained ground and was finally fixed and naturalized in the language. There are some other Latin idioms which authors tried to imitate, but which have always been felt as unnatural, so that now they have been dropped, for instance *who* for *he who* or *those who* as in 'sleeping found by whom they dread' (Milton, *P.L.*, I, 1333), further such interrogative and relative constructions as those found in the following quotations : 'To do what service am I sent for hither?' (Shakesp. R 2, IV, 1, 176) and 'a right noble and pious lord, who had he not sacrific'd his life . . . we had not now mist and bewayl'd a worthy patron' (Milton, *Areop.*, 51).

126. Latin grammar was the only grammar taught in those days, and the only grammar found worthy of study and imitation. 'That highly disciplined syntax which Milton favoured from the first, and to which he tended more and more, was in fact the classical syntax, or, to be more exact, an adaptation of the syntax of the Latin tongue,' says D. Masson,[1] and when he adds, 'It could hardly fail to be so . . . Even now, questions in English syntax are often settled best practically, if a settlement is wanted, by a reference to Latin construction', he expressed a totally erroneous conception which has been, and is, unfortunately too common, although very little linguistic culture would seem to be needed to expose its fallacy. Nowhere, perhaps, has this misconception been more strongly expressed than in Dryden's preface to *Troilus and Cressida*, where he writes : 'How barbarously we yet write and speak your Lordship

---

[1] *Poetical Works of Milton*, 1890, vol. III, p. 74-5.

knows, and I am sufficiently sensible in my own
English. For I am often put to a stand in considering
whether what I write be the idiom of the tongue, or
false grammar and nonsense couched beneath that
specious name of Anglicism, and have no other way
to clear my doubts but by translating my English into
Latin, and thereby trying what sense the words will
bear in a more stable language.' I am afraid that
Dryden would never have become the famous writer
he is, had he employed this practice as often as he
would have us imagine. But it was certainly in
deference to Latin syntax that in the later editions of
his *Essay on Dramatic Poesy* he changed such phrases
as 'I cannot think so contemptibly of the age I live
in' to 'the age in which I live'; he speaks somewhere[1]
of the preposition at the end of the sentence as a
common fault with Ben Jonson 'and which I have but
lately observed in my own writings'. The construction Dryden here reprehends is not a 'fault' and is not
confined to Ben Jonson, but is a genuine English idiom
of long standing in the language and found very frequently in all writers of natural prose and verse.
The omission of the relative pronoun, which Dr. Johnson terms 'a colloquial barbarism' and which is found
only seven or eight times in all the writings of Milton,
and according to Thum only twice in the whole of
Macaulay's History, abounds in the writings of such
authors as Shakespeare, Bunyan, Swift, Fielding,
Goldsmith, Sterne, Byron, Shelley, Dickens, Thackeray, Tennyson, Ruskin, etc., etc. In Addison's well-
known *Humble Petition of Who and Which*[2] these two
pronouns complain of the injury done to them by the
recent extension of the use of *that*. 'We are descended
of ancient Families, and kept up our Dignity and
Honour many Years till the Jacksprat *that* supplanted
us.' Addison here turns all historical truth topsy-

[1] I quote this second-hand, see J. Earle, *English Prose*, 267;
Hales, Notes to Milton's *Areopagitica*, p. 103.

[2] The *Spectator*, No. 78, May 30, 1711.

turvy, for *that* is much older as a relative than either
who or *which* ; but the real reason of his predilection
for the latter two was certainly their conformity with
Latin relative pronouns, and there can be no doubt
that his article, assisted by English grammars and the
teaching given in schoolrooms, has contributed very
much to restricting the use of *that* as a relative word
—in writing at least. Addison himself, when editing
the *Spectator* in book-form, corrected many a natural
that into a less natural *who* or *which*.

127. As to the more general effect of classical studies
on English style, I am very much inclined to think that
Darwin and Huxley are right as against most schoolmasters. Darwin 'had the strongest disbelief in the
common idea that a classical scholar must write good
English ; indeed, he thought that the contrary was
the case'.[1] Huxley wrote to *The Times*, Aug. 5, 1890[2] :
'My impression has been that the Genius of the
English language is widely different from that of Latin;
and that the worst and the most debased kinds of
English style are those which ape Latinity. I know of
no purer English prose than that of John Bunyan and
Daniel Defoe; I doubt if the music of Keats's verse has
ever been surpassed; it has not been my fortune to hear
any orator who approached the powerful simplicity,
the limpid sincerity, of the speech of John Bright. Yet
Latin literature and these masters of English had little
to do with one another.' As 'in diesem Bund der dritte'
might be mentioned Herbert Spencer, who expressed
himself strongly to the same effect in his last book.[3]

128. To return to the vocabulary. We may now
consider the question : Is the Latin element on the
whole beneficial to the English tongue or would it have
been better if the free adoption of words from the
classical languages had been kept within much narrower limits? A perfectly impartial decision is not easy
but it is hoped that the following may be considered a

---

[1] *Lie and Letters* of Ch. Darwin, 1887, I, p. 155.

[2] Quoted by J. Earle, *English Prose*, 487.

[3] *Facts and Comments*, 1902, p. 70.

fair statement of the most important pros and cons. The first advantage that strikes the observer is the enormous addition to the English vocabulary. If the English boast that their language is richer than any other, and that their dictionaries contain a far greater number of words than German and French ones, the chief reason is, of course, the greater number of foreign and especially of French and Latin words adopted. 'I trade,' says Dryden, 'both with the living and the dead for the enrichment of our native language.'

129. But this wealth of words has its seamy side too. The real psychological wealth is wealth of ideas, not of mere names. 'We have more words than notions, half a dozen words for the same thing,' says Selden (*Table Talk*, LXXVI). Words are not material things that can be heaped up like money or stores of food and clothes, from which you may at any time take what you want. A word to be yours must be learnt by you, and possessing it means reproducing it. Both the process of learning and that of reproducing it involve labour on your part. Some words are easy to handle, and others difficult. The number of words at your disposal in a given language is, therefore, not the only thing of importance ; their quality, too, is to be considered, and especially the ease with which they can be associated with the ideas they are to symbolize and with other words. Now many of the Latin words are deficient in that respect, and this entails other drawback to speakers of English, as will presently appear.

130. It will be argued in favour of the classical elements that many of them fill up gaps in the native stock of words, so that they serve to express ideas which would have been nameless but for them. To this it may be objected that the resources of the original language should not be underrated. In most, perhaps in all, cases it would have been possible to find an adequate expression in the vernacular or to coin one. The tendency to such economy in Old English and the ease with which felicitous terms for new ideas were then framed by means of native

speech-material, have been mentioned above. But
little by little English speakers lost the habit of looking first to their own language and utilizing it to the
utmost before going abroad for new expressions.
People who had had their whole education in Latin
and had thought all their best thoughts in that
language to an extent which is not easy for us moderns
to realize, often found it easier to write on abstract or
learned subjects in Latin than in their own vernacular,
and when they tried to write on these things in English
Latin words would constantly come first to their
minds. Mental laziness and regard to their own
momentary convenience therefore led them to retain
the Latin word and give it only an English termina-
tion. Little did they care for the convenience of their
readers, if they should happen to be ignorant of the
classics, or for that of unborn generations, whom they
forced by their disregard for their own language to
carry on the burden of committing to memory words
and expressions that were really foreign to their idiom.
If they have not actually dried up the natural sources
of speech—for these run on as fresh as ever—yet they
have accustomed their countrymen to cross the stream
in search of water, to use an expressive Danish locution.

131. There is one class of words which seems to be
rather sparingly represented in the native vocabulary,
so that classical formations are extremely often
resorted to, namely, the adjectives. It is, in fact,
surprising how many pairs we have of native nouns
and foreign adjectives, e.g. mouth : *oral* ; nose : *nasal* ;
eye : *ocular* ; mind: *mental* ; son : *filial* ; ox : *bovine* ;
worm : *vermicular* ; house : *domestic* ; the middle
ages : *medieval* ; book : *literary* ; moon : *lunar* ; sun :
solar ; star : *stellar* ; town : *urban* ; man : *human,* ;
virile, etc., etc. In the same category we may class
such pairs as money : *monetary, pecuniary* ; letter :
epistolary ; school : *scholastic,* as the nouns, though
originally foreign, are now for all practical purposes
to be considered native. We may note here English

proper names and their Latinized adjectives, e.g.
Dorset : *Dorsetian* ; Oxford : *Oxonian* ; Cambridge :
Cantabrigian ; Gladstone : *Gladstonian*. Lancaster
has even two adjectives, *Lancastrian* (in medieval
history) and *Lancasterian* (schools, Joseph Lancaster,
1771–1838). It cannot be pretended that all these
adjectives are used on account of any real deficiency
in the English language, as it has quite a number of
endings by which to turn substantives into adjectives :
-en (silken), *-y* (flowery), *-ish* (girlish), *-ly* (fatherly),
-like (fishlike), *-some* (burdensome), *-ful* (sinful), and
these might easily have been utilized still more than
they actually have been. In point of fact, we possess
not a few native adjectives by the side of more
learned ones, e.g. *fatherly* : *paternal* ; *motherly* :
maternal ; *brotherly* : *fraternal* (but only *sisterly*, as
sororal is so rare as to be left out of account) ; further
watery : *aquatic* or *aqueous* ; *heavenly* : *celestial* ;
earthy, earthly, earthen : *terrestrial* ; *timely* : *temporal* ;
daily : *diurnal* ; *truthful* : *veracious* ; etc. In some cases
the meanings of these have become more or less
differentiated, the English words having often lost an
abstract sense which they formerly had and which
might have been retained with advantage. If the
word *sanguinary* is now extensively used it is due to
the curious twisting of the meaning of *bloody* in vulgar
speech (cf. 244). *Kingly, royal* and *regal* : who is able
to tell exactly how these adjectives differ in signification? And might not English like other languages (*royal*
in French, *kongelig* in Danish, *königlich* in German)
have been content with one word instead of three?

132. Besides, in a great many cases it is really contrary to the genius of the language to use an adjective
at all. Where Romanic and Slavic languages very
often prefer a combination of a noun and an adjective
the Germanic languages combine the two ideas into a
compound noun. *Birthday* is much more English than
natal day (which is used, for instance, in Wordsworth's
75th Sonnet), and *eyeball* than *ocular globe*, but

physiologists think it more dignified to speak of the
gustatory nerve than of the *taste nerve* and will even say
mental nerve (Lat. mentum 'chin') instead of *chin
nerve* in spite of the unavoidable confusion with the
familiar adjective *mental*. Mere position before another
noun is really the most English way of turning a noun
into an adjective, e.g. the *London* market, a *Wessex*
man, *Yorkshire* pudding, a strong *Edinburgh* accent, a
Japan table, *Venice* glasses, the *Chaucer* Society, the
Droeshout picture, a *Gladstone* bag, *imitation* Astra-
khan, 'Every *tiger* madness muzzled, every *serpent* passion kill'd' (Tennyson).[1] It is worth noting that the
English adjective corresponding to *family* is not
familiar, which has been somewhat estranged from its
kindred, but *family*; family reasons, family affairs,
family questions, etc. The unnaturalness of forming
Latin adjectives is, perhaps, also shown by the vacillation often found between different endings, as in *feuda-
tary* and *feudatory*, *festal* and *festive*. From *labyrinth* no
less than six adjectives have been found : *labyrinthal,
labyrinthean, labyrinthian, labyrinthic, labyrinthical* and
labyrinthine. Many adjectives are quite superfluous ;
Shakespeare never used either *autumnal, hibernal,
vernal* or *estival*, and he probably never missed them.
Instead of *hodiernal* and *hesternal* we have luckily other
expressions (to-day's post ; the questions of the day ;
yesterday's news). Most of us can certainly do without
gressorial (birds), *avuncular* (a favourite with Thackeray: 'Clive, in the avuncular gig'; 'the avuncular bank-
ing house'; 'the avuncular quarrel', all from *The Newcomes*), *osculatory* (processes = kissing; ib.), *lachrymat-
ory* (he is great in the l. line; ib.), *aquiline* ('What! am I
an eagle too? I have no aquiline pretensions at all', ib.[2])
—and a great many similarly purposeless adjectives.

133. More than in anything else the richness of the
English language manifests itself in its great number of

---

[1] Shakespeare did not scruple to write 'the Carthage queen',
'Rome gates', 'Tiber banks', even 'through faire Verona streets'.
Cf. below, § 194, and *Mod. Engl. Grammar*, II, ch. XIII.

[2] Thus used in a different manner from the familiar *aquiline* nose.

synonyms, whether we take this word in its strict sense of words of exactly the same meaning or in the looser sense of words with nearly the same meaning. It is evident that the latter class must be the most valuable, as it allows speakers to express subtle shades of thought. *Juvenile* does not signify the same thing as *youthful, ponderous* as *weighty, portion* as *share, miserable* as *wretched. Legible* means 'that can be read', *readable* generally 'worth reading'. Sometimes the Latin word is used in a more limited, special or precise sense than the English, as is seen by a comparison of *identical* and *same, science* and *knowledge, sentence* and *saying, latent* or *occult* and *hidden. Breath* can hardly now be called a synonym of *spirit* ('The spirit does not mean the breath', Tennyson), and similarly *edify*, which is still used by Spenser in the concrete sense of 'building up', is now used exclusively with a spiritual signification, which its former synonym *build* can never have. *Homicide* is the learned, abstract, colourless word, while *murder* denotes only one kind of *manslaughter*, and *killing* is the everyday word with a much vaguer signification (being applicable also to animals); there is a very apposite quotation from Coleridge in the NED.: '[He] is acquitted of murder—the act was manslaughter only, or it was justifiable homicide.' The learned word *magnitude* is more specialized than *greatness* or *size* (which is now thoroughly English, but is a very recent development of *assize* in a curiously modified sense). *Popish* has an element of contempt which the learned *papal* does not share. The Latin *masculine* is more abstract than the English *manly*, which generally implies an emotional element of praise, the French *male* has not exactly the same import as either, and the Latin *virile* represents a fourth shade, while for the other sex we have *female, feminine, womanly* and *womanish*, the differences between which are not parallel to those between the first series of synonyms.

134. These examples will suffice to illustrate the synonymic relations between classical and other words.

It will be seen that it is not always easy to draw a line
or to determine exactly the different shades of meaning
attached to each word ; indeed, a comparison of the
definitions given in various essays on synonyms and in
dictionaries, and especially a comparison of these
definitions with the use as actually found in various
writers, will show that it is in many cases a hopeless
task to assign definite spheres of signification to these
words. Sometimes the only real difference is that one
term is preferred in certain collocations and another in
others. Still, it is indubitable that very often the existence of a double or triple assortment of expressions will
allow a writer to express his thoughts with the greatest
precision imaginable. But on the other hand, only
those whose thoughts are accurate and well disciplined
attain to the highest degree of linguistic precision, and
the use in speech and writing of the same set of words
by loose and inexact thinkers will always tend to blur
out any sharp lines of demarcation that may exist
between such synonymous terms as do not belong to
their everyday stock of language.

135. However, even where there is no real difference
in the value of two words or where the difference is
momentarily disregarded, their existence may not be
entirely worthless, as it enables an author to avoid a
trivial repetition of the same word, and variety of
expressions is generally considered one of the felicities
of style. We very often see English authors use a native
and a borrowed word side by side simply, it would
seem, to amplify the expression, without modifying its
meaning. Thus 'of blind *forgetfulnesse* and dark *oblivion*'
(Shakespeare, in Buckingham's strongly rhetorical
speech, R 3, III, 7, 129). 'The *manifold multiform*
flower' (Swinburne, *Songs bef. Sunr.*, 106). A perfectly
natural variation of three expressions is seen in: 'the
Bushman story is just the *sort* of *story* we *expect* from
Bushmen, whereas the Hesiodic story is not at all the
kind of *tale* we *look for* from Greeks'. (A. Lang, *Custom
and Myth*, 54). Further examples: 'I *went upstairs* with

my candle directly. It appeared to my childish fancy, as I *ascended* to the bedroom . . .' 'He asked me if it would suit my convenience to have the light *put out*; and on my answering "yes", instantly *extinguished it.*' 'The phantom slowly *approached*. When it *came near* him, Scrooge bent down'; 'they are *exactly unlike*. They are *utterly dissimilar* in all respects' (all these from Dickens). 'We who boast of our *land* of *freedom*, we who live in the *country* of *liberty*.' 'I could not repress a *half smile* as he said this; a similar *demi-manifestation of feeling* appeared at the same moment on Hunsden's lips.' This kind of variation evidently does not *always* lead to the highest excellence of style. I quote from Minto[1] Samuel Johnson's comparison between punch and conversation: 'The spirit, volatile and fiery, is *the proper emblem* of vivacity and wit ; the acidity of the lemon will very *aptly figure* pungency of raillery and acrimony of censure ; sugar is the *natural representative* of luscious adulation and gentle complaisance ; and water is the *proper hieroglyphic* of easy prattle, innocent and tasteless.' This is not far from Mr. Micawber's piling up of words ('to the best of my knowledge, information and belief . . . to wit, in manner following, that is to say'), which gives Dickens the occasion for the following outburst :

'In the taking of legal oaths, for instance, deponents seem to enjoy themselves mightily when they come to several good words in succession, for the expression of one idea ; as, that they utterly detest, abominate, and abjure, or so forth ; and the old anathemas were made relishing on the same principle. We talk about the tyranny of words, but we like to tyrannize over them too ; we are fond of having a large superfluous establishment of words to wait upon us on great occasions ; we think it looks important, and sounds well. As we are not particular about the meanings of our liveries on state occasions, if they be but fine and numerous enough, so the meaning or necessity of our

---

[1] *Manual of English Prose Literature*, 3rd ed., 1896, p. 418.

words is a secondary consideration if there be but a
great parade of them. And as individuals get into
trouble by making too great a show of liveries, or as
slaves when they are too numerous rise against their
masters, so I think I could mention a nation that has
got into many great difficulties, and will get into many
greater, from maintaining too large a retinue of
words.' (*David Copperfield*, p. 702.)[1]

136. No doubt many of the synonymous terms introduced from Latin and Greek had best been let
alone. No one would have missed *pharos* by the side
of *lighthouse*, or *nigritude* by the side of *blackness*. The
native words *cold, cool, chill, chilly, icy, frosty* might
have seemed sufficient for all purposes, without any
necessity for importing *frigid, gelid,* and *algid*, which
as a matter of fact are found neither in Shakespeare
nor in the Authorized Version of the Bible nor in the
poetical works of Milton, Pope, Cowper and Shelley.

137. Apart from the advantage of being able constantly to make a choice between words possessing a
different number of syllables and often also presenting
a difference in the place of the accent, poets will often
find the sonorous Latin words better for their purposes
than the short native ones. In some kinds of prose
writing, too, they are felt to heighten the tone, and add
dignity, even majesty, to the structure of the sentence.
The chief reason of this seems to be that the long word
takes up more time. Instead of hurrying the reader or
listener on to the next idea, it allows his mind to dwell
for a longer time upon the same idea ; it gives time for
his reflexion to be deeper and especially for his
emotion to be stronger. This seems to me more important than the two other reasons given by H. Spencer (*Essays*, II, p. 14) that 'a voluminous, mouth-
filling epithet is, by its very size, suggestive of large-
ness or strength' and that 'a word of several syllables

---

[1] Mr. Micawber also has the following delightful piece of bathos :
'It is not an avocation of a remunerative description—in other
words, it does *not* pay.'

admits of more emphatic articulation (?); and as emphatic articulation is a sign of emotion, the unusual impressiveness of the thing named is implied by it'. Let me quote here also a quaint passage (not to be taken too seriously) from Howell (*New English Grammar*, 1662, p. 40): 'The Spanish abound and delight in words of many syllables and where the English expresseth himself in one syllable, he doth in 5 or 6, as thoughts pensamientos, fray levantamiento, &c., which is held a part of wisdom, for while they speak they take time to consider of the matter.'

138. It is often said that the classical elements are commendable on the score of international intelligibility, and it is certain that many of them, even of those formed during the last century on more or less exact Latin and Greek analogy, are used in many other civilized countries as well as in England. The utility of this is evident in our days of easy communication between the nations; but on the whole its utility should not be valued beyond measure. If the thing to be named is one of everyday importance, national convenience should certainly be considered before international ease: therefore *to wire* and *a wire* are preferable to *telegraph* and *telegram*.[1] Scientific nomenclature is to a great extent universal, and there is no reason why each nation should have its own name for *foraminifera* or *monocotyledones*. But so much of science is now becoming more and more the property of everybody and influences daily life so deeply that the endeavour should rather be to have popular than learned names for whatever in science is not intended exclusively for the specialist. *Sleeplessness* is a better name than *insomnia*, and foreigners who know English enough to read a medical treatise in it will be no more perplexed by the word than an Englishman reading German is by *Schlaflosigkeit*. Foreign phoneticians have had no difficulty in understanding

---

[1] Nowadays also *wireless* both as a noun and as a verb: 'I sent him a wireless'; 'they wirelessed for help'.

Melville Bell's excellent nomenclature and have even
to a great extent adopted the English terms of *front,
mixed, back,* etc., in preference to the more cumbersome *palatal, gutturopalatal,* and *guttural.* It is a pity
that *half-vowel* (Googe, 1577) and *half-vowelish* (Ben
Jonson) should have been superseded by *semi-vowel*
and *semi-vowel-like.* Among English words that have
been in recent times adopted by many foreign languages may be mentioned *cheque, box* (in a bank), *trust,
film* (in photography), *sport, jockey, sulky, gig, handi-
cap, dock, waterproof, tender, coke* (German and Danish
koks or sometimes with pseudo-English spelling *coaks*),
so that even to obtain international currency a word
need not have a learned appearance or be derived from
Greek and Latin roots. Besides, many of the latter
class are not quite so international as might be supposed, as their English significations are unknown on
the continent (*pathos, physic, concurrent, competition,
actual, eventual, injury*) ; sometimes, also, the ending
is different, as in *principle* (Fr. principe, etc.), *individual* (Fr. individu, Dan. individ, German In-
dividuum), *chemistry* (chimie, chemie), *botany* (botan-
ique), *fanaticism* (fanatisme).

139. It is possible to point out a certain number of
inherent deficiencies which affect parts of the vocabulary borrowed from the classical language. Mention has
already been made (§ 26) of the stress-shifting which is
so contrary to the general spirit of Germanic tongues
and which obscures the relation between connected
words, especially in a language where unstressed syllables are generally pronounced with such indistinct
vowel sounds as in English. Compare, for instance,
solid and *solidity, pathos* and *pathetic, pathology* and
pathologic, pacify and *pacific* (note that the first two
syllables of *pacification,* where the strongest stress is on
the fourth syllable, vacillate between the two corresponding pronunciations). The incongruity is especially
disagreeable when native names are distorted by
means of a learned derivative ending, as when *Milton*

has the stress shifted on to the second syllable and the vowel changed (in two different ways) in *Miltonic* and *Miltonian* ; cf. also *Baconian, Dickensian, Taylorian, Spenserian, Canadian, Dorsetian,* etc.

140. Another drawback is shown in the relation between *emit* and *immit, emerge* and *immerge*. While in Latin *emitto* and *immitto, emergo* and *immergo* were easily kept apart, because the vowels were distinct and double consonants were rigorously pronounced double and so kept apart from single ones, the natural English pronunciation will confound them, just as it confounds the first syllables of *immediate* and *emotion.* Now, as the meaning of *e-* is the exact opposite of *in-*, the two pairs do not go well together in the same language. The same is true of *illusion* and *elusion*.[1] A still greater drawback arises from the two meanings of initial *in*, which is sometimes the negative prefix and sometimes the preposition. According to dictionaries *infusible* means (1) that may be infused or poured in, (2) incapable of being fused or melted. *Importable*, which is now only used as derived from *import* (capable of being imported), had formerly also the meaning 'unbearable', and *improvable* similarly had the meaning of 'incapable of being proved' though it only retains that of 'capable of being improved'. What Shakespeare in one passage (Temp. II, 1, 37) expresses in accordance with modern usage by the word *uninhabitable* he elsewhere calls *inhabitable* ('Even to the frozen ridges of the Alpes, Or any other ground inhabitable', R 2, I, 1, 65), and the ambiguity of the latter word has now led to the curious result that the positive adjective corresponding to *inhabit* is *habitable* and the negative *uninhabitable.* The first syllable of *inebriety* is the preposition *in-*, so that it means the same thing as the rare *ebriety* 'drunken-

---

[1] Illiterate spellers will often write *illicit* for *elicit, enumerable* for *innumerable,* etc. Many words have had, and some still have, two spellings, with *en-* (*em-*, from the French, and with *in-* (*im-*) from the Latin (*enquire, inquire,* etc.).

ness', but T. Hook mistook it for the negative prefix
and so, subtracting *in-*, made *ebriety* mean 'sobriety'.[1]
Illustrious is used in Shakespeare's Cymb. I, 6, 109,
as the negative of *lustrous*, while elsewhere it has the
exactly opposite signification. Fortunately this ambiguity is limited to a comparatively small portion
of the vocabulary.[2]

141. Loan-words do not necessarily make a language inharmonious. In Finnish, for instance, in spite
of numerous loans from a variety of languages, the
prevailing impression is one of unity, apart perhaps
from some of the most recent Swedish words. The
foreign elements have been so assimilated in sound
and inflexion as to be recognizable as foreign only to
the eye of a philologist. The same may be said of the
pre-Conquest borrowings from Latin into English, of
the Scandinavian and of the most important among
the French loans, nay even of a great many recent
loans from exotic languages. *Wine* and *tea, bacon* and
eggs, orange and *sugar, plunder* and *war, prison* and
judge—all are not only indispensable, but harmonious
elements of English. But while most people are aston-
ished on first hearing that such words have not
always belonged to their language, no philological
training is required to discover that *phenomenon* or
diphtheria or *intellectual* or *latitudinarian* are out of
harmony with the real core or central part of the
language. Every one must feel the incongruity of such
sets of words as *father—paternal—parricide*, or of the
abnormal plurals which break the beautiful regularity
of nearly all English substantives—*phenomena, nuclei,
larvæ, chrysalides, indices*, etc. The occasional occurrence of such blundering plurals as *animalculæ* and
ignorami is an unconscious protest against the prevalent pedantry of schoolmasters in this respect.[3]

---

[1] See quotation in Davies, *Supplementary English Glossary*, 1881.

[2] If *invaluable* means generally 'very valuable' and sometimes
'valueless', the case is obviously different from the above.

[3] 'He may also see giraffes, lions or rhinoceros. The mention of
this last word reminds me of a problem, which has tormented

142. The unnatural state into which the language has been thrown by the wholesale adoption of learned words is further manifested by the fact that not a few of them have no fixed pronunciation ; they are, in fact, eye-words that do not really exist in the language. Educated people freely write them and understand them when they see them written, but are more or less puzzled when they have to pronounce them. Dr. Murray relates how he was once present at a meeting of a learned society, where in the course of discussion he heard the word *gaseous* systematically pronounced in six different ways by as many eminent physicists. (NED., Preface). *Diatribist* is by Murray and the CenturyDictionary stressedon the first, byWebster on the second syllable, and the same hesitation is found with *phonotypy,photochromy,* and many similar words. This is, however, beaten by two so well-known words as *hegemony* and *phthisis*, for each of which dictionaries record no less than nine possible pronunciations without being able to tell us which of these is the prevalent or preferable one. I doubt very much whether analogous waverings can be found in any other language.

143. The worst thing, however, that can be said against the words that are occupying us here is their difficulty and the undemocratic character which is a natural outcome of their difficulty. A great many of them will never be used or understood by anybody that has not had a classical education.[1] There are

---

me all the time that I have been in East Africa, namely, what is the plural of rhinoceros? The conversational abbreviations, "rhino", "rhinos", seem beneath the dignity of literature, and to use the sporting idiom by which the singular is always put for the plural is merely to avoid the difficulty. Liddell and Scott seem to authorize "rhinocerotes" which is pedantic, but "rhinoceroses" is not euphonious.' Sir Charles Eliot, *The East Africa Protectorate* (1905), 266. Cf. *Mod. Engl. Grammar* II, ch. III.

[1] Sometimes they are not even understood by the erudite themselves. *Gestic* in Goldsmith's 'skill'd in gestic lore' (*Traveller*, 253) is taken in many dictionaries as meaning 'legendary, historical' as if from *gest*, OFr. *geste*, 'story, romance' ; but the context shows conclusively that 'pertaining to bodily movement, esp. dancing'

usually no associations of ideas between them and the
ordinary stock of words, and no likenesses in root or
in the formative elements to assist the memory. We
have here none of those invisible threads that knit
words together in the human mind. Their great number in the language is therefore apt to form or rather
to accentuate class divisions, so that a man's culture
is largely judged by the extent to which he is able
correctly to handle these hard words in speech and in
writing—certainly not the highest imaginable standard of a man's worth. No literature in the world
abounds as English does in characters made ridiculous
to the reader by the manner in which they misapply or distort 'big' words. Shakespeare's Dogberry
and Mrs. Quickly, Fielding's Mrs. Slipslop, Smollet's
Winifred Jenkins, Sheridan's Mrs. Malaprop, Dickens's
Weller senior, Shillaber's Mrs. Partington, and foot-
men and labourers innumerable made fun of in novels
and comedies might all of them appear in court as
witnesses for the plaintiff in a law-suit brought
against the educated classes of England for wilfully
making the language more complicated than necessary and thereby hindering the spread of education
among all classes of the population.

144. Different authors vary very greatly with
regard to the extent to which they make use of such
'choice words, and measured phrase above the reach
of ordinary men'. So much is said on this head in
easily accessible textbooks on literature that I need
not repeat it here. Unfortunately the statistical calculations given there of the percentage of native and
of foreign words in different writers are not quite to
the point, for while they generally include Scandinavian loans among native words, they reckon together

(NED.) must be the meaning ; cf. Lat. *gestus,* 'gesture'. *Aristarchy*
has been wrongly interpreted in most dictionaries as 'a body of
good men in power', while it is derived from the proper name
Aristarch and means 'a body of severe critics' (Fitzedward Hall,
Modern English, 143).

all words of classical origin, although such popular
words as *cry* or *crown* have evidently quite a different
standing in the language from learned words like
auditory or *hymenoptera*. The culmination with regard
to the use of learned words in ordinary literary style
was reached in the time of Dr. Samuel Johnson. I can
find no better example to illustrate the effect of
extreme 'Johnsonese' than the following :

'The proverbial oracles of our parsimonious ancestors have informed us, that the fatal waste of our
fortune is by small expenses, by the profusion of sums
too little singly to alarm our caution, and which we
never suffer ourselves to consider together. Of the
same kind is the prodigality of life ; he that hopes to
look back hereafter with satisfaction upon past years,
must learn to know the present value of single minutes
and endeavour to let no particle of time fall useless
to the ground.'[1]

145. In his Essay on Madame D'Arblay, Macaulay
gives some delightful samples of this style as developed
by that ardent admirer of Dr. Johnson. Sheridan
refused to permit his lovely wife to sing in public,
and was warmly praised on this account by Johnson.
'The last of men,' says Madame D'Arblay, 'was
Doctor Johnson to have abetted squandering the
delicacy of integrity by nullifying the labours of
talent.' To be starved to death is 'to sink from in-
anition into nonentity'. Sir Isaac Newton is 'the
developer of the skies in their embodied movements',
and Mrs. Thrale, when a party of clever people sat
silent, is said to have been 'provoked by the dulness
of a taciturnity that, in the midst of such renowned
interlocutors, produced as narcotic a torpor as could
have been caused by a death the most barren of all

---

[1] Minto (*Manual of Engl. Prose Lit.*, 422) translates this as follows : 'Take care of the pennies', says the thrifty old proverb,
'and the pounds will take care of themselves.' In like manner we
might say, 'Take care of the minutes, and the years will take care
of themselves'.

human faculties'. (Macaulay, *Essays*, Tauchn. ed. V.,
p. 65.)[1]

146. In the nineteenth century a most happy
reaction set in in favour of 'Saxon' words and natural
expressions ; and it is highly significant that Tennyson,
for instance, prides himself on having in the *Idylls of
the King* used Latin words more sparingly than any
other poet. But still the malady lingers on, especially
with the half-educated. I quote from a newspaper
the following story : The young lady home from
school was explaining. 'Take an egg,' she said, 'and
make a perforation in the base and a corresponding
one in the apex. Then apply the lips to the aperture,
and by forcibly inhaling the breath the shell is entirely discharged of its contents.' An old lady who was
listening exclaimed : 'It beats all how folks do things
nowadays. When I was a gal they made a hole in each
end and sucked.' To a different class belongs that
master of Saxon English, Charles Lamb, who begins
his 'Chapter on Ears' in the following way : 'I have
no ear. Mistake me not, reader, nor imagine that I
am by nature destitute of those exterior twin appen-
dages, hanging ornaments, and (architecturally speaking) handsome volutes to the human capital. Better
my mother had never borne me. I am, I think, rather
delicately than copiously provided with those con-
duits ; and I feel no disposition to envy the mule for
his plenty, or the mole for her exactness, in those
labyrinthine inlets—those indispensable side-intelli-
gencers.'

147. Of course, the author of the last sample aims
here at a certain humorous effect, and very often
similar circumlocutions are consciously resorted to in
conversation to obtain a ludicrous effect, as 'he am-
putated his mahogany' (cut his stick, went off), 'to
agitate the communicator' (ring the bell), 'a sanguin-

---

[1] 'My brother and I meet every week, by an alternate recipro-
cation of intercourse, as Sam Johnson would express it' (Cowper,
Letters, I, 18).

ary nasal protuberance', 'the Recent Incision' (the New Cut, a street in London), 'the Grove of the Evangelist' (St. John's Wood in London), etc. When Mr. Bob Sawyer asked 'I say, old boy, where do you hang out?' Mr. Pickwick replied that he was at present *suspended* at the George and Vulture. (Dickens, *Pickw.* II, 13). *Punch* somewhere gives the following paraphrases of well-known proverbs : 'Iniquitous intercourses contaminate proper habits. In the absence of the feline race, the mice give themselves up to various pastimes. Casualties will take place in the most excellently conducted family circles. More confectioners than are absolutely necessary are apt to ruin the potage.' (Quoted in Fitzgerald's *Miscellanies*, p. 166). Similarly 'A rolling stone gathers no moss' is paraphrased 'Cryptogamous concretion never grows on mineral fragments that decline repose'. Some Latin and Greek words will scarcely ever be used except in jocular or ironical speech, such as *sapient* (wise), *histrion* (actor), *a virgin aunt* (maiden aunt), *hylactism* (barking), *edacious* (greedy), the *genus Homo* (mankind), etc.

148. But how many words are there not which belong virtually to the same class, but are used in dead earnest by people who know that many big words are found in the best authors and who want to show off their education by avoiding plain everyday expressions and couching their thoughts in a would-be refined style? When Canning wrote the inscription graven on Pitt's monument in the London Guildhall, an Alderman felt much disgust at the grand phrase, 'he died poor', and wished to substitute 'he expired in indigent circumstances' (quoted by Kington Oliphant).[1] James Russell Lowell, in the Introduction

[1] Cf. the following passage from Arnold Bennett's *Clayhanger* : Edwin began to write : 'Dear James, my father passed peacefully away at —' Then, with an abrupt movement, he tore the sheet in two and began again : 'Dear James, my father died quietly at eight o'clock to-night.' Which of the two bills is preferable, 'Expectoration is strictly prohibited' or 'Don't spit'?

to the Second Series of his *Biglow Papers*, has a list
of what he calls the old and the new styles of newspaper writing, which I find so characteristic that I
select a few samples :

Old Style.	New Style.
A great crowd came to see.	A vast concourse was assembled to witness.
Great fire	Disastrous conflagration.
The fire spread.	The conflagration extended its devastating career.
Man fell.	Individual was precipitated.
Sent for the doctor.	Called into requisition the services of the family physician.
Began his answer.	Commenced his rejoinder.
He died.	He deceased, he passed out of existence, his spirit quitted its earthly habitation, winged its way to eternity, shook off its burden, etc.

149. I do not deny that somewhat parallel instances
of stilted language might be culled from the daily press
of most other nations, but nowhere else are they found
in such plenty as in English, and no other language
lends itself by its very structure to such vile stylistic
tricks as English does. Wordsworth writes : 'And
sitting on the grass partook The fragrant beverage
drawn from China's herb', to which Tennyson remarked : 'Why could he not have said, "And sitting
on the grass had tea"?'[1] Gissing in one of his novels
says of a clergyman : 'One might have suspected that
he had made a list of uncommon words wherewith to
adorn his discourse, for certain of these frequently
recurred. "Nullifidian", "mortific", "renascent",
were among his favourites. Once or twice he spoke of
"psychogenesis", with an emphatic enunciation which

---

[1] *Life and Letters*, III, 60.

seemed to invite respectful wonder.'[1] And did not
little Thomas Babington Macaulay, when four years
old, reply to a lady who took pity on him after he
had spilt some hot coffee over his legs, 'Thank you,
madam, the agony is abated'? And does not a language which possesses, besides the natural expression
for each thing, two or three sonorous equivalents,
tempt a writer into what Lecky hits off so well when
he says of Gladstone : 'He seemed sometimes to be
labouring to show with how many words a simple
thought could be expressed or obscured'?[2]

150. To sum up : the classical words adopted since
the Renaissance have enriched the English language
very greatly and have especially increased its number
of synonyms. But it is not every 'enrichment' that
is an advantage, and this one comprises much that is
really superfluous, or worse than superfluous, and has,
moreover, stunted the growth of native formations.
The international currency of many words is not a full
compensation for their want of harmony with the core
of the language and for the undemocratic character
they give to the vocabulary. While the composite
character of the language gives variety and to some
extent precision to the style of the greatest masters,
on the other hand it encourages an inflated turgidity
of style. Without siding completely with Milton's
teacher Alexander Gill, who says that classical studies
have done the English language more harm than ever
the cruelties of the Danes or the devastations of the
Normans,[3] we shall probably be near the truth if we
recognize in the latest influence from the classical
languages 'something between a hindrance and a
help'.

---

[1] *Born in Exile*, p. 380.

[2] *Democracy and Liberty*, I, p. xxi.

[3] 'Ad Latina venio. Et si uspiam querelæ locus, hîc est; quòd
otium, quòd literæ, maiorem cladem sermoni Anglico intulerint
quam ulla Danorum sævitia, ulla Normannorum vastitas unquam
inflixerit.' *Logonomia Anglica*, 1621 (Jiriczek's reprint, Strassburg
1903, p. 43).

Chapter VII

Various Sources

151. Although English has borrowed a great many words from other languages than those mentioned in the preceding chapters, these borrowings need not occupy us long here. For only Scandinavian, French and Latin have left a mark on English deep enough to modify its character and to change its structure, and the language would remain the same in every essential respect even were all the other loan-words to disappear to-morrow.

There is, of course, nothing peculiarly English in the adoption of words denoting animals, plants, products, or institutions originally peculiar to one part of the world, but later known in many countries, such as *gondola*, *maccaroni* and *lava* from Italian, *matador*, *siesta* and *sherry* from Spanish, *steppe* and *verst* from Russian, *caravan* and *dervish* from Persian, *hussar* and *shako* from Hungarian, *bey* and *caftan* from Turkish, *harem* and *mufti* from Arabic, *bamboo* and *orang-outang* from Malay, *taboo* from Polynesian, *boomerang* and *wombat* from Australian, *chocolate* and *tomato* from Mexican, *moccasin*, *tomahawk* and *totem* from other American languages. As a matter of fact, all these words now belong to the whole of the civilized world : like such classical or pseudo-classical words as *nationality*, *telegram* and *civilization*, they bear witness to the sameness of modern culture everywhere : the same products and to a great extent the same ideas are now known all over the globe and many of them have in many languages identical names.

With regard to these as well as to other loan-words

it should always be remembered that the ultimate
origin of a word is not always the source whence it has
penetrated into English. Many exotic words have
come to England through Spanish or Portuguese.
Paradise, originally a Persian word, has come through
French ; so have *shallop*, *chaloupe*, originally Dutch
sloep, in English spelt *sloop*, and *fuchsia*, as shown by
the pronunciation : it is derived from the name of a
German botanist Fuchs.

152. It will be worth our while to consider the loans
from a few languages, as they have great cultural importance. First the Dutch.[1] It is significant that this
word in English means not German (deutsch), but the
inhabitants and the language of the Netherlands, with
which the English came into more intimate relations
than with the Germans themselves. The Dutch have
always been a seafaring nation ; hence it is no wonder
that many nautical words have come from that
source : *yacht*, *yawl*, *schooner*, *bowline*, *deck*, *cruise*,
iceberg ; *euphroe*, a learned spelling of Du. *juffrouw*
'a crowfoot dead-eye', must have been taken over by
word of mouth. There are also some military words :
furlough, *tattoo*, *onslaught*. But the most interesting
group of Dutch words relates to the fine arts, which
flourished in the Low Countries in the 16th and 17th
centuries and exercised a strong influence on English
artists. Hence such words as *easel*, *etch*, *sketch*, *mual-
stick*, *landscape* (whence such English new-formed
words as *seascape*, *cloudscape*, and finally the isolated
scape). On South African words see § 160.

153. This leads us naturally to the other great
influence on the artistic vocabulary, namely Italian.[2]

---

[1] See J. F. Bense, *The Anglo-Dutch Relations* ('s-Gravenhage,
1924) ; Bense, *A Dictionary of the Dutch Element in the English
Vocabulary* (The Hague, 1926–1935. A standard work, not yet
finished) ; E. C. Llewellyn, *The Influence of Low Dutch on the English
Vocabulary* (Oxford, 1936 ; based chiefly on Bense) ; G. N. Clark, *The
Dutch Influence on the English Vocabulary* (S.P.E., 44, Oxford, 1935).

[2] See Mario Praz, *The Italian Element in English* (Essays and
Studies, XV, 20 ff.).

Attention has already been called to the great number of musical terms derived from Italian (§ 31). A great many terms of architecture and of the fine arts in general derive from Italy : *balcony, colonnade, cornice, corridor, grotto, loggia, mezzanine, niche, parapet, pilaster, profile* ; further *fresco, miniature* ; *improvisatore, dilettante, opera, sonnet.* From related cultural domains we may mention *casino, carnival, milliner* (orig. modistes from Milan). Commercial relations have given us such words as *traffic, risk, magazine, bank* and what belongs to that : *bankrupt* (Latinized from *bancarotta*), *agio, Lombard.* Among military terms may be mentioned *alarm, colonel* (the pronunciation goes back to the form *coronel*), *arsenal, pistol.*

154. From Spanish we may mention the military words *armada, escapade* and *embargo*, further designations for persons like *don* (note the curious use in English universities) and *hidalgo* ; *padre* obtained a certain vogue during the first world war. In the world of games we have *quadrille, spade* and other terms for cards. Commerce brought *anchovy, cargo, cordovan* and *lime* (the fruit). In recent times the Californian *cafeteria* has proved exceedingly productive in linguistic offspring : *drugteria, sodateria, fruiteria, shaveteria, shoeteria*, and other more or less ridiculous American words.

155. Among Arabic words in English[1]—some of them easily recognizable through the definite article *al*—we must specially mention those relating to mathematics, astronomy, and science in general : *algebra, cipher, zero, nadir, zenith, alchemy, alcohol, alkali, bismuth, elixir, natron.* Some English scientific terms are Arabic in meaning, but not in form, thus the mathematical *sine* from Latin *sinus* 'fold', translating Arabic *jaib* ; x as a sign for an unknown quantity 'was no doubt used first in Spain because it is the letter corresponding etymologically in Spanish to Arabic *shin,* used in this sense as an abbreviation of the word

---

[1] Walt Taylor, *Arabic Words in English* (S.P.E., 38, Oxford, 1933).

shai thing'. Other Arabic words are *alcove, sofa, sash, caraway, sherbet.*

156. The British Empire has caused contact with a great many peoples and in consequence loans from many languages. From India we have, among other words, *sahib, begum, maharajah, pundit, baboo* (the curious language spoken by some Hindus is often called Baboo English), *thug ; durbar, Swaraj ; cot, bungalow, pucka, coolie, pariah, chit, Choki,* originally meaning customs-house, is used for 'prison' (folk-etymological connexion with E. choke?). For articles of apparel we have *topi, pyjamas* and *bandana. Loot* is an interesting parallel to *plunder* (§ 157). The notorious *dumdum* bullets are named from a place Dum Dum, near Calcutta. Some originally Indian words have come to English through Persian : *divan, khaki, zenana, purdah.* From African languages we have, e.g., *impi* 'regiment', *indaba* 'conference'. From Chinese *kowtow.* But some of these words can hardly be said to belong to ordinary English.

157. There are surprisingly few German loan-words in English,[1] and very little can be inferred from them with regard to cultural relations, apart, perhaps, from some philosophical terms the meaning of which was stamped by Kant and his English followers. *Plunder* is due to the English soldiers in the thirty years' war, and *swindler* is said to have been introduced by German Jews ab. 1726. Some mining terms, such as *feldspar, gneiss* and *quartz,* come from Germany. There are some translation-loans, e.g. *home-sickness* and *one-sided,* also the place-name the *Black Forest,* but otherwise the tendency is to swallow German words raw, even where a translation would have been easy : the *Siebengebirge* and the *Riesengebirge* are much more commonly used than the *Seven Mountains* and the *Giant Mountains.* Thus we have *kindergarten* unchanged, while for the same institution Danish has the

[1] See Charles T. Carr, *The German Influence on the English Vocabulary* (S.P.E., 42, Oxford, 1934).

literal translation *börnehave* and Norwegian *barne-
have*. Similarly English has *rinderpet, landsturm,
zollverein, weltpolitik, weltanschauung* and *hinterland*
—which may even be used as in 'a residential hinterland' (of a town, Kaye Smith, *Tamarisk Town*, 105),
and 'a vast hinterland of thoughts and feelings'
(Wells, *Marriage*, 2, 121). Here we have come upon
something which seems to be characteristic of the
English in their relation to foreign words.

158. An interesting contrast may be seen between
the linguistic behaviour of the Dutch and the English
in South Africa. The former, finding there a great
many natural objects which were new to them, designated them either by means of existing Dutch words
whose meanings were, accordingly, more or less
modified, or else by coining new words, generally
compounds. Thus *sloot* 'ditch' was applied to the
peculiar dry rivers of that country, *veld* 'field' to the
open pasturages, and *kopje* 'a little head or cup' to
the hills, etc.; different kinds of animals were called
roodebok 'red-buck', *steenbok* 'stonebuck', *springbok*
'hopbuck', *springhaas* 'hop-hare', *hartebeest* 'hart-
beast'; a certain bird was called *slangvreter* 'serpent-
eater', a certain large shrub *spekboom* 'bacon-tree',
etc. The English, on the other hand, instead of imitating this principle, have simply taken over all these
names into their own language, where they now figure[1]
together with some other South African Dutch words,
among which may be mentioned *trek* and *spoor* in the
special significations of 'colonial migration' and 'track
of wild animal', while the Dutch words are much less
specialized (*trekken* 'to draw, pull, travel, move';
spoor 'trace, track, trail'). These examples of borrowings might easily be multiplied from other domains,
and we may say of the English what Moth says of
Holofernes and Sir Nathaniel that 'they have been at

---

[1] *Roodebok* often spelt in accordance with the actual Dutch
pronunciation *rooibok, rooyebok*. *Sloot* often appears in the un-
Dutch spelling *sluit*.

a great feast of languages, and stolen the scraps'
(Love's L. L. V, 1, 39). It will therefore be natural
to inquire into the cause of this linguistic omnivorous-
ness.

159. It would, of course, be irrational to ascribe the
phenomenon to a greater natural gift for learning
languages, for in the first place, the English are not
usually credited with such a gift, and secondly the
best linguists are generally inclined to keep their own
language pure rather than adulterate it with scraps of
other languages. Consequently, we should be nearer
the truth if we were to give as a reason the linguistic
incapacity of the average Englishman. As a traveller
and a colonizer, however, he is thrown into contact
with people of a great many different nations and thus
cannot help seeing numerous things and institutions
unknown in England. R. L. Stevenson says somewhere about the typical John Bull, that 'his is a
domineering nature, steady in fight, imperious to
command, but neither curious nor quick about the
life of others'.[1] And perhaps the loan-words we are
considering testify to nothing but the most super-
ficial curiosity about the life of other nations and
would not have been adopted if John Bull had really
in his heart cared any more than this for the foreigners
he meets. He is content to pick up a few scattered
fragments of their speech—just enough to impart a
certain local colouring to his narratives and political
discussions, but he goes no further.

160. The tendency to adopt words from other
languages is due, then, probably to a variety of causes.
Foremost among these I think it is right to place the
linguistic laziness mentioned in § 159 and fostered
especially by the preference for words from the classical languages. That the borrowing is not occasioned
by an inherent deficiency in the *language* itself is
shown by the ease with which new terms actually *are*
framed whenever the need of them is really felt,

---

[1] *Memories and Portraits*, p. 3.

especially by uneducated people who are not tempted to go outside their own language to express their thoughts. Interesting examples of this natural inventiveness may be found in Mr. Edward E. Morris's *Austral English, A dictionary of Australasian words, phrases and usages.* As Mr. Morris says in his preface, 'Those who, speaking the tongue of Shakespeare, of Milton, and of Dr. Johnson, came to various parts of Australasia, found a Flora and a Fauna waiting to be named in English. New birds, beasts and fishes, new trees, bushes and flowers, had to receive names for general use. It is probably not too much to say that there never was an instance in history when so many new names were needed, and that there never will be such an occasion again, for never did settlers come, nor can they ever again come, upon Flora and Fauna so completely different from anything seen by them before.' The gaps were filled partly by adopting words from the aboriginal languages, e.g. *kangaroo, wombat,* partly by applying English words to objects bearing a real or fancied resemblance to the objects denoted by them in England, e.g. *magpie, oak, beech,* but partly also by new English formations. Accordingly, in turning over the leaves of Mr. Morris's Dictionary we come across numerous names of birds like *friar-bird, frogs-mouth, honey-eater, ground-lark, forty-spot,*[1] of fishes like *long-fin, trumpeter,* of plants like *sugar-grass, hedge-laurel, ironheart, thousand-jacket.* Most of these show that 'the settler must have had an imagination. Whip-bird, or Coach-whip, from the sound of the note, Lyre-bird from the appearance of the outspread tail, are admirable names.' (Morris, l. c.). It certainly seems

---

[1] One story of a curious change of meaning must be recounted in Mr. Morris's words : 'The settler heard a bird laugh in what he thought an extremely ridiculous manner, its opening notes suggesting a donkey's bray—he called it the "laughing jackass". His descendants have dropped the adjective, and it has come to pass that the word "jackass" denotes to an Australian something quite different from its meaning to other speakers of our English tongue.'

a pity that book-learned people when wanting to
enrich their mother tongue have not, as a rule, drawn
from the same source or shown the same talent for
picturesque and 'telling' designations.

161. Many of our times' new inventions and other
innovations have enriched the language.[1] Cinemato-
graph is generally shortened into *cinema*, even *cine*,
but people often speak of the *movies*. We have the
curious differentiation of *radium* and *radio* : the latter
has given a new sense to the old *broadcast* (B.B.C.=
British Broadcasting Corporation). For *automobile* the
simple word *car* is generally said, or else *motor-car*.
We have *aeroplane*, for which some people prefer the
form *airplane* ; it is also shortened into *plane*, and we
have the new *aquaplane* and *seaplane* ; further,
airship, aircraft, airman, etc., also *aerodrome* ; *taxi* is
used for crawling along the ground before or after
alighting in a plane. Some of the new words introduced with these inventions have taken some time,
before their spoken forms in English were quite fixed :
chauffeur from [ʃouˈfɔˑ] has now usually become
[ˈʃoufɔ] ; *hangar* and *garage* were at first spoken with
long [aˑ] in the last syllable, but now they are generally
Anglicized [hæŋgɔ] or [hæŋɔ], [gæridʒ]. The learned *tele-
vision* has brought about the verb *televise*, and *televisor*
for the apparatus. Let me finally mention *tango* and *jazz*.

162. A great many words are nowadays coined by
tradespeople to designate new articles of merchandise.
Very little regard is generally paid to correctness of
formation, the only essential being a name that is
good for advertising purposes. Sometimes a mere
arbitrary collection of sounds or letters is chosen, as
in the case of *kodak*, and sometimes the inventor
contents himself with some vague resemblance to
some other word, which may assist the buyer to

---

[1] Recent linguistic innovations are dealt with in H. Spies, *Kultur
und Sprache im neuen England* (Leipzig, 1925) ; R. Hittmair, *Wort-
bildende Kräfte im heutigen Englisch* (Leipzig, 1937) ; W. E. Collinson,
Contemporary English (Leipzig, 1927).

remember the name. A few examples may be given :
bovril (Latin bos + vril, an electrical fluid mentioned
in an old novel by Lytton), *vapo-cresolene* (cresolene
vaporized), *harlene* (hair), *wincarnis* (a tonic, wine,
Latin caro?), *rinso* (for cleaning, rinse), *redux* (reducing herbal tea), *yeast-vite* (tonic), *ceilingite* (white-
wash), *elasto* . . . Sometimes these trade names are
merely ordinary words disguised by fancy spellings,
e.g. *Phiteesi* boots, *Stickphast*, *Uneeda* cigar (= you
need a cigar) in England, *Uneeda* biscuit in America.
Many such names are very short-lived, but some are
there to stay and may even pass into common use
outside the sphere for which they were originally
invented. This is the case with *kodak*.[1]

163. The Great War (1914–1918) left its mark on
language as on everything.[2] It introduced a certain
number of foreign words, e.g. *camouflage* (in English
also as a verb = Fr. camoufler), in the navy called
dazzle-painting ; from German we had *u-boat* = sub-
marine, and the stupid *strafe* (from 'Gott strafe
England', at the time often pronounced [streif] ; the
curious *blighty* is from Hindu *bilayati* 'foreign', used
by soldiers on foreign service for 'home, i.e. England'.
Old words were provided with new meanings : *ace* like
Fr. *as* came to mean an airman who had brought
down a certain number of foreign men ; *bus* = aeroplane, further *gas* (be gassed) and *tank* ; *go west* was
used as a euphemism for 'die, be lost'. The war even
produced a new numeral : *umpteen*, used to disguise
the number of a brigade, later in the sense of a considerable number. The tendency to shorten words (cf. 186)
is seen in *conchy* = conscientious objector, *zepp* =
Zeppelin, etc. But most of the war words belong to
slang and as such fall outside the scope of this work.

---

[1] Additional examples in Louise Pound, *Word-Coinage and
Modern Trade Names* (Dialect Notes, LV, 1913), and H. L. Mencken,
The American Language, 4th ed., 171 ff.

[2] See besides the works by Spies, Collinson and Hittmair mentioned
above, A. Smith, *New Words Self-Defined* (New York, 1920).

Chapter VIII

Native Resources

164. However important foreign loan-words are, the chief enrichment of the language is due to those regular processes which are so familiar that any new word formed by means of them seems at once an old acquaintance. The whole history of English word-formation may be summed up as follows—that some formative elements have been gradually discarded, especially those that presented some difficulty of application, while others have been continually gaining ground, because they have admitted of being added to all or nearly all words without occasioning any change in the kernel of the word. Among the former I shall mention *-en* to denote female beings (cf. German *-in*). In Old English this had already become very impracticable because sound changes had occurred which obscured the connexion between related words. Corresponding to the masculine *þegn* 'retainer', *þeow* 'slave', *wealh* 'foreigner', *scealc* 'servant', *fox*, we find the feminine *þignen*, *þiewen*, *wielen*, *scielcen*, *fyxen*. It seems clear that new generations would find difficulties in forming new feminines on such indistinct analogies, so we cannot wonder that the ending ceased to be productive and that the French ending *-ess*, which presented no difficulties, came to be used extensively (107). Of the words in *-en* mentioned, *fyxen* is the only one surviving, and its connexion with *fox* is now loosened, both through the form *vixen* (with its *v* from Southern dialects) and through the meaning, which is now most often 'a quarrelsome woman'.

165. A much more brilliant destiny was reserved for the Old English ending *-isc*. At first it was added only to nouns indicating nations, whose vowel it changed by mutation ; thus *Englisc*, now *English*, from *Angle*, etc. In some adjectives, however, no mutation was possible, e.g. *Irish*, and by analogy the vowel of the primitive word was soon introduced into some of the adjectives, e.g., *Scottish* (earlier *Scyttisc*), *Danish* (earlier *Denisc*). The ending was extended first to words whose meaning was cognate to these national names, *heathenish*, OE. *folcisc* or *þeodisc* 'national' (from *folc* or *þeod* 'people') ; then gradually came *childish*, *churlish*, etc. Each century added new extensions; *foolish* and *feverish*, for instance, date from the 14th, and *boyish* and *girlish* from the 16th century, until now *-ish* can be added to nearly any noun and adjective (swinish, bookish, greenish, biggish, etc.).

166. We shall see in a later section (§ 206) that the ending *-ing* has still more noticeably broken the bounds of its originally narrow sphere of application. Another case in point is the verbal suffix *-en*. It is now possible to form a verb from any adjective fulfilling certain phonetic conditions by adding *-en* (harden, weaken, sweeten, sharpen, lessen). But this suffix was not used very much before 1500, indeed most of the verbs formed in *-en* belong to the last three centuries. Another extensively used ending is *-er*. Old English had various methods of forming substantives to denote agents ; from the verb *huntan* 'hunt' it had the noun *hunta* 'hunter' ; from *beodan* 'announce', *boda* 'messenger, herald' ; from *wealdan* 'rule', *weada* ; from *beran* 'bear', *bora* ; from *sceppan* 'injure', *sceapa* ; from *weorcan* 'work', *wyrhta* 'wright' (in *wheelwright*, etc.), though some of these were used in compounds only ; some nouns were formed in *-end* : *rædend* 'ruler', *scieppend* 'creator', and others in *-ere* : *blawere* 'one who blows', *blotere* 'sacrificer', etc. But it seems as if there were many verbs from which it was impossible to form any agent-noun at all, and the reader will have noticed that even the formation in *a* presented some difficulties, as the vowel was modified according to complicated rules. When the want of new substantives was felt, it was, therefore, more and more the ending *-ere* that was resorted to. But the curious thing is that the function of this ending was at first to make nouns, not from verbs, but from other nouns, thus OE. *bocere* 'scribe' from *boc* 'book' (already Gothic *bokareis*), compare modern *hatter*, *tinner*, *Londoner*, *New Englander*, *first-nighter*. As, however, such a word as *fisher*, OE. *fiscere*, which is derived from the noun a *fish*, OE. *fisc*, might just as well be analysed as derived from the corresponding verb to *fish*, OE. *fiscian*, it became usual to form new agent-denoting nouns in *-er* from verbs, and in some cases these supplanted older formations (OE. *hunta*, now *hunter*). *Now* we do not hesitate to make new words in *-er* from any verb, e.g., a *snorer*, a *sitter*, odd *comers* and *goers*, a total *abstainer*, etc. Combinations with an adverb (a *diner-out*, a *looker-on*) go back to Chaucer (A somnour is a renner up and down With mandements for fornicacioun, D. 1284), but do not seem to be very frequent before the Elizabethan period. Note also the extensive use of the suffix to denote instruments and things, as in *slipper*, *rubber*, *typewriter*, *sleeper* (American = sleeping car). A variant of *-er* is *-eer*, which is liable, but only after *t*, to impart a disparaging meaning : this starts perhaps from *garreteer* and *pamphleteer*, hence the contemptuous *sonneteer*, *profiteer*, famous or infamous during the war, and *patrioteering* (my *Language*, p. 388, not in NED.). Another variant of *-er* is *-ster*,[1] which is often wrongly supposed to be a specially feminine suffix, though from the earliest times it has been used of men as well as of women, from the old *demestre*, now *deemster* or *dempster* 'a judge', and family names like *Baxter*, *Webster*, down to the more modern *punster*, *gangster*, *fibster*, *youngster*, etc. A *spinster* originally

---

[1] Jespersen, *Linguistica* (Copenhagen, 1933), p. 420 ff.

meant one who spins, but is now restricted to unmarried (old) maids. Special feminines are formed in
-*stress* : *seamstress* (*sempstress*), *songstress*.

167. Other much-used suffixes for substantives are :
-*ness* (goodness, truthfulness), -*dom* (Christendom,
boredom, 'Swelldom', Thackeray), -*ship* (ownership,
companionship, horsemanship), for adjectives : -*ly*
(lordly, cowardly), -*y* (fiery, churchy, creepy), -*less*
(powerless, dauntless), -*ful* (powerful, fanciful), and
-*ed* (blue-eyed, good-natured, renowned, conceited,
talented ; broad-breasted ; level-browed, like the
horizon ; —thighed and shouldered like the billows ;
— footed like their stealing foam', Ruskin). Prefixes
of wide application are *mis-*, *un-*, *be-*, and others.
By means of these formatives the English vocabulary
has been and is being constantly enriched with thousands and thousands of useful new words.

168. There is one manner of forming verbs from
nouns and vice versa which is specifically English and
which is of the greatest value on account of the ease
with which it is managed, namely that of making them
exactly like one another. In Old English there were
a certain number of verbs and nouns of the same
'root', but distinguished by the endings. Thus 'I
love' through the three persons singular ran *lufie*,
lufast, lufaþ, plural *lufiaþ* ; the infinitive was *lufian*,
the subjunctive *lufie*, pl. *lufien*, and the imperative was
lufa, pl. *lufiaþ*. The substantive 'love' on the other
hand was *lufu*, in the other cases *lufe*, plural *lufa* or
lufe, lufum, lufena or *lufa*. Similarly 'to sleep' was
slǽpan, pres. *slǽpe, slǽpest, slǽp(e)þ, slǽpaþ*, subjunctive *slǽpe, slǽpen*, imperative *slǽp, slǽpaþ*, while
the substantive had the forms *slǽp, slǽpe* and *slǽpes*
in the singular and *slǽpas, slǽpum, slǽpa* in the plural.
If we were to give the corresponding forms used in the
subsequent centuries, we should witness a gradual
simplification which had as a further consequence the
mutual approximation of the verbal and nominal
forms. The -*m* is changed into -*n*, all the vowels of

the weak syllables are levelled to one uniform *e*, the
plural forms of the verbs in -*þ* give way to forms in
-*n*, and all the final *n*'s eventually disappear, while in
the nouns *s* is gradually extended so that it becomes
the only genitive and almost the only plural ending.
The second person singular of the verbs retains its
distinctive -*st*, but towards the end of the Middle
English period *thou* already begins to be less used,
and the polite *ye*, *you*, which becomes more and more
universal, claims no distinctive ending in the verb.
In the fifteenth century, the *e* of the endings, which
had hitherto been pronounced, ceased to be sounded,
and somewhat later *s* became the ordinary ending of
the third person singular instead of *th*. These changes
brought about the modern scheme :

noun : *love loves—sleep sleeps*
verb : *love loves—sleep sleeps*

where we have perfect formal identity of the two parts
of speech, only with the curious cross-relation between
them that *s* is the ending of the plural in the nouns
and of the singular (third person) in the verbs—an
accident which might almost be taken as a device for
getting an *s* into most sentences in the present tense
(the lover love*s* ; the lover*s* love) and for showing by the
place of the *s* which of the two numbers is intended.

169. As a great many native nouns and verbs had
thus come to be identical in form (e.g. *blossom, care,
deal, drink, ebb, end, fathom, fight, fish, fire*), and as the
same thing happened with numerous originally French
words (e.g., *accord*, OFr. acord and acorder, *account,
arm, blame, cause, change, charge, charm, claim, combat,
comfort, copy, cost, couch*), it was quite natural that the
speech-instinct should take it as a matter of course
that whenever the need of a verb arose, it might be
formed without any derivative ending from the corresponding substantive.[1] Among the innumerable nouns

---

[1] It is often said, even by some of the most famous recent writers,
that Modern English has given up the sharp division into different
parts of speech which was characteristic of the earlier stages of

from which verbs have been formed in this manner, we
may mention a few : *ape, awe, cook, husband, silence,
time, worship.* Nearly every word for the different
parts of the body has given rise to a homonym verb,
though true it is that some of them are rarely used :
eye, nose ('you shall nose him as you go up the staires',
Hamlet), *lip* (= kiss, Shakesp.), *beard, tongue, brain* 'such
stuffe as madmen tongue and braine not', Shakesp.
Cymbeline), *jaw* (= scold, etc.), *ear* (rare = give ear to),
chin (American = to chatter), *arm* (= put one's arm
round), *shoulder* (arms), *elbow* (one's way through the
crowd), *hand, fist* ('fisting each other's throat',
Shakesp.), *finger, thumb, breast* (= oppose), *body* (forth),
skin, stomach, limb ('they limb themselves', Milton),
knee (= kneel, Shakesp.), *foot.* It would be possible in
a similar way to go through a great many other
categories of words ; everywhere we should see the
same facility of forming new verbs from substantives.

170. The process is also very often resorted to for
'nonce-words' in speaking and in writing. Thus, a
common form of retort is exemplified by the following
quotations : 'Trinkets ! a bauble for Lydia ! . . . So
this was the history of his trinkets ! I'll *bauble* him !'
(Sheridan, *Rivals*, V, 2). 'I was explaining the Golden
Bull to his Royal Highness.' 'I'll *Golden Bull* you, you
rascal !' roared the Majesty of Prussia (Macaulay,
Biographical Ess.). 'Such a savage as that, as has just

---

our family of speech. This is entirely wrong : even if the same
form *love* or *sleep* may be said to belong to more than one word-
class, this is true of the isolated form only : in each separate case
in which the word is used in actual speech it belongs definitely to
one class and to no other. The form *round* is a substantive in 'a
round of the ladder', 'he took his daily round', an adjective in
'a round table', a verb in 'he failed to round the lamp-post', an
adverb in 'come round to-morrow', and a preposition in 'he walked
round the house'. Many people will say that in the sentence 'we
tead at the vicarage' we have a case of a substantive used as a verb.
The truth is that we have a real verb, just as real as *dine* or *eat*,
though derived from the substantive *tea*, and derived without any
distinctive ending in the infinitive. Cf. *Philosophy of Grammar*,
p. 52 and 61f.

come home from South Africa. Diamonds indeed !
I'd *diamond* him' (Trollope, *Old Man's Love*)—
and in a somewhat different manner : 'My gracious
Uncle.—Tut, tut, Grace me no Grace, nor Uncle me
no Uncle (Shakesp. R 2, cf. also Romeo III, 5, 143).
'I heartily wish I could, but—' 'Nay, but me no
buts—I have set my heart upon it' (Scott, *Antiq.*,
ch. XI). 'Advance and take thy prize, The diamond ;
but he answered, Diamond me No diamonds ! For
God's love, a little air ! Prize me no prizes, for my
prize is death' (Tennyson, *Lancelot and Elaine*).

171. A still more characteristic peculiarity of the
English language is the corresponding freedom with
which a form which was originally a verb is used
unchanged as a substantive. This was not possible till
the disappearance of the final *-e* which was found in
most verbal forms, and accordingly we see an ever
increasing number of these formations from about
1500. I shall give some examples in chronological
order, adding the date of the earliest quotation for the
noun in the NED.: *glance* 1503, *bend* 1529, *cut* 1530,
fetch 1530, *hearsay* 1532, *blemish* 1535, *gaze* 1542, *reach*
1542, *drain* 1552, *gather* 1555, *burn* 1563, *lend* 1575,
dislike 1577, *frown* 1581, *dissent* 1585, *fawn* (a servile
cringe) 1590, *dismay* 1590, *embrace* 1592, *hatch* 1597,
dip 1599, *dress* (personal attire) 1606, *flutter* 1641,
divide 1642, *build* 1667 (before the 19th century
apparently used by Pepys only), *harass* 1667, *haul*
1670, *dive* 1700, *go* 1727 (many of the most frequent
applications date from the 19th century), *hobble*
1727, *lean* (the act or condition of leaning) 1776, *bid*
1788, *hang* 1797, *dig* 1819, *find* 1825 (in the sense of
that which is found, 1847), *crave* 1830, *kill* (the act of
killing) 1825, (a killed animal) 1878. It will be seen
that the 16th century is very fertile in these nouns,
which is only a natural consequence of the phono-
logical reason given above. As, however, some
of the verb-nouns found in Elizabethan authors have
in modern times disappeared or become rare, some

grammarians have inferred that we have here a phenomenon peculiar to that period and due to the general exuberance of the Renaissance which made people more free with their language than they have since been. A glance at our list will show that this is a wrong view ; indeed, we use a great many formations of this kind which were unknown to Shakespeare ; he had only the substantive *a visitation*, where we say *a visit*, nor did he know our *worries*, our *kicks*, and *moves*, etc., etc.

172. In some cases a substantive is formed in this manner in spite of there being already another noun derived from the same verb ; thus *a move* has nearly the same meaning as *removal, movement* or *motion* (from which latter a new verb *to motion* is formed) ; *a resolve* and *resolution*, a *laugh* and *laughter* are nearly the same thing (though an *exhibit* is only one of the things found at an *exhibition*). Hence we get a lively competition started between these substantives and forms in *-ing* : *meet* (especially in the sporting world) and *meeting, shoot* and *shooting, read* (in the afternoon I like a rest and a read) and *reading*,[1] *row* (let us go out for a row) and *rowing* (he goes in for rowing), *smoke* and *smoking, mend* and *mending, feel* (there was a soft feel of autumn in the air) and *feeling*. The *build* of a house and the *make* of a machine are different from the *building* of the house and the *making* of the machine. The *sit* of a coat may sometimes be spoilt at one *sitting*, and we speak of *dressing*, not of *dress*, in connexion with a salad, etc. The enormous development of these convenient differentiations belongs to the most recent period of the language. Compared with the sets of synonyms mentioned above (§ 133 : one of the words borrowed from Latin, etc.) this class

---

[1] Darwin says in one of his letters : 'I have just finished, after several reads, your paper' ; this implies that he did not read it from beginning to end at one sitting ; if he had written 'after several readings' he would have implied that he had read it through several times.

of synonyms shows a decided superiority, because
here small differences in sense are expressed by small
differences in sound, and because all these words are
formed in the most regular and easy manner ; consequently there is the least possible strain put on the
memory.

173. In early English a noun and the verb corresponding to it were often similar, although not exactly
alike, some historical reason causing a difference in
either the vowel or the final consonant or both. In
such pairs of words as the following the old relation is
kept unchanged : a *life*, to *live* ; a *calf*, to *calve* ; a *grief*,
to *grieve* ; a *cloth*, to *clothe* ; a *house*, to *house* ; a *use*,
to *use*—in all these the noun has the voiceless and the
verb the voiced consonant. The same alternation has
been imitated in a few words which had originally the
same consonant in the noun as in the verb ; thus *belief*,
proof, and *excuse* (with voiceless *s*) have supplanted
the older substantives in -*ve* and voiced -*se* and
inversely the verb *grease* has now often voiced *s* [z]
alternating with a voiceless *s*. But in a far greater
number of words the tendency to have nouns and
verbs of exactly the same sound has prevailed, so
that we have to *knife*, to *scarf* (Shakesp.), to *elf* (id.),
to *roof*, and with voiceless *s*, to *loose*, to *race*, to *ice*,
to *promise*, while the nouns *repose*, *cruise* (at sea), to
reprieve, owe their voiced consonants to the corresponding verbs. In this way we get some interesting
doublets. Besides the old noun *bath* and verb *bathe*
we have the recent verb to *bath* (will you bath baby
to-day?) and the substantive *bathe* ('I walked into the
sea by myself and had a very decent bathe', Tennyson). Besides *glass* (noun) and *glaze* (verb) we have
now also *glass* as a verb and *glaze* as a noun ; so also
in the case of *grass* and *graze*, *price* and *prize* (where
praise verb and noun should be mentioned as etymologically the same word).

174. The same forces are at work in the smaller class
of words in which the distinction between the noun

and the verb is made by the alternation of *ch* and *k*, as
in *speech—speak*. Side by side with the old *batch* we
have a new noun a *bake*, besides the noun *stitch* and
the verb *stick* we have now also a verb to *stitch* (a
book, etc.) and the rare noun a *stick* (the act of stick-
ing) ; besides the old noun *stench* we have a new one
from the verb *stink*. The modern word *ache* (in
toothache, etc.) is a curious cross of the old noun,
whose spelling has been kept, and the old verb, whose
pronunciation (with k) has prevailed. Baret (1573)
says expressly, '*Ake* is the verb of this substantive
ache, *ch* being turned into *k* '. In the Shakespeare
folio of 1623 the noun is always spelt with *ch* and the
verb with *k* ; the verb rimes with *brake* and *sake*.
The noun was thus sounded like the name of the letter
h ; and Hart (*An Orthographie*, 1569, p. 35) says expressly, 'We abuse the name of h, calling it ache,
which sounde serveth very well to expresse a head-
ache, or some bone ache'. Indeed, the identity in
sound of the noun and the name of the letter gave rise
to one of the stock puns of the time ; see for instance
Shakespeare (Ado III, 4, 56) ; 'by my troth I am
exceeding ill, hey ho.—For a hauke, a horse, or a
husband?—For the letter that begins them all, H, '
and a poem by Heywood : 'It is worst among letters
in the crosse row, For if thou find him other [= either]
in thine elbow, In thine arme, or leg . . . Where ever
you find ache, thou shalt not like him.'

175. Numerous substantives and verbs have the
same consonants, but a difference in the vowels, due
either to gradation (ablaut) or to mutation (umlaut).
But here, too, the creative powers of language may
be observed. Where in old times there was only a
noun *bit* and a verb to *bite*, we have now in addition
not only a verb to *bit* (a horse, to put the bit into its
mouth) as in Carlyle's 'the accursed hag "dyspepsia"
had got me bitted and bridled' and in Coleridge's
witty remark (quoted in the NED.) : 'It is not
women and Frenchmen only that would rather have

their tongues bitten than bitted'—but also a noun
bite in various meanings, e.g. in 'his bite is as dangerous as the cobra's' (Kipling) and 'she took a bite out
of the apple' (Anthony Hope). From the noun *seat*
(see above, § 72) we have the new verb to *seat* (to
place on a seat), while the verb to *sit* has given birth
to the noun *sit* (cf. § 172). No longer content with the
old *sale* as the substantive corresponding to *sell*, in
slang we have the new noun *a* (fearful) *sell* (an imposition) ; cf. also the American substantive *tell*
(according to their tell, see Farmer and Henley).
As *knot* (n.) was to *knit* (v.), so was *coss* to *kiss*, but
while of the former pair both forms have survived
and have given rise to a new verb to *knot* and a new
noun, *a knit* (he has a permanent knit of the brow,
NED.), from the latter the *o*-form has disappeared,
the noun being now formed from the verb : *a kiss*.
We have the old *brood* (n.) and *breed* (v.) and the new
brood (v.) and *breed* (n.) ; a new verb to *blood* exists by
the side of the old to *bleed*, and a new noun *feed* by the
side of the old *food*. It is obvious that the language
has been enriched by acquiring all these newly formed
words ; but it should also be admitted that there has
been a positive gain in ease and simplicity in all those
cases where there was no occasion for turning the
existing phonetic difference to account by creating
new verbs or nouns in new significations, and where,
accordingly, one of the phonetic forms has simply
disappeared, as when the old verbs *sniwan*, *scrydan*,
swierman have given way to the new *snows*, *shroud*,
swarm, which are like the nouns, or when the noun
swat, *swot* (he swette blodes swot, *Ancrene Riwle*) has
been discarded in favour of *sweat*, which has the same
vowel as the verb.

176. In some cases the place of the stress serves to
distinguish substantives from verbs, the former having
initial and the latter final stress. Thus some native
words with prefixes : |*forecast* sb., *fore*|*cast* vb.,
similarly *overthrow*, *underline*. In the same way a

great many Romanic words are differentiated, the substantives (adjectives) having fore-stress, the corresponding verbs end-stress : e.g. *absent, accent, conduct, frequent, object, present, rebel, record, subject, interdict.* Words like *compliment, experiment* have an obscure vowel [ə] in the sb., but a full vowel [e] in the vb., even if the final syllable has not full stress.

177. Among the other points of interest presented by the formations occupying us here I may mention the curious oscillation found in some instances between noun and verb. *Smoke* is first a noun (the smoke from the chimney), then a verb (the chimney smokes, he smokes a pipe) ; then a new noun is formed from the verb in the last sense (let us have a smoke). Similarly *gossip* (a) noun : godfather, intimate friend, idle talker, (b) verb : to talk idly, (c) new noun : idle talk ; *dart* (a) a weapon, (b) to throw (a dart), to move rapidly (like a dart), (c) a sudden motion ; *brush* (a) an instrument, (b) to use that instrument, (c) the action of using it : your hat wants a brush ; *sail* (a) a piece of canvas, (b) to sail, (c) a sailing excursion ; *wire* (a) a metallic thread, (b) to telegraph, (c) a telegram ; so also *cable* ; in vulgar language a verb is formed to *jaw* and from that a second noun a *jaw* ('what speech do you mean?' 'Why that grand jaw that you sputtered forth just now about reputation', F. C. Philips). Sometimes the starting point is a verb, e.g., *frame* (a) to form, (b) noun : a fabric, a border for a picture, etc., (c) verb : to set in a frame ; and sometimes an adjective, e.g. *faint* (a) weak, (b) to become weak, (c) a fainting fit.

178. To those who might see in the obliteration of the old distinctive marks of the different parts of speech a danger of ambiguity, I would answer that this danger is more imaginary than real. I open at random a modern novel and count on one page 34 nouns which can be used as infinitives without any change, and 38 verbs the forms of which can be used as nouns,[1] while only 22 nouns and 9 verbs cannot be thus used. As some of the ambiguous nouns and verbs occur more than once, and as the same page contains adverbs, prepositions, and conjunctions[2] which are identical with nouns (adjectives) or verbs, or both, the theoretical possibilities of mistakes arising from confusion of parts of speech would seem to be very numerous. And yet no one reading that page would feel the slightest hesitation about understanding every word correctly, as either the ending or the context shows at once whether a verb is meant or not. Even such an extreme case as this line, which is actually found in a modern song, 'Her eyes like angels watch them still', is not obscure, although *her* might be both accusative and possessive, *eyes* both noun and verb, *like* adjective, conjunction, and verb, *watch* noun and verb, and *still* adjective, verb and adverb. A modern Englishman, realizing the great advantage his language possesses in its power of making words serve in new functions, might make Shakespeare's lines his own in a different sense :

> So all my best is dressing old words new,
> Spending againe what is already spent.[3]

179. Word-composition plays a very important part in English. Compounds are either fixed or free, i.e. such that when the need arises any speaker can form new compounds after the pattern of already existing combinations. The former tend to be felt as independent units, isolated from the component parts in

---

[1] Answer, brother, reply, father, room, key, haste, gate, time, head, pavement, man, waste, truth, thunder, clap, storey, bed, book, night, face, point, shame, while, eye, top, hook, finger, bell, land, lamp, taper, shelf, church,—whisper, wait, return, go, keep, call, look, leave, reproach, do, pass, come, cry, open, sing, fall, hurry, reach, snatch, lie, regard, creep, lend, say, try, steal, hold, swell, wonder, interest, see, choke, shake, place, escape, ring, take, light. (I have not counted auxiliary verbs).

[2] Back, down, still, out, home, except, like, while, straight.

[3] Sonnet 76.

sound and (or) in meaning. *Daisy* was originally *dayes eye*, but no one nowadays connects the word with either *day* or *eye*. *Woman* was originally *wīf + man* ; a reminder of the [i]-sound is kept in the plural *women* ; *nostril*, OE. *nosu-þyrel* (the latter part means 'hole'), *fifteen, Monday, Christmas* show shortening of the first element as compared with *nose, five, moon, Christ*. Compare the treatment of the second element in the numerous place-names in *-ton*, from *town*, and in *-mouth*, pronounced [-meþ]. *Cupboard* is pronounced [kʌbəd]. Sometimes there is re-composition as a reaction against isolation : OE. *hūs + wif* in course of time lost *w*, both vowels were shortened, *s* was sounded [z], and *f* became *v* or was even lost ; in the derived meanings 'needle-case' and 'jade' we find the forms *huzzif, huzzive*, and *huzzy*. But in the original sense the word was constantly revived : *housewife*. With free compounds we may have even long strings, like *railway refreshment room, New Year Eve fancy dress ball*, his *twopence a week pocket-money*, etc.

180. With regard to the logical relation of the parts of a compound very few are of the same type as *tiptoe* = tip of the toe. In the majority the first part determines the second : a *garden flower* is a kind of flower, but a *flower garden* a kind of garden. The relation of the two parts may be very different, and is left to be inferred from the meaning of each. Compare for instance *lifeboat* on the one hand with *life-insurance life member, lifetime, life class* (class of painters drawing from life) and on the other hand *steamboat, pilot boat, iron boat*, etc. *Home letters* (from h.), *home voyage* (to), *home life* (at). Sometimes a compound means 'at the same time A and B' : *servantman* = man *servant, queen-dowager, deaf-mute* = deaf and dumb.

181. A special type of compounds is exemplified in *pick-pocket* = 'one who picks pockets'. This type (verb + object) seems to have originated in Romanic languages, but has in modern times proved very fertile in English : *cut-purse, know-nothing, sawbones, break-*

water, stopgap, scare-crow, etc. Such compounds are
very often used as first parts of new compounds, in
which case they may be considered adjectives : *break-
neck* pace, a very *tell-tale* face, a *lack-lustre* eye, a
make-shift dinner.[1]

182. While in the old type of fixed compounds the
first part had strong and the second weak stress, the
stress tends in free compounds, such as *gold coin, coat
tail, lead pencil, headmaster*, to be more level, so that
it often varies rhythmically according to the context.
Each part of the compound is felt as independent of
and of equal weight with the other. As an adjective
before a substantive is now just as uninflected as a
substantive forming the first part of a compound, the
two combinations are also made syntactically equal.
They are co-ordinated in 'her Christian and *family*
name', 'all national, *State, county*, and municipal
offices', 'a *Boston* young lady'. The prop-word *one*
may be used as in 'two *gold* watches and a *silver* one',
'give me a paper, one of the *Sunday* ones'. The like-
ness with adjectives is made even more obvious when
an adverb is used as in 'from a too exclusively *London*
standpoint', 'in purely *Government* work', 'in the most
matter-of-fact way'. From being often used as first
parts of compounds some substantives have really
become regular adjectives and are recognized as such
by everybody : *chief, choice, commonplace* ; they may
even form adverbs : *choicely*, and substantives like
commonplaceness. Dainty, originally a substantive
meaning a delicacy (Old French *daintie* from L.
dignitatem), and *bridal* (originally *brydealu* 'bride-ale')
are now practically nothing but adjectives : note in
both their seemingly adjectival endings.[2]

183. Having thus considered the modes of forming
new words by adding something to existing words, by
adding to them nothing at all, and by composition, we
shall end this chapter by some remarks on the forma-

---

[1] MEG. II, 8, 6 and 14, 7.
[2] See MEG. II, ch. XI.

tion of new words by subtracting something from old
ones.[1] Such 'back-formations', as they are very
conveniently termed by Dr. Murray, owe their origin
to one part of a word being mistaken for some derivative suffix (or, more rarely, prefix). The adverbs
sideling, groveling and *darkling* were originally formed
by means of the adverbial ending *-ling*, but in such
phrases as *he walks sideling, he lies groveling*, etc., they
looked exactly like participles in *-ing*, and the consequence was that the new verbs to *sidle*, to *grovel*,
and to *darkle* were derived from them by the subtraction of *-ing*. The *Banting* cure was named after
one Mr. Banting ; the occasional verb to *bant* is,
accordingly, a back-formation. The ending *-y* is often
subtracted ; from *greedy* is thus formed the noun *greed*
(about 1600), from *lazy* and *cosy* the two verbs *laze*
and *cose* (Kingsley), and from *jeopardy* (French *jeu
parti*) the verb *jeopard*. The old adjective corresponding to *difficulty* was *difficile* as in French, but
about 1600 the adjective *difficult* (= the noun minus
y) makes its appearance. *Puppy* from French *poupée*
was thought to be formed by means of the petting
suffix *y*, and thus *pup* was created ; similarly I think
that *cad* is from *caddy, caddie* = Fr. *cadet* (a youngster)
and *pet* from *petty* = Fr. *petit*, the transition in meaning
from 'little' to 'favourite' being easily accounted for.
Several verbs originate from nouns in *-er* (*-ar, -or*),
which were not originally 'agent nouns' ; *butcher* is
the French *boucher*, derived from *bouc* 'a buck, goat'
with no corresponding verb, but in English it has
given rise to the rare verb to *butch* and to the noun a
butch-knife. Similarly *harbinger, rover, pedlar, burglar,
hawker*, and probably *beggar*, call into existence the
verbs to *harbinge* (Whitman), *rove, peddle, burgle, hawk*,
and *beg* ; and the Latin words *editor, donator, vivi-*

---

[1] Otto Jespersen, 'Om subtraktionsdannelser, særligt på dansk
og engelsk', in *Festskrift til Vilh Thomsen* (Copenhagen, 1894). I have
treated a few classes of back-formations in *Engl. Studien* 70, p. 117 ff.
On the subtraction of *s*, as if it were a plural sign, see below, § 198.

sector, produce the un-Latin verbs to *edit, donate* (American), *vivisect* (Meredith), etc., which look as if they came from Latin participles.[1] Some of these back-formations have been more successful than others in being generally recognized in Standard English.

184. It is not usual in Germanic languages to form compounds with a verb as the second, and an object or a predicative as the first, part. Hence, when we find such verbs as to *housekeep* (Kipling, Merriman), the explanation must be that -*er* has been subtracted from the perfectly legitimate noun a *housekeeper* (or -*ing* from *housekeeping*). The oldest examples I know of this formation are to *backbite* (1300), to *partake* (parttake, 16th c.) and to *soothsay* and *conycatch* (Shakesp.); others are to *hutkeep*, common in Australia, *book-keep* (Shaw), to *dressmake*, to *matchmake* (women will match-make, you know, A. Hope), to *thoughtread* (Why don't they thoughtread each other? H. G. Wells), to *typewrite* (I could typewrite if I had a machine, id., also in B. Shaw's *Candida*), to *merrymake* (you merrymake together, Du Maurier). It will be seen that most of these are nonce-words. The verbs to *henpeck* and to *sunburn* are back-formations from the participles *henpecked* and *sunburnt*; and Browning even says '*moonstrike* him!' (*Pippa Passes*) for 'let him be moonstruck'.

185. We have seen (§ 7 ff.) that monosyllabism is one of the most characteristic features of modern English, and this chapter has shown us some of the morphological processes by which the original stock of monosyllables has been in course of time considerably increased. It may not, therefore, be out of place here briefly to give an account of some of the other modes by which such short words have been developed. Some are simply longer words which have been shortened by regular phonetic development (cf. *love*, § 163); e.g. *eight* OE. *eahta, dear* OE. *deore, fowl* OE. *ugol, hawk* OE. *hafoc, lord* OE. *hlaford, not* and *nought* OE. *nawiht, pence* OE. *penigas, ant* OE. *æmette,* etc.

Miss before the names of unmarried ladies is a some-what irregular shortening of 'missis' (mistress); though found here and there in the seventeenth century, *Miss* was not yet recognized in the middle of the eighteenth century (cf. Fielding's Mrs. Bridgit, Mrs. Honour, etc.).

186. This leads us to the numerous popular clippings of long foreign words, of which rarely the middle (as in *Tench* 'the House of *Detention*' and *teck* 'detective') or the end (as in *bus* 'omnibus', *baccer, baccy* 'tobacco', *phone*, 'telephone'), but more often the beginning only subsists. Some of these stump-words have never passed beyond slang, such as *sov* 'sovereign', *pub* 'public-house', *confab* 'confabulation', *pop* 'popular concert', *vet* 'veterinary surgeon', *Jap* 'Japanese', *guv* 'Governor', *Mods* 'Moderations', an Oxford examination, *matric* 'matriculation', *prep* 'preparation', and *impot* or *impo* 'imposition' in schoolboys' slang, *sup.* 'supernumerary', *props* 'properties' in theatrical slang, *perks* 'perquisites', *comp* 'compositor', *caps* 'capital letters', etc., etc. Some are perhaps now in a fair way to become recognized in ordinary speech, such as *exam* 'examination', and *bike* 'bicycle'; and some words have become so firmly established as to make the full words pass completely into oblivion, e.g. *cab* (cabriolet), *fad* (fadaise), *navvy* (navigator in the sense of canal-digger and later railway labourer) and *mob* (mobile vulgus).

187. A last group of English monosyllables comprises a certain number of words the etymology of which has hitherto baffled all the endeavours of philologists. At a certain moment such a word suddenly comes into the language, nobody knowing from where, so that we must feel really inclined to think of a creation *ex nihilo*. I am not particularly thinking of words denoting sounds or movements in a more or less onomatopoetic way, for their origin is psychologically easy to account for, but of such words as the following some of which belong now to the most indispensable speech material : *bad*,[1] *big*,[2] *lad* and *lass*, all appearing towards the end of the thirteenth century ; *fit* adjective and *fit* substantive, probably two mutually independent words, the adjective dating from 1440, the substantive in the now current sense from 1547 ; *dad* 'father', *jump*, *crease* 'fold, wrinkle', *gloat*, and *bet* from the sixteenth century; *job*, *fun* (and *pun*), *blight*, *chum* and *hump* from the seventeenth century ; *fuss*, *jam* verb and substantive, and *hoax* from the eighteenth, and *slum*, *stunt* and *blurb* from the nineteenth and twentieth centuries. Anyone who has watched small children carefully must have noticed that they sometimes create some such word without any apparent reason ; sometimes they stick to it only for a day or two as the name of some plaything, etc., and then forget it ; but sometimes a funny sound takes lastingly their fancy and may even be adopted by their playmates or parents as a real word.[3] Without pretending that such is the origin of all the words just mentioned I yet venture to throw out the suggestion that some of them may be due to children's playful inventiveness—while others may have sprung from the corresponding linguistic playfulness of grown-up people which forms the fundamental essence of the phenomenon called *slang*.

---

[1] See Zupitza's attempt at an explanation in the NED., which does not account for the origin of *bœddel*.

[2] The best explanation is Björkman's, see *Scand. Loan Words*, p. 157 and 259 ; but even he does not claim to have solved the mystery completely.

[3] Cf. my book *Language*, p. 151 ff. On the general theory of slang see ib. 298 ff., and *Mankind, Nation and Individual*, p. 149 ff.

Chapter IX

Grammar

188. The preceding chapter has already brought us near to our present province or rather has crossed its boundary, for word-formation is rightly considered one of the main divisions of grammar. In the other divisions a survey of the historical development shows us the same general tendency as word-formation does (§ 164), the tendency, as we might call it, from chaos towards cosmos. Where the old language had a great many endings, most of them with very vague meanings and applications, Modern English has but few, and their sphere of signification is more definite. The number of irregularities and anomalies, so considerable in Old English, has been greatly reduced so that now the vast majority of words are inflected regularly. It has been objected that most of the old strong verbs are still strong, and that this means irregularity in the formation of the tenses : *shake, shook, shaken* is just as irregular as Old English *scacan, scoc, scacen.* But it must be remembered, first, that there is a complete disappearance of a great many of those details of inflexion which made every Old English paradigm much more complicated than its modern successor, such as distinctions of persons and numbers, and nearly all differences between the infinitive, the imperative, the indicative, and the subjunctive ; secondly that the number of distinct vowels has been reduced in many verbs ; compare thus *beran, bireþ, bær, bæron, boren* with *bear, bears, bore, bore, born* ; *feohtan, fieht, feaht, fuhton, fohten* with *fiyht, fights, fought, fought, fought* ; *bindan, band, bunden* with *bind, bound, bound,* *berstan, bærst, burston, borsten* with *burst, burst, burst, burst*; and thirdly, that the consonant change found in many verbs (*ceas, curon, snap, snidon, teah, tugon*) has been abolished altogether except in the single case of *was, were*. The greatest change towards simplicity and regularity is seen in the adjectives, where one form now represents the eleven different forms used by the contemporaries of Alfred. But it must not be imagined that the development has in every minute particular made for progress; nothing has been gained, for instance, by the modern creation of *mine* and *thine* as primary possessive pronouns by the side of *my* and *thy*. It is only when we compare the entire linguistic structure of some remote period with the structure in modern times that we observe that the gain in clearness and simplicity has really been enormous.

189. This grammatical development and simplification has taken place not suddenly and from one cause, but gradually and from a variety of causes, most of these the same that have worked and are working similar changes in other languages. It cannot be said that 'the chief impulse to such changes is due to progressive thinking and advancing culture which made the traditional forms insufficient for the abundance of ideas in their mutual relations' (Morsbach), for some of the changes took place with greatest rapidity in centuries when culture was at a low ebb. Chief among the general causes of the decay of the Old English apparatus of declensions and conjugations must be reckoned the manifold incongruities of the system : if the same vowel did not everywhere denote the same shade of meaning, speakers would naturally tend to indulge in the universal inclination to pronounce weak syllables indistinctly (and the OE. flexional endings were all unstressed) : thus *a, i, u* of the endings were levelled in the one colourless vowel *e*, and this could even after some time be dropped altogether in most cases. The same want of system would also favour the analogical extension of those endings which were clearest in their forms and in their sphere of employment, thus in substantives the *s*-forms both as genitives and as plurals.[1] But beside this general cause we must in each separate case inquire into those special causes that may have been at work, and even such a seemingly small step as that by which the old declension of *ye* (nominative) and *you* (accusative and dative) has given way to the modern use of *you* in all cases, has been the result of the activity of many moving forces. In the following sections I shall select a few points of grammar which seem to me illustrative of the processes of change in general, and (as regards some of them) of the progressive tendency I have mentioned.

190. (I.) The *s*-ending in nouns : In Old English the *genitive* was formed in *es* in most masculines and neuters, but beside this a variety of other endings were in use with the different stems, in *-e*, in *-re*, in *-an* ; some words had no separate ending in the genitive, and some formed a mutation-genitive (*boc* 'book', gen. *bec*). Besides, the genitive of the plural never ended in *-s* but in *-a* or *-ra* or *-na* (*-ena*, *-ana*). With regard to syntax, the genitive case filled a variety of functions, possessive, subjective, objective, partitive, definitive, descriptive, etc. It was used not only to connect two substantives, but also after a great number of verbs and adjectives (rejoice at, fear, long for, remember, fill, empty, weary, deprive of, etc.) ; it sometimes stood before and sometimes after the governing word. In short, the rules for the formation as well as for the employment of that case were complicated to a very high degree. But gradually a greater regularity and simplicity prevailed in accidence as well as in syntax ;

---

[1] This is the view I have held since 1891 and expressed more or less explicitly in various publications; see now *Language*, books III and IV, also *Chapters on English*. On the influence of speech-mixture on the rapidity of movement see above (§ 79) ; on the rapidity of change due to wars, pestilences, etc., in the fourteenth and fifteenth centuries, see *Language*, p. 261.

the *s*-genitive was extended to more and more nouns and to the plural as well as the singular number, and now it is the only genitive ending used in the language though in the plural it is in the great majority of cases hidden away behind the *s* used to denote the plural number (*kings'*, cf. *men's*). The position of the genitive now is always immediately before the governing word, and this in connexion with the regularity of the formation of the case has been intrumental in bringing about the modern group-genitive, where the *s* is tacked on to the end of a word-group, with no regard to the logic of the older grammar : *the King of England's power* (formerly 'the kinges power of England'), *the bride and bridegroom's return, somebody else's hat*, etc.[1]

191. As for the use of the genitive, it has been in various ways encroached upon by the combination with *of*. First, its use is now in ordinary prose almost restricted to personal beings, and even such phrases as 'society's hard-drilled soldiery' (Meredith), where *society* is personified, are felt as poetical ; still more so, of course, 'thou knowst not golds effect', (Sh.) or 'setting out upon life's journey' (Stevenson). But in some set phrases the genitive is still established, e.g. out of *harm's* way ; he is at his *wits'* (or *wit's*) end ; so also in the stock quotation from Hamlet, in my *mind's* eye, etc. Then to indicate measure, etc.: at a *boat's* length from the ship, and especially time : an *hour's* walk, a good *night's* rest, *yesterday's* post ; and this is even extended to such prepositional combinations as *to-day's* adventures, *to-morrow's* papers.

192. Secondly, the genitive (of names of persons) is now chiefly used possessively, though this word must be taken in a very wide sense, including such cases as 'Shelley's works', 'Gainsborough's pictures', 'Tom's enemies', 'Tom's death', etc. The subjective genitive, too, is in great vigour, for instance in 'the King's arrival', 'the Duke's invitation', 'the Duke's inviting

---

[1] See the detailed historical account of the group-genitive, *Chapters on English*, 1918, ch. III.

him', 'Mrs. Poyser's repulse of the squire' (G. Eliot).
Still there is, in quite recent times, a tendency towards
expressing the subject by means of the preposition *by*,
just as in the passive voice, for instance in 'the accidental discovery by Miss Knag of some correspondence' (Dickens); 'the appropriation by a settled
community of lands on the other side of an ocean'
(Seeley), 'the massacre of Christians by Chinese'.
'Forster's Life of Dickens' is the same thing as
'Dickens's Life, by Forster'. The objective genitive
was formerly much more common than now, the
ambiguity of the genitive being probably the reason
of its decline. Still, we find, for instance, 'his expulsion
from power by the Tories' (Thackeray), 'What was
thy pity's recompense?' (Byron). 'England's wrongs'
generally means the wrongs done to England; thus
also 'my cosens wrongs' in Shakespeare's R 2, II,
3, 141, but 'your foule wrongs' (in the same play, III,
1, 15) means the wrongs committed by you. In 'my
sceptre's awe' (ib. I, 1, 118) we have an objective, but
in 'thy free awe pays homage to us' (Hamlet IV,
3, 63) a subjective genitive. But on the whole such
obscurity will occur less frequently in English than in
other languages, where the genitive is more freely
used.

193. Now, *of* has so far prevailed that there are very
few cases where a genitive cannot be replaced by it,
and it is even used to supplant a possessive pronoun in
such stock phrases as 'not for the death of me' (cf.
Chaucer's 'the blood of me', LGW. 848). *Of* is required
in a great many cases, such as 'I come here at the
instance of your colleague, Dr. H. J. Henry Jekyll'
(Stevenson), and it is often employed to avoid tacking
on the *s* to too long a series of words, as in 'Will
Wimble's is the case of many a younger brother of a
great family' (Addison) or 'the wife of a clergyman of
the Church of England' (Thackeray), where most
Englishmen will resent the iteration of *of*'s less than
they do the repeated *s*'s in Mrs. Browning's 'all the

hoofs of King Saul's father's asses' or in Pinero's
'He is my wife's first husband's only child's godfather'.
Even long strings of prepositions are tolerated, as in
'on the occasion of the coming of age of one of the
youngest sons of a wealthy member of Parliament',
or 'Swift's visit to London in 1707 had for its object
the obtaining for the Irish Church of the surrender by
the Crown of the First-Fruits and Twentieths' (Aitken)
or 'that sublime conception of the Holy Father of a
spiritual kingdom on earth under the sovereignty of
the Vicar of Jesus Christ himself' (Hall Caine). I
suppose that very few readers of the original books
have found anything heavy or cumbersome in these
passages, even if they may here, where their attention
is drawn to the grammatical construction.

194. Speaking of the genitive, we ought also to mention the curious use in phrases like 'a friend of my
brother's'. This began in the fourteenth century with
such instances as 'an officere of the prefectes' (Chaucer
G 368), where *officers* might be supplied (= one of the
prefect's officers) and 'if that any neighebor of mine
(= any of my neighbours) Wol nat in chirche to my
wyf enclyne' (id. B 3091). In the course of a few centuries, the construction became more and more
frequent, so that it has now long been one of the
fixtures of the English language. A partitive sense is
still conceivable in such phrases as 'an olde religious
unckle of mine' (Sh. As III, 3, 362) = one of my uncles,
though it will be seen that it is impossible to analyse
it as being equal to 'one of my old religious uncles'.
But it is not at all certain that *of* here from the first
was partitive ;[1] it is rather to be classed with the
appositional use in *the three of us* = 'the three who are
we' ; *the City of Rome* = 'the City which is Rome'.
The construction is used chiefly to avoid the juxtaposition of two pronouns, 'this hat of mine, that ring
of yours' being preferred to 'this my hat, that your

[1] See *Mod. Engl. Grammar*, III, p. 15 ff.

ring', or of a pronoun and a genitive, as in 'any ring of Jane's', where 'any Jane's ring' or 'Jane's any ring' would be impossible ; compare also 'I make it a rule of mine', 'this is no fault of Frank's', etc. In all such cases the construction was found so convenient that it is no wonder that it should soon be used extensively where no partitive sense is logically possible, as in 'nor shall [we] ever see That face of hers againe' (Shakespeare, Lear I, 1, 267), 'that flattering tongue of yours' (As IV, 1, 188), 'Time hath not yet so dried this bloud of mine' (Ado IV, 1, 195), 'If I had such a tyre, this face of mine Were full as lovely as is this of hers' (Gent. IV, 4, 190), 'this uneasy heart of ours' (Wordsworth), 'that poor old mother of his', etc. When we now say 'he has a house of his own', no one could think of this as meaning 'he has one of his own houses'.

195. In the *nominative plural* the Old English declensions present the same motley spectacle as the genitive singular. Most masculines have the ending *as*, but some have *e* (Engle, etc.), some *a* (suna, etc.) and a great many *an* (guman, etc.) ; some nouns have no ending at all, and most of these change the vowel of the kernel (fet, etc.), while a few have the plural exactly like the singular (hettend). Feminine words formed their plural in *a* (giefa), in *e* (bene), in *an* (tungan) or without any ending (sweostor ; with mutation bec). Neuters had either no ending (word) or else *u* (hofu) or *an* (eagan). From the oldest period the ending *as* (later *es*, *s*) has been continually gaining ground, first among those masculines that belonged to other declensional classes, later on also in the other genders. The *an*-ending, which was common to a very great number of substantives from the very beginning, also showed great powers of expansion and at one time seemed as likely as (*e*)*s* to become the universal plural ending. But finally (*e*)*s* carried the day, probably because it was the most distinctive ending, and possibly under Scandinavian influence (§ 79).

In the beginning of the modern period *eyen, shoon,* and
hosen, housen, peasen still existed, but they were
doomed to destruction, and now *oxen* is the only real
plural in *n* surviving, for *children* as well as the biblical
kine and *brethren* are too irregular to count as plurals
made by the addition of *n.* The mutation plural has
survived in some words whose signification causes the
plural to occur more frequently than, or at least as
frequently as, the singular : *geese, teeth, feet, mice, lice,
men* and *women.* In all other words the analogy of the
plurals in *s* was too strong for the old form to be preserved.

196. Instead of the ending *-ses* we often find a
single *s* ; in some cases this may be the continued use
of the French plural form without any ending (*cas*
sg. and pl.), as in *sense* (their sense are shut, Sh.),
corpse (pl. Sh.), etc. In Coriolanus III, 1, 118, *voyce
voyces* occur, both of them to be read as one syllable :
'Why shall the people give One that speakes thus,
their voyce?—Ile give my reasons, More worthier than
their voyces. They know the corne.' But when Shakespeare uses *princesse* and *balance* as plurals (Tp. I,
2, 173 ; Merch. IV, 1, 255), the forms admit of no other
explanation than that of haplology (pronouncing the
same sound once instead of twice). Thus also in the
genitive case : 'his mistresse eye-brow' (As. II, 7, 149),
'your Highness' pleasure', etc. Now it is more usual
to give the full form *mistress's,* etc., yet in *Pears' soap*
the juxtaposition of three *s*'s is avoided by means of
the apostrophized form. The genitive of the plural is
now always haplologized : 'the Poets' Corner', except
in some dialects : 'other folks's children' (George
Eliot), 'the bairns's clease' (Murray, *Dial. of Scotl.,*
164). Wallis (1653) expressly states that the gen. pl.
in *the Lord's House* (by him written *Lord's*) stands
instead of *the Lords's House* (duo *s* in unum coinci-
dunt). A phenomenon of the same order is the omission of the genitive sign before a word beginning with
s, now chiefly before *sake* : for fashion sake, etc.

197. Sometimes an *s* belonging to the stem of the word is taken by the popular instinct to be a plural ending.[1] Thus in *alms* (ME. *almesse, elmesse,* pl. *almesses* ; OE. *œlmesse* from Gr. *eleemosune*) ; it is significant that the word is very often found in connexions where it is impossible from the context to discover whether a singular or a plural is intended (ask alms, give alms, etc.). In the Authorized Version the word occurs eleven times, but eight of these are ambiguous, two are clearly singular (asked an almes, gave much almes) and one is probably plural (Thy praiers and thine almes are come up). Nowadays the association between the *s* of the *alms* and the plural ending has become so firm that *an alms* is said and written very rarely indeed, though it is found in Tennyson's *Enoch Arden. Riches* is another case in point ; Chaucer still lays the stress on the second syllable (*richésse* as in French) and uses the plural *richesses* ; but as subsequently the final *e* disappeared, and as the word occurred very often in such a way that the context does not show its number ('Thou bearst thy heavie riches but a journie', Sh. Meas. III, 1, 27), thus in fourteen out of the 24 places where Shakespeare uses it, it is no wonder that the form was generally conceived as a plural, thus 'riches are a power' (Ruskin). The singular use (the riches of the ship is come on shore, Sh. Oth. II, 1, 83, too much riches, R 2, III, 4, 60) is now wholly obsolete.

198. A further step is taken in those words that lose the *s* originally belonging to their stem, because it is mistakenly apprehended as the sign of plural.[2] Latin *pisum* became in OE. *pise,* in ME. *pese,* pl. *pesen* ; Butler (1633) still gives *peas* as sg. and *peasen* as pl., but he adds, 'the singular is most used for the plural : as . . . a peck of peas ; though the Londoners seem to make it a regular plural, calling a *peas* a *pea*'. In compounds like *peaseblossom, peaseporridge* and *pease-*

---

[1] Cf. *Mod. Engl. Grammar,* II, ch. V.
[2] Cf. the other back-formations mentioned above (§ 183).

soup (Swift, Lamb) the old form was preserved long after *pea* had become the recognized singular. Similarly *a cherry* was evolved from a form in *s* (French *cerise*), *a riddle* from *riddles* ; *an eaves* (OE. *efes*, cf. Got. *ubizwa*, ON. *ups*) is often made *an eave*, and vulgarly *a pony shay* is said for *chaise* ; compare also Bret Harte's 'heathen *Chinee*' and the parallel forms *a Portuguee, a Maltee*. An interesting case in point is *Yankee*, if H. Logeman's ingenious explanation is to be accepted. The term was originally applied to the inhabitants of the Dutch colonies in North America (New Amsterdam, now New York, etc.). Now *Jan Kees* is a nickname still applied in Flanders to people from Holland proper. *Jan* of course is the common Dutch name corresponding to English John, and *Kees* may be either the usual pet form of the name Cornelis, another Christian name typical of the Dutch, or else a dialectal variation of *kaas* 'cheese' in allusion to that typically Dutch product, or—what is most probable—a combination of both. *Jankees* in English became *Yankees*, where the *s* was taken as the plural ending and eventually disappeared, and *Yankee* became the designation of any inhabitant of New England and even sometimes of the whole of the United States.

199. We have a different class of back-formations in those cases in which the *s* that is subtracted is really the plural ending, while one part of the word is retained which is logically consistent with the plural idea only. It is easily conceivable that most people ignorant of the fact that the first syllable of *cinque-ports* means 'five', have no hesitation in speaking of Hastings as a *cinque-port* ; but it is more difficult to see how the signification of the numeral in *nine-pins* should be forgotten, and yet sometimes each of the 'pins' used in that play is called *a ninepin*, and Gosse writes 'the author sets up his four ninepins'.

200. In some words the *s* of the plural has become fixed, as if it belonged to the singular, thus in *means*. As is shown by the pun in Shakespeare's *Romeo*, 'no

sudden meane of death, though nere so meane' the old
form was still understood in his time, but the modern
form too is used by him (*by that meanes*, Merch.; *a
means*, Wint.). Similarly : *too much pains, an honour-
able amends, a shambles, an innings*, etc., sometimes
a scissors, a tweezers, a barracks, a golf links, etc., where
the logical idea of a single action or thing has proved
stronger than the original grammar.

201. It is not, however, till a new plural has been
formed on such a form that the transformation from
plural to singular has been completed. This phenomenon, which might be termed plural raised to the
second power, will naturally occur with greater facility
when the original singular is not in use or when the
manner of forming the plural is no longer perspicuous.
Thus OE. *broc* formed its plural *brec* (cf. *gos, ges*,
goose, geese), but *broc* became obsolete, and *brec,
breech* was free to become a singular and to form a
new plural *breeches*. Similarly *invoices, quinces,
bodices*, and a few others have a double plural ending ;
but then the unusual sound of the first ending (voiceless *s*, where the ordinary ending is voiced, as in
joys, sins) facilitated the forgetting of the original
function of the *s* (written -*ce*). *Bodice* is really nothing
but a by-form of *bodies*. The old pronunciation of
bellows and *gallows* had also a voiceless *s*, which helps
to explain the vulgar plurals *belowses* and *gallowses*.
But in the occasional plural *mewses* (from *a mews*,
orig. *a mue*) the new ending has been added in spite
of the first *s* being voiced. These plurals raised to the
second power, to which must be added *sixpences,
threepences*, etc., are particularly interesting because
there really are cases where the want is felt of expressing the plural of something which is in itself
plural, either formally or logically ; cf. *many (pairs of)
scissors*. Generally one plural ending only is used,[1]
but occasionally the logically correct double ending is

---

[1] 'Then ensued one of the most lively ten minutes that I can
remember' (Conan Doyle), plural of 'a lively ten minutes'.

resorted to, especially among uneducated people ;
Thackeray makes his flunkey write : 'there was 8 sets
of chamberses' (*Yellowplush Papers*, p. 39), and a
London schoolboy[1] once wrote : 'cats have clawses'
(one cat has claws !) and again 'cats have 9 liveses'
(each cat has nine lives !). Dr. Murray[2] mentions a
double plural sometimes formed in Scotch dialect
from such words as *schuin* (one person's shoes), *feit*
'feet' and *kye* 'cows', *schuins* meaning more than one
pair of shoes, and he ingeniously suggests that this
may illustrate such plurals as *children, brethren, kine* ;
the original plurals were *childer, brether, ky* (still
preserved in the northern dialect), which may have
'come to be used collectively for the offspring or
members of a single family, the herd of a single owner,
so that a second plural inflection became necessary to
express the *brethren* and *children* of many families, the
ky-en of many owners . . . In modern English we
restrict *brothers*, which replaces *brether*, to those of one
family, using *brethren* for those who call each other
brother, though of different families.'

202. Most of the words that make their plural like
the singular are old neuters, the *s*-ending belonging
originally to masculines only and having only gradually been extended to the other two genders ; thus,
swine, deer, sheep. In some cases a difference sprang
up between the singular in speaking of the mass and
an individual plural (in *-s*), as seen most clearly in
Shakespeare's 'Shee hath more *haire* then wit, and
more faults then *hairs*' (Gent. III, 1, 362) and Milton's
'which thou from Heaven Feigndst at thy birth was
giv'n thee in thy *hair*, Where strength can least abide,
though all thy *hairs* Were bristles' (*Sams. Ag.*, 1136).
This difference was transferred to some old masculines,
like *fish, fowl* ; and a great many names of particular
fishes and birds, especially those generally hunted and
used for food, are now often unchanged in the plural

---

[1] *Very Original English*, by Barker (London, 1889), p. 71.
[2] *Dialect of the Southern Counties of Scotland* (London, 1873), p. 161.

(*snipe, plover, trout, salmon*, etc.), though with a great deal of vacillation. It is also noticeable that *much fruit = many fruits* and *much coal = many coals*. When we say 'four *hundred* men', but *hundreds* of men', 'two *dozen* collars', but '*dozens* of collars' and similarly with *couple, pair, score*, and some other words, we have an approach to the rule prevailing in many languages, e.g. Magyar, where the plural ending is not added after a numeral, because that suffices in itself to show that a plural is intended.[1]

203. (II) Disappearance of the old *word-gender*.[2] In Old English, as in all the old cognate languages, each substantive, no matter whether it referred to animate beings or things or abstract notions, belonged to one or other of the three gender-classes. Thus masculine pronouns and endings were found with names of a great many things which had nothing to do with male sex (e.g. *horn, ende* 'end', *ebba* 'ebb', *dæg* 'day') and similarly feminine pronouns and endings with many words without any relation to female sex (e.g. *sorh* 'sorrow', *glof* 'glove', *plume* 'plum', *pipe*). Anyone acquainted with the intricacies of the same system (or want of system) in German will feel how much English has gained in clearness and simplicity by giving up these distinctions and applying *he* only to male, and *she* only to female, living beings. The distinction between animate and inanimate now is much more accentuated than it used to be, and this has led to some other changes, of which the two most important are the creation (about 1600) of the form *its* (before that time *his* was neuter as well as masculine) and the restriction of the relative pronoun *which* to things : its old use alike for persons and things is seen in 'Our father *which* art in Heaven'.

204. (III) *Numerals*. While the cardinal numerals

---

[1] Cf. *Mod. Engl. Gr.*, II, ch. III., Unchanged plurals, and ch. V, Mass-words.

[2] On the relation between gender and sex, see *Philosophy of Grammar*, ch. XVII.

show very little change during the whole life of the
language, except what is a consequence of ordinary
phonetic development,[1] the ordinals have been much
more changed so that their formation is now completely regular, with the exception of the first three.
First has ousted the old *forma* (corresponding to Latin
primus), and the French *second* has been called in to
relieve *other* of one of its significations, so that a useful
distinction has been created between the definite and
the indefinite numeral. As for the numbers from 4
upwards, the regularization has affected both the
stem and the ending of the numeral. In Old English
the *n* had disappeared from *seofoða, nigoða and teoða*
(*feowerteoða,* etc.), but now it has been analogically
reintroduced : *seventh, ninth, tenth (fourteenth,* etc.), the
only survival of the older forms being *tithe,* which is
now a substantive differentiated from the numeral, as
seen particularly clearly in the phrase 'a tenth part
of the tithe' (Auth. Version, Num. 18, 26). In *twelfth*
and *fifth* we have the insignificant anomaly of *f* (which
in the former is often mute) instead of *v,* and the
consonant-group in the latter has shortened the vowel,
but elsewhere there is complete correspondence
between each cardinal and its ordinal. As for the
ending, it used according to a well-known phonetic
rule to be *-ta* (later *-te, -t*) after voiceless open consonants, thus *fifta, fift, sixta, sixt, twelfta, twelft* ; and
these are still the only forms in Shakespeare (*Henry
the Fift,* etc.)[2] and Milton. The regular forms in *th*
evidently were used in writing before they became
prevalent in speaking, for Schade in 1765 laid down

---

[1] Note that in Old and Middle English the cardinals had an *e-*
when used absolutely (*fif* men ; they were *five*), and that it is this
form that has prevailed. If the old conjoint form had survived,
five and *twelve* would have ended in *f,* and *seven, nine* and *eleven*
would have had no *-n*.

[2] *Twelfth Night* is in the folio of 1623 called *Twelfe Night* and
similarly we have *twelfe day,* where the middle consonant of a
difficult group has been discarded, just as in *the thousand part*
(As IV. 1, 46).

the rule that *th* was to be pronounced *t* in *twelfth* and
fifth. Eighth, which would be more adequately written
eightth, is also a modern form ; the old editions of
Shakespeare have *eight.* The formation in *-th,* which
is now beautifully regular, has also been extended in
recent times to a few substantives : *the hundredth,
thousandth, millionth,* and *dozenth.*

205. (IV). The *pronominal system* has been reinforced by some new applications of old material. *Who*
and *which,* originally interrogative and indefinite
pronouns, are now used also as relatives. *Self* has
entered into the compounds *myself, himself,* etc., and
has developed a plural, *ourselves, themselves,* which
was new in the beginning of the sixteenth century.
With regard to the use of these *self*-forms, it may be
remarked that their frequency first increased and then
in certain cases decreased again : *he dressed him*
became *he dressed himself,* and this is now giving way
to *he dressed. One* has come to serve several purposes ;
as an indefinite pronoun (in 'one never can tell') it
dates from the fifteenth century, and as a prop-word
('a little one', 'the little ones') the modern usage goes
no further back than to the sixteenth century.

206. (V). The history of the forms in *ing* is certainly
one of the most interesting examples of the growth
from a very small beginning of something very important in the economy of the language. The *ing,*
as I shall for shortness call the form with that ending,
began as a pure substantive,[1] restricted as to the
number of words from which it might be formed and
restricted as to its syntactical functions. It seems to
have been originally possible to form it only from
nouns, cf. modern words like *schooling, shirting,
stabling* ; as some of the nouns from which ings were
derived had corresponding weak verbs, the ings came
to be looked upon as derived from these verbs, and
new ings were made from other weak verbs. (Also
from French verbs, cf. above § 106). But it was a long

---

[1] The Old English ending was *ung* as well as *ing.*

time before ings were made from strong verbs ; a few
occur in the very last decades of the Old English
period, but most of them did not creep into existence
till the twelfth or thirteenth century or even later, and
it is not, perhaps, till the beginning of the fifteenth
century that the formation had taken such a firm root
in the language that an ing could be formed unhesitat-
ingly from any verb whatever (apart from the auxiliaries *can, may, shall, must,* etc., which have no ings).

207. With regard to its syntactical use the old ing
was a substantive and was restricted to the functions
it shared with all other substantives. While keeping
all its substantival qualities, it has since gradually
acquired most of the functions belonging to a verb.
It was, and is, inflected like a substantive ; now the
genitive case is rare and scarcely occurs outside of
such phrases as 'reading for reading's sake' ; but the
plural is common : his comings and goings ; feelings,
drawings, leavings, weddings, etc. Like any other
substantive it can have the definite or indefinite
article and an adjective before it : a beginning, the
beginning, a good beginning, etc., so also a genitive :
Tom's savings. It can enter into a compound noun
either as the first or as the second part : a walking-
stick ; sight-seeing. The ing can be used in a sentence
in every position occupied by an ordinary substantive.
It is the subject and the predicative nominative in
'complimenting is lying', the object in 'I hate lying' ;
it is governed by an adjective in 'worth knowing', and
governed by a preposition in 'before answering', etc.
But we shall now see how several of the peculiar
functions of verbs are extended to the ing. The
coalescence in form of the verbal substantive and of
the present participle is, of course, one of the chief
factors of this development.

208. When the ing was a pure substantive the *object*
of the action it indicated could be expressed in one
of three ways : it might be put in the genitive case
('sio feding þara sceapa', the feeding of the sheep

Alfred), or it might form the first part of a compound
(blood-letting) or—the usual construction in Middle
English—it might be added after *of* (in magnifying of
his name, Chaucer). The first of these constructions
has died out ; the last is in our days especially frequent
after the article (since the telling of those little fibs,
Thackeray). But from the fourteenth century we find
a growing tendency to treat the ing like a form of the
verb, and accordingly, to put the object in the accusative case. Chaucer's words, 'in getinge of your
richesses and in usinge hem' (B 2813) show both
constructions in juxtaposition ; so also 'Thou art so
fat-witted with drinking of olde sacke, and unbutton-
ing thee after supper' (Henry IV A, 1, 2, 2). Chaucer's
'In liftinge up his hevy dronken cors' (H 67) shows
a double deviation from the old substantival construction, for an ordinary substantive cannot in this
way be *followed by an adverb*, and in the old language
the adverb was joined to the ing in a different way
(up-lifting, in-coming, down-going). In course of time
it became more and more usual to join any kind of
adverb to the ing, e.g. 'a man shal not wyth *ones*
[once] over redying fynde the ryght understandyng'
(Caxton), 'he proposed our *immediately* drinking a
bottle together' (Fielding), 'nothing distinguishes
great men from inferior men more than their *always*,
whether in life or in art, knowing the ways things are
going' (Ruskin).

209. A substantive does not admit of any indication
of *time* ; *his movement* may correspond in meaning to
'he moves (is moving)', 'he moved (was moving)', or
'he will move'. Similarly the ing had originally, and
to a great extent still has, no reference to time : 'on
account of his coming' may be equal to 'because he
comes' or 'because he came' or 'he will come', according to the connexion in which it occurs. 'I intend
seeing the king' refers to the future. 'I remember
seeing the king' to the past, or rather the ing as such
implies neither of these tenses. But since the end of

the sixteenth century the ing has still further approximated to the character of a verb by developing a composite perfect. Shakespeare, who uses the new tense in a few places, e.g. Gent. I, 3, 16 ('To let him spend his time no more at home ; Which would be great impeachment to his age, In *having knowne* no travaile in his youth') does not always use it where it would be used now ; for in 'Give order to my servants that they take No note at all of our *being* absent hence' *being* corresponds in meaning to *having been*, as shown by the context (Merch. of Ven. V, 120). Like other nouns the ing was also at first incapable of expressing the verbal distinction between *the active* and *the passive voice*. The simple ing is still often neutral in this respect, and in some connexions assumes a passive meaning, as in 'it wants mending', 'the story lost much in the telling'. This is extremely frequent in old authors, e.g. 'Use everie man after his desart, and who should scape whipping' (Hamlet II, 2, 554), 'Shall we . . . excuse his throwing into the water?' (Wiv. III, 3, 206 = his being, or having been, thrown), 'An instrument of this your calling backe' (Oth. IV, 2, 45). But about 1600 a new form came into existence, as the old one would often appear ambiguous, and it was felt convenient to be able to distinguish between 'foxes enjoy hunting' and 'foxes enjoy being hunted'. The new passive is rare in Shakespeare ('I spoke . . . of being taken by the insolent foe', Oth. I, 3, 136), but has now for a long time been firmly established in the language.

210. Still another step must be mentioned in this long development of a form at first purely substantival into one partly substantival and partly verbal in function. The *subject* of the ing, like that of any verbal noun (for instance *Cæsar's* conquests, *Pope's* imitations of Horace), is for the most part put in the genitive case—nearly always when it is a personal pronoun (in spite of *his* saying so), and generally when it indicates a person (in spite of *John's* saying so). But

a variety of circumstances led to the use in many
instances of the common case before the ing.[1] Here
I must content myself with quoting a few instances of
the new construction : 'When we talk of this man or
that woman being no longer the same person' (Thackeray), 'besides the fact of those three being there, the
drawbridge is kept up' (A. Hope), 'When I think of
this being the last time of seeing you' (Miss Austen),
'the possibility of such an effect being wrought by such
a cause' (Dickens), 'he insisted upon the Chamber
carrying out his policy' (Lecky), 'I have not the least
objection in life to a rogue being hung' (Thackeray ;
here evidently no participle), 'no man ever heard of
opium leading into delirium tremens' (De Quincey),
'the suffering arises simply from people not understanding this truism' (Ruskin). These examples will
show that the construction is especially useful in those
cases where for some reason or other it is impossible to
use the genitive case, but that it is also found where no
such reason could be adduced. Let me sum up by saying that when an Englishman now says, 'There is some
probability of the place having never been inspected
by the police', he deviates in four points from the
constructions of the ing that would have been possible
to one of his ancestors six hundred years ago ; *place* is
in the crude form, not in the genitive ; the adverb ; the
perfect ; and the passive. Thanks to these extensions
the ing has clearly become a most valuable means
of expressing tersely and neatly relations that must
else have been indicated by clumsy dependent clauses.

211. (VI). We proceed to the *verbal ending -s* (*he
loves*, etc). In Old English *-th* (þ) was used in the
ending of the third person singular and in all persons
in the plural of the present indicative, but the vowel
before it varied, so that we have for instance :

---

[1] See *Society for Pure English*, Tract XXV (1926), p. 147 ff.
(against H. W. Fowler's view of 'Fused Participles'). Van der Gaaf,
in *Engl. Studies*, X (1928) is probably wrong in attributing the construction to imitation of Old French.

infinitive	*3rd sg.*	*pl.*
sprecan	spricþ	sprecaþ
bindan	bindeþ, bint	bindaþ
nerian	nereþ	neriaþ
lufian	lufaþ	lufiaþ

But in the Northumbrian dialect of the tenth century *s* was substituted for þ (singular *bindes*, plural *bindas*), and as all unstressed vowels were soon after levelled, the two forms became identical (*bindes*). As in the same dialect the second person singular too ended in *s* (as against the *-st* of the South), all persons sounded alike except the first singular. But the development was not to stop there. In Old English a difference is made in the plural, according as the verb precedes *we* or *ge* ('ye') or not (*binde we, binde ge, but we bindaþ, ge bindaþ*). This is the germ of the more radical difference now carried through consistently in the Scotch dialect, where the *s* is only added when the verb is not accompanied by its proper pronoun—but in that case it is used in all persons. Murray gives the following sentences among others[1]:

aa *cum* fyrst—yt's mey at *cums* fyrst.
wey *gang* theare—huz tweae quheyles *gangs* theare, they *cum* an' *teake* them—the burds *cums* an' *pæcks* them. (I come first; it is I that come first; we go there; we two sometimes go there; they come and take them; the birds come and pick them.)

In the other parts of the country the development was different. In the Midland dialect the *-en* of the subjunctive and of the preterit was transferred to the present of the indicative, so that we have the following forms in the standard language:

14th century	*16th century*
I falle	I fall
he falleth	he fall(e)th
we fallen (falle)	we fall

---

[1] *Dial. of the Southern Counties of Scotland*, 1873, p. 212, where quotations from the earlier literature are also given.

This is the only dialect in which the third person singular is kept clearly distinct from the other persons.

In the South of England, finally, the *th* was preserved in the plural, and was even extended to the first person singular. Old people in the hilly parts of Somersetshire and Devonshire still say not only [i wɔ·kþ] 'he walks', but also [ðei zeþ, ai zeþ] 'they say, I say'. In most cases, however, *do* is used, which is made [də] without any *th* through the whole singular as well as plural.[1]

212. But the northern *s*'s wandered southward. Three solitary examples are found in Chaucer for the sake of the rime.[2] A century later Caxton used the *th*-ending (eth, ith, yth) exclusively, and this remained the usual form in writing till the 16th century, when *s* began to be used in poetry. In Marlowe *s* is by far the commoner ending, except after hissing consonants (passeth, opposeth, pitcheth, presageth, etc., *Tamburlaine* 68, 845, 1415, 1622). Spenser prefers *s* in poetry. In the first four cantos of the *Faerie Queene* I have counted 94 *s*'s as against 24 *th*'s (besides 8 *has*, 18 *hath*, 15 *does*, and 31 *doth*. But in his prose *th* predominates even much more than *s* does in his poetry. In the introductory letter to Sir W. Raleigh there is only one *s* (it needs), but many *th*'s ; and in his book on 'the Present State of Ireland' all the third persons singular end in *th*, except a small number of phrases (*me seems*, several times, but *it seemeth* ; *what boots it* ; *how comes it*, and perhaps a few more) that seem to be characteristic of a more colloquial tone than the rest of the book. Shakespeare's practice is not easy to ascertain. In a great many passages the folio of 1623 has *th* where the earlier quartos have *s*. In the prose

---

[1] Elworthy, *Grammar of the Dialect of West Somerset*, p. 191 ff.

[2] *Telles* : *elles* Duch. 73, Fame 426 ; *falles* : *halles* Duch. 257. In the Reves Tale the *s*-forms are used to characterize the North of England dialect of the two students (*gas* for Chaucer's ordinary *gooth*, etc.).

parts of his dramas *s* prevails,[1] and the rule may be
laid down that *th* belongs more to the solemn or dignified speeches than to everyday talk, although this is
by no means carried through everywhere. In Macbeth
I, 7, 29 ff., Lady Macbeth is more matter-of-fact than
her husband (Lady : He *has* almost supt ... Macbeth :
Hath he ask'd for me? Lady : Know you not he *ha's*.
Macbeth : ... He *hath* honour'd me of late ...), but
when his more solemn mood seizes her, she too puts
on the buskin (Was the hope drunke, Wherein you
drest your selfe? *Hath* it slept since?). Where Mer-
cutio mocks Romeo's love-sickness (II, 1, 15), he has
the line : He *heareth* not, he *stirreth* not, he *moveth* not,
but in his famous description of Queen Mab (I, 4, 53
ff.) he has 18 verbs in *s* and only two in *th*, *hath* and
driveth, of which the latter is used for the sake of the
metre.

213. Contemporary prose, at any rate in its higher
forms, has generally *th* ; the *s*-ending is not at all found
in the Authorized Version of 1611, nor in Bacon's
Atlantis (though in his *Essays* there are some *s*'s).
The conclusion with regard to Elizabethan usage as
a whole seems to be that the form in *s* was a colloquialism and as such was allowed in poetry and
especially in the drama. This *s* must, however, be
considered a licence wherever it occurs in the higher
literature of that period. But in the first half of the
seventeenth century *s* must have been the ending
universally used in ordinary conversation, and we
have evidence that it was even usual to read *s* where
the book had *th*, for Richard Hodges (1643) gives in his
list of words pronounced alike though spelt differently
among others *boughs boweth bowze*; *clause claweth
claws* ; *courses courseth corpses* ; *choose cheweth*,[2] and

---

[1] Franz, *Shakespeare-Grammatik*, 3rd ed., p. 151 : In Much Ado
(Q 1600) *th* is not found at all in the prose parts and only twice in
the poetical parts ; the Merry Wives, which is chiefly in prose, has
only one *th*.

[2] See Ellis, *Early English Pronunciation*, IV, 1018.

in 1649 he says 'howsoever wee write them thus,
leadeth it, maketh it, noteth it, we say lead's it, make's
it, note's it'. The only exception seems to have been
hath and *doth*, where the frequency of occurrence pro-
tected the old forms from being modified analogically,[1]
so that they were prevalent till about the middle of the
eighteenth century. Milton, with the exceptions just
mentioned, always writes *s* in his prose as well as in
his poetry, and so does Pope. No difference was then
felt to be necessary between even the most elevated
poetry and ordinary conversation in that respect.
But it is well worth noting that Swift, in the Introduction to his *Polite Conversation*, where he affects a
quasi-scientific tone, writes *hath* and *doth*, while in the
conversations themselves *has* and *does* are the forms
constantly used.[2]

214. At church, however, people went on hearing
the *th*-forms, although even there the *s*'s began to
creep in.[3] And it must certainly be ascribed to
influence from biblical language that the *th*-forms
again began to be used by poets towards the end of the
eighteenth century ; at first apparently this was done
rather sparingly, but nineteenth century poets employ
th to a greater extent. This revival of the old form
affords the advantage from the poet's point of view of
adding at discretion a syllable, as in Wordsworth's

> In gratitude to God, Who *feeds* our hearts
> For His own service ; *knoweth, loveth* us (Prelude 13, 276)

---

[1] This applies, partially at least, to *saith* as well.

[2] In the *Journal to Stella*, all verbs have *s*, except *hath*, which is,
however, less frequent than *has*. Further details on *th* and *s* in E.
Holmqvist, *History of the Engl. Pres. Inflections* (Heidelberg, 1922)
and H. C. Wyld, *A History of Mod. Colloquial English* (2nd ed.,
London, 1936), p. 332 ff. Wyld may be right in thinking that the
extremely common auxiliary *is* contributed to the popularity of
the *s*-ending.

[3] See the Spectator, No. 147 (Morley's ed., p. 217), 'a set of
readers [of prayers at church] who affect, forsooth, a certain gentle-
man-like familiarity of tone, and mend the language as they go on,
crying instead of pardoneth and absolveth, pardons and absolves'.

or in Byron's

> Whate'er she *loveth*, so she *loves* thee not,
> What can it profit thee? (Heaven and Earth, I, sc. 2.)

Sometimes the *th*-form comes more handy for the rime (as when *saith* rimes with *death*), and sometimes the following sound may have induced a poet to prefer one or the other ending, as in

> . . . Coleridge *hath the* sway,
> And Wordsworth *has supporters*, two or three,[1]

but in a great many cases individual fancy only decides which form is chosen. In prose, too, the *th*-form begins to make its reappearance in the nineteenth century, not only in biblical quotations, etc., but often with the sole view of imparting a more solemn tone to the style, as in Thackeray's 'Not always *doth* the writer know whither the divine Muse *leadeth* him'.

215. The nineteenth century has even gone so far as to create a double-form in one verb, making a distinction between *doth* [pronounced dʌþ] as an auxiliary verb and *doeth* [pronounced duˑiþ] as an independent one. The early printers used the two forms indiscriminately, or rather preferred *doth* where *doeth* would make the line appear too closely packed, and *doeth* where there was room enough. Thus in the Authorized Version of 1611 we find 'a henne *doeth* gather her brood under her wings' (Luke XIII, 34), and 'he that *doth* the will of my father' (Matth. VII, 21), where recent use would have reversed the order of the forms, but in 'whosoever heareth these sayings of mine, and *doeth* them' (Matth. VII, 24), the old printer happens to be in accordance with the rule of our own days. When the *th*-form was really living, *doeth* was certainly always pronounced in one syllable (thus in Shakespeare). I give a few examples of the modern differentiation.[2] J. R. Lowell writes (*My*

---

[1] *Don Juan* XI., 69.

[2] Which has not been noticed in N.E.D., though it mentions the corresponding differences between *dost* and *doest* as 'in late use'.

Love, Poems, 1849, I, 129 = Poetical Works in one
volume, p. 6) 'She *doeth* little kindnesses . . . Her life
doth rightly harmonize . . . And yet *doth* ever flow
aright.' Rider Haggard has both forms in the same
sentence (*She*, 199), 'Man *doeth* this and *doeth* that,
but he knows not to what ends his sense *doth* prompt
him'; cf. also Tennyson's *The Captain* : 'He that only
rules by terror, *Doeth* grievous wrong.'

216. To sum up. If the *s* of the third person singular
comes from the North, this is true of the outer form
only ; the 'inner form.', to use the expression of some
philologists, is the Midland one, that is to say, *s* is used
in those cases only where the Midland dialects had *th*,
and is not extended according to the northern rules.
In vulgar English, *s* is used in the first person singular :
I wishes ; says I, etc., as in *Rehearsal* (1671) : 'I makes
'em both speak fresh' (Arber's reprint, p. 53). But it
will be seen that this is in direct opposition to the
northern usage where the *s* is never found by the side
of the personal pronoun.

217. (VII). A notable feature of the history of the
English language is the building up of a rich system
of *tenses*[1] on the basis of the few possessed by Old
English, where the present was also a sort of vague
future, and where the simple preterit was often employed as a kind of pluperfect, especially when sup-
ported by *ær*, 'ere, before'. The use of *have* and *had* as
an auxiliary for the perfect and pluperfect began in the
Old English period, but it was then chiefly found with
transitive verbs, and the real perfect-signification had
scarcely yet been completely evolved from the original
meaning of the connexion : *ic hæbbe þone fisc gefan-
genne* meant at first 'I *have* the fish (as) caught' (note
the accusative ending in the participle). By and by a
distinction was made between 'I had mended the
table' and 'I had the table mended', 'he had left

---

[1] See my *Modern Engl. Gr.*, vol. IV, especially chs. 12–14 (Expanded tenses) and 15–21 (will, shall, would, should), *Philosophy
of Grammar*, chs. 19 and 20, *Essentials of Engl. Gr.*, chs. 23–25.

nothing' and 'he had nothing left'. In Middle English *have* came to be used extensively in the perfect of intransitive verbs as well as transitive ; *I have been* does not seem to occur earlier than 1200. With such verbs as *go* and *come, I am* was usual in the perfect for several centuries, where now *I have gone* and *I have come (returned,* etc.) are the ordinary expressions. The verbs *will* and *shall* have in many contexts come to be auxiliaries serving to express pure futurity, the original meaning of volition and obligation being more or less effaced ; but owing partly to the fact that to express the three distinct ideas of obligation, volition, and simple futurity we have only those two verbs as against German *sollen, wollen* and *werden,* the actual rules for the employment of the two verbs are somewhat complicated, and where strict grammarians require *shall* (I shall, shall you ; he thinks that he shall die, he = shifted first person), the verb *will* (and the shortened form 'll) is now more and more used, even in the South of England. In Scotland, Ireland and North America, *will* has long been almost exclusively used as auxiliary. The present rules may be stated roughly thus : To indicate pure, colourless future *will* is used everywhere, except in those cases in which it might be misunderstood as implying actual will. Often the unambiguous *is going to* is used, and in many cases the simple present suffices : *I start to-morrow if it is fine.* To express obligation or necessity we have the unambiguous expressions *must, has to,* and to express volition *want, intend, mean, choose* are often preferred where *will* was formerly used. The expanded tenses *I am reading, I was reading, I have been reading, I shall be reading,* were not fully developed even in Shakespeare's time ; the distinction between the simple and the expanded tenses is now a wonderful means of expressing temporal and emotional nuances.[1]

---

[1] The latest and best treatment of the expanded forms is F. Mossé, *Histoire de la Forme Périphrastique être + participe présent* II (Paris, 1938).

The passive construction (*the house is being built*) is an innovation dating from the very end of the eighteenth century.[1] Before that time the phrase was *the house is building*, i.e., *a-building* 'is in construction', and the new phrase had to fight its way against much violent opposition in the nineteenth century before it was universally recognized as good English. Macaulay used it inadvertently a few times in letters in his youth, but avoided it in his books. A still more recent innovation is the use of *is being* before an adjective : After all, he was being sensible (Wells), i.e. was at that particular moment sensible. While the number of tenses has increased, the number of moods has tended to diminish, the subjunctive having now very little vital power left. Most of its forms have become indistinguishable from those of the indicative, but the loss is not a serious one, for the thought is just as clearly expressed in 'if he died', where *died* may be either indicative or subjunctive, as in 'if he were dead', where the verb has a distinctively subjunctive form.

218. It will be seen that the development of new tenses sketched in the preceding section greatly increased the number of sentences formed after the same pattern that we had already in the case of some small verbs, chief of which were *can, may, must.* First we have a small, in itself insignificant verb and afterwards the really important verb either in the infinitive (*can see, will see, could see,* etc.) or in some participle (*is seeing, has seen, was seeing, had seen*). The number of sentences belonging to this type was enormously increased by the gradual development of the periphrastic *do.*[2] This verb was in OE. and early ME. used as a pro-verb to avoid the repetition of a verb just used, and as a causative, e.g. 'to do me live or

---

[1] The alleged earlier examples are shown by Mossé, p. 149, to be wrong.

[2] The latest and fullest treatment is V. Engblom, *On the Origin and Early Development of the Auxiliary do* (Lund, 1938), with bibliography and criticism of other writers.

deye' (Chaucer). In the latter sense it disappeared
and was replaced by *make*. In ME. it came to be used
more and more as an auxiliary and may as such be
placed by the side of the other lesser verbs, as in
'Though this good man can not see it : other men
can see it, and haue sene it, and daily do see it' (Sir
T. More). At first it was used indiscriminately without any definite grammatical purpose. In some poets
such as Lydgate, in the beginning of the fifteenth
century, it served chiefly to fill up the line and to make
it possible to place the infinitive at the end as a convenient rime-word. Sometimes it serves to make the
tense clear in those verbs that are alike in the present
and preterit : we do set, did set. Cf. also 'the holy
spyryte dyd and dothe remayne and shall remayne'
(J. Fisher, ab. 1535). The culmination was reached in
the sixteenth century, when it might almost seem as
if all full verbs were 'stripped of all those elements
which to most grammarians constitute the very
essence of a verb, namely, the marks of person,
number, tense, and mood' (*Progress in Lang.* 124),
leaving them to lesser verbs placed before them.

219. But then a reaction set in and gradually
restricted the use of *do* to those cases that are well
known from grammars of Present English, and in
which it serves a definite grammatical purpose. It is
used (1) for the sake of emphasis, especially in contrast : 'Shelley, when he did laugh, laughed heartily' ;
thus in earnest requests : 'Do tell me', even with *be* :
'Do be quiet !' (2) in negative sentences with *not*.
Here it ends a long development. The earliest negative
adverb is *ne*, placed before the verb, OE. *ic ne secge*.
But frequently this was strengthened by the addition
of *noht* (from *nawiht, nowiht,* meaning 'nothing') after
the verb ; *noht* became *not* ; and the typical ME. form
thus was *I ne seye not*. Here *ne* was pronounced with
so little stress that it was apt to be dropped altogether
and the fifteenth century form was *I say not*. This
survived for some centuries in *I know not* and a few

other now obsolete combinations, as well as with all the formerly mentioned lesser verbs. By means of *do* that word-order is obtained which in most languages is thought the most felicitous, *not* being placed before the really significant verb : *I do not say*, just as *I cannot say*, etc. In this position, however, *not* tends to be weakened, and so we get the colloquial forms *I don't say, can't say*, etc. (3) In such questions as are not introduced by a pronominal subject, which naturally has to stand first, the use of *do* as well as of the other lesser verbs effects a compromise between the ordinary interrogative word-order (verb before the subject) and the universal tendency to have the subject before the verb (that is, the verb that really means something) : *Did he come?* just as *Must he come?*

220. Now the curious thing is that a similar construction of sentences is often made possible by means of the verbal substantives mentioned in 171. These are placed after verbs of small intrinsic meaning, to which are attached the marks of person and tense, of negation and question, in such familiar phrases as have a look (peep) at, have a wash, a shave, a try, have a care, take care, take a drive, a walk, a rest ; give a glance, look, kick, push, hint ; make (pay) a call, make a plunge, make use of, he made his bow to the hostess, etc.

221. (VIII). There are some important innovations in the syntax of the *infinitive*. In such a sentence as 'it is good for a man not to touch a woman', the noun with *for* was originally in the closest connexion with the adjective : 'What is good for a man?' 'Not to touch a woman.' But by a natural shifting this came to be apprehended as 'it is good | for a man not to touch a woman', so that *for a man* was felt to be the subject of the infinitive, and this manner of indicating the subject gradually came to be employed where the original construction is excluded. Thus in the beginning of a sentence : 'For us to levy power Proportionate to th'enemy, is all impossible' (Shakespeare), and

after *than* : 'I don't know, what is worse than for such wicked strumpets to lay their sins at honest men's doors' (Fielding) ; further, 'What I like best, is for a nobleman to marry a miller's daughter. And what I like next best, is for a poor fellow to run away with a rich girl' (Thackeray), 'it is of great use to healthy women for them to cycle.'[1] Another recent innovation is the use of *to* as what might be called a pro-infinitive instead of the clumsy *to do so* : 'Will you play?' 'Yes, I intend to.' 'I am going to.' This is one among several indications that the linguistic instinct now takes *to* to belong to the preceding verb rather than to the infinitive, a fact which, together with other circumstances, serves to explain the phenomenon usually mistermed 'the split infinitive.' This name is bad because we have many infinitives without *to*, as 'I made him go.' *To* therefore is no more an essential part of an infinitive than the definite article is an essential part of a nominative, and no one would think of calling 'the good man' a split nominative. Although examples of an adverb between *to* and the infinitive occur as early as the fourteenth century, they do not become very frequent till the latter half of the nineteenth century. In some cases they decidedly contribute to the clearness of the sentence by showing at once what word is qualified by the adverb. Thackeray's and Seeley's sentences 'she only wanted a pipe in her mouth *considerably* to resemble the late Field Marshal' and 'the poverty of the nation did not allow them *successfully* to compete with the other nations' are not very happily built up, for the reader at the first glance is inclined to connect the adverb with what precedes. The sentences would have been clearer if the authors had ventured to place *to* before the adverb, as Burns does in 'Who dar'd to nobly stem tyrannic pride', and Carlyle in 'new Emissaries are

---

[1] See my article in *Festschrift Viëtor* (Marburg, 1910), p. 85 ff., and *Philos. of Grammar*, 118, where a Slavic parallel is mentioned.

trained, with new tactics, to, if possible, entrap him, and hoodwink and handcuff him'.

222. This rapid sketch of a certain number of grammatical changes, though necessarily giving only a fraction of the material on which it is based, has yet, I hope, been sufficiently full to show that such changes are continually going on and that it would be a gross error to suppose that any deviation from the established rules of grammar is necessarily a corruption. Those teachers who know least of the age, origin and development of the rules they follow, are generally the most apt to think that whatsoever is more than these cometh of evil, while he who has patiently studied the history of the past and trained himself to hear the linguistic grass grow in the present age will generally be more inclined to see in the processes of human speech a wise natural selection, through which while nearly all innovations of questionable value disappear pretty soon, the fittest survive and make human speech ever more varied and flexible, and yet ever more easy and convenient to the speakers. There is no reason to suppose that this development has come to a stop with the beginning of the twentieth century : let us hope that in the future the more and more almighty schoolmaster may not nip too many beneficial changes in the bud.

Chapter X

Shakespeare and the Language of Poetry

223. In this chapter I shall endeavour to characterize the language of the greatest master of English
poetry and make some observations in regard to his
influence on the English language as well as in regard
to poetic and archaic language generally. But it must
be distinctly understood that I shall concern myself
with *language* and not with literary *style*. It is true
that the two things cannot be completely kept apart,
but as far as possible I shall deal only with what are
really philological as opposed to literary problems.

224. Shakespeare's vocabulary is often stated to be
the richest ever employed by any single man. It has
been calculated to comprise 21,000 words ('rough cal-
culation, found in Mrs. Clark's Concordance . . . without counting inflected forms as distinct words',
Craik), or, according to others, 24,000 or 15,000. In
order to appreciate what that means we must look a
little at the various statements that have been given
of the number of words used by other authors and by
ordinary beings, educated and not educated. Unfortunately these statements are in many cases given and
repeated without any indication of the manner in
which they have been arrived at.[1] Milton's vocabulary
is said to comprise 7,000 or 8,000 words, that of the
Iliad and Odyssey taken together 9,000, that of the

---

[1] Max Müller, *Wissenschaft der Sprache*, I, 360, and *Lectures on
the Science of Language*, 6th ed., I, 309. Wood, *Journal of Germanic
Philology*, I, 294. Smedberg, *Svenska landsmålen*, XI, 9 (57), 1896.

Old Testament 5,642, and that of the New Testament 4,800 ; A. S. Cook (in *The Nation*, Sept. 12, 1912) computes the vocabulary of the English Authorized Version at 6,568 words, or at 9,884, if inflected forms of nouns, pronouns, or verbs are included.

225. Max Müller says that a farm-labourer uses only 300 words, and Wood that 'the average man uses about five hundred words' (adding 'it is appalling to think how pitiably we have degenerated from the copiousness of our ancestors'), and the same statements are found in writings by Abel, Sütterlin and other philologists. But both figures are obviously wrong. One two-year-old girl had 489 and another 1,121 words (see Wundt), while Mrs. Winfield S. Hall's boy used in his seventeenth month 232 different words and, when six years old, 2,688 words, at least, for it is probable that the mother and her assistants who noted down every word they heard the child use, even so did not get hold of its whole vocabulary. Now, are we really to believe that the linguistic range of a grown-up man, however humble, is considerably smaller than that of a two-year-old child of educated parents or is only one-seventh of that of a six-year-old boy ! Any one going through the lists given by Mrs. Hall will feel quite certain that no labourer contents himself with so scanty a vocabulary. School-books for teaching foreign languages often include some 700 words in the first year's course ; yet on how few subjects of everyday occurrence are our pupils able to converse after one year's teaching. Sweet also contradicts the statement about 300 words, saying

---

Marius Kristensen, *Aarbog for dansk kulturhistorie*, 1897. E. H. Babbitt, *Common Sense in Teaching Modern Languages* (New York, 1895), 11, and *Popular Science Monthly*, April 1907 (cf. E. A. Kirkpatrick, ibid., Febr. 1907). Sweet, *History of Language*, 1900, 139. Weise, *Unsere Muttersprache*, 1897, 205. Mrs. Winfield S. Hall, *Child Study*, Monthly, March 1897, and *Journal of Childhood and Adolescence*, January 1902. G. H. M'Knight, *Modern English in the Making*, 1928, p. 186. W. Wartburg, *Evolution et Structure de la Langue Française*, 1934, p. 238. M. Nice in *American Speech*, 2, 1.

'When we find a missionary in Tierra del Fuego compiling a dictionary of 30,000 words in the Yaagan language—that is, a hundred times as many—we cannot give any credence to this statement, especially if we consider the number of names of different parts of a waggon or a plough, and all the words required in connexion even with a single agricultural operation, together with names of birds, plants, and other natural objects'. Smedberg, who has investigated the vocabulary of Swedish peasants and who emphasizes its richness in technical terms, arrives at the result that 26,000 is probably too small a figure, and the Danish and French dialectologists Kristensen and Duraffour completely endorse this view. Professor E. S. Holden tested himself by a reference to all the words in Webster's Dictionary, and found that his own vocabulary comprised 33,456 words. And E. H. Babbitt writes : 'I tried to get at the vocabulary of adults and made experiments, chiefly with my students, to see how many English words each knew. . . . My plan was to take a considerable number of pages from the dictionary at random, count the number of words on those pages which the subject of the experiment could define without any context, and work out a proportion to get an approximation of the entire number of words in the dictionary known. The results were surprising for two reasons. In the size of the vocabulary of such students the outside variations were less than 20 per cent, and their vocabulary was much larger than I had expected to find. The majority reported a little below 60,000 words.' People who had never been to college, but, with an ordinary common school education, were regular readers of books and periodicals, according to the same writer reported generally from 25,000 to 35,000 words, though some went higher, even to 50,000.

226. These statements are easily reconciled with the ascription of 20,000 words to Shakespeare. For it must be remembered that in the case of each of us there is a

great difference between the words *known* (especially those of which he has a reading knowledge) and the words actually *used* in conversation. And then, there must always be a great many words which a man will use readily in conversation, but which will never occur in his writings, simply because the subjects on which a man addresses the public are generally much less varied than those he has to talk about every day.[1] How many authors have occasion to use in their books even the most familiar names of garden tools or common dishes or kitchen implements? If Milton as a poet uses only 8,000 against Shakespeare's 20,000 words, this is a natural consequence of the narrower range of his subjects, and it is easy to prove that his vocabulary really contained many more than the 8,000 words found in a Concordance to his poetical works. We have only to take any page of his prose writings, and we shall meet with a great many words not in the Concordance.[2]

227. The greatness of Shakespeare's mind is therefore not shown by the fact that he was acquainted with 20,000 words, but by the fact that he wrote about so great a variety of subjects and touched upon so many human facts and relations that he needed this number of words in his writings.[3] His remarkable familiarity

---

[1] Inversely, many authors will use some (learned or abstract) words in writing which they do not use in conversation ; their number, however, is rarely great.

[2] Thus, on p. 30 of *Areopagitica*, I find the following 21 words, which are not in Bradshaw's Concordance : Churchman, competency, utterly, mercenary, pretender, ingenuous, evidently, tutor, examiner, scism, ferular, fescu, imprimatur, grammar, pedagogue, cursory, temporize, extemporize, licencer, commonwealth, foreiner. And p. 50 adds 18 more words to the list : writing, commons, valorous, rarify, enfranchise, founder, formall, slavish, oppressive, reinforce, abrogate, mercilesse, noble (n.), Danegelt, immunity, newnes, unsutableness, customary.

[3] I have amused myself with making up the following sentences of words not used by Shakespeare though found in the language of that time : In Shakespeare we find no *blunders*, although *decency* and *delicacy* had *disappeared* ; *energy* and *enthusiasm* are not in

with technical expressions in many different spheres has often been noticed, but there are other facts with regard to his use of words that have not been remarked or not sufficiently remarked. His reticence about religious matters, which has given rise to the most divergent theories of his religious belief, is shown strikingly in the fact that such words as *Bible, Holy Ghost* and *Trinity* do not occur at all in his writings, while *Jesus* (Jesu), *Christ* and *Christmas* are found only in some of his earliest plays ; *Saviour* occurs only once (in Hamlet), and *Creator* only in two of the dubious plays (H 6 C and Troilus).[1]

228. Of far greater importance is his use of language to individualize the characters in his plays. In this he shows a much finer and subtler art than some modern novelists, who make the same person continually use the same stock phrase or phrases. Even where he resorts to the same tricks as other authors he varies them more ; Mrs. Quickly and Dogberry do not misapply words from the classical languages in the same way. The everyday speech of the artisans in *A Midsummer Night's Dream* is comic in a different manner from the diction they use in their play within the play, which serves Shakespeare to ridicule some linguistic artifices employed in good faith by many of his contemporaries (alliteration, bombast). Shakespeare is not entirely exempt from the fashionable affectation of his days known as Euphuism,[2] but it must be noticed that he is superior to its worst aberrations and he satirizes them, not only in *Love's Labour's Lost*, but also in many other places. Euphuistic expressions

---

existence, and we see no *elegant expressions* nor any *gleams* of *genius* etc.

[1] The act against profane language on the stage (see below, § 254) is not sufficient to explain this reticence.

[2] The various kinds of affected court style have been carefully distinguished by M. Basse. *Stijlaffectatie bij Shakespeare*, vooral uit het oogpunt van het Euphuisme (Université de Gand, 1895). Cf. also L. Morsbach, *Shakespeare und der Euphuismus*, Gesellsch. d. Wiss (Göttingen, 1908), S. 600 ff.

are generally put in the mouth of some subordinate
character who has nothing to do except to announce
some trifling incident, relate a little of the circumstances that lead up to the action of the play, deliver
a message from a king, etc. It is not improbable that
the company possessed some actor who knew how to
make small parts funny by imitating fashionable
affectation, and we can imagine that it was he who
acted Osric in *Hamlet*, and by his vocabulary and
appearance exposed himself to the scoffs of the
Danish prince, and the nameless gentleman in *Lear*,
III, sc. 1, and IV, sc. 3.[1] But the messenger from
Antony in *Julius Cæsar* (III, 1, 122) speaks in a
totally different strain and gives us a sort of foretaste
of Antony's eloquence. And how different again—I
am speaking here of subordinate parts only—are the
gardeners in *Richard the Second* (III, sc. 4) with their
characteristic application of botanical similes to
politics and vice versa. And thus one might go on,
for no author has shown greater skill in adapting
language to character.

229. A modern reader, however, is sure to miss
many of the *nuances* that were felt instinctively by the
poet's contemporaries. A great many words have now
another value than they had then ; in some cases it is
only a slightly different colouring, but in others the
diversity is greater, and only a close study of Elizabethan usage can bring out the exact value of each
word. A *bonnet* then meant a man's cap or hat ;
Lear walks unbonneted. To *charm* always implied
magic power, to make invulnerable by witchcraft, to
call forth by spells, etc.; 'charming words' were
magic words and not simply delightful words as in our
days. *Notorious* might be used in a good sense as
'well-known'; *censure*, too, was a colourless word
('And your name is great In mouthes of wisest censure'
Oth. II, 3, 193). The same is true of *succeed* and

---

[1] See my interpretation of the well-known crux in that scene,
1, 19 ff., in *Linguistica*, 1933, p. 430.

success, which now imply what Shakespeare several times calls 'good success', whereas he also knows 'bad success'; cf. 'the effects he writes of succeede unhappily', Lear I, 2, 157. *Companion* was often used in a bad sense, like *fellow* now, and inversely *sheer*, which is now used with such words as 'folly, nonsense', had kept the original meaning of 'pure', as in 'thou sheere, immaculate, and silver fountaine' (R 2, V, 3, 61). *Politician* seems always to imply intriguing or scheming, and *remorse* generally means pity or sympathy. *Accommodate* evidently did not belong to ordinary language, but was considered affected; *occupy* and *activity* were at least half-vulgar, while on the other hand *wag* (vb.) was then free from its present trivial or ludicrous associations ('Untill my eielids will no longer wag', Hamlet V, 1, 290, see Dowden's note to this passage). *Assassination* (only Macbeth I, 7, 2) would then call up the memory of the 'Assasines, a company of most desperat and dangerous men among the Mahometans' (Knolles, *Hist. Turks*, 1603) or 'That bloudy sect of Sarazens, called Assassini, who, without feare of torments, undertake . . . the murther of any eminent Prince, impugning their irreligion' (Speed, 1611, quoted NED.).

230. Even adverbs might then have another colouring than their present signification. *Now-a-days* was a vulgar word; it is used by no one in Shakespeare except Bottom, the grave-digger in *Hamlet*, and a fisherman in *Pericles*. The adverb *eke*, in the nineteenth century a poetic word, seems to have been a comic expression; it occurs only three times in Shakespeare (twice in the *Merry Wives*, used by Pistol and the Host, once by Flute in *Midsummer Night's Dream*); Milton and Pope avoid the word. The synonym *also* is worth noticing. Shakespeare uses it only 22 times, and nearly always puts it in the mouth of vulgar or affected persons (Dogberry twice in *Ado*, the Clown once in *Wint.*, the Second Lord in *As* II, sc. 2, the Second Lord in *Tim.* III, sc. 6, the affected

Captain in *Tw.* I, sc. 2 ; the knight in *Lear* I, 4, 66,
may belong here too; further Pistol twice in grandil-
oquent speeches, H 4 B II, 4, 171 and V, 3, 145, and
two of Shakespeare's Welshmen, Evans three times,
and Fluellen twice). It is used twice in solemn and
official speeches (H 5 I, 2, 77, where Canterbury
expounds lex Salica, and IV, 6, 10), and it is, therefore,
highly characteristic that Falstaff uses the word twice
in his Euphuistic impersonation of the king (H 4
A II, 4, 440 and 459) and twice in similar speeches in
the *Merry Wives* (V, 1, 24, and V, 5, 7).[1]

231. Shylock is one of Shakespeare's most interesting creations, even from the point of view of language.
Although Sir Sidney Lee has shown that there were
Jews in England in those times and that, consequently, Shakespeare need not have gone outside his
own country in order to see models for Shylock, the
number of Jews cannot have been sufficient for his
hearers to be very familiar with the Jewish type, and
no Anglo-Jewish dialect or mode of speech had
developed which Shakespeare could put into Shylock's

---

[1] The only passages not accounted for above are Gent. III, 2,
25, where the metre is wrong, Hamlet V, 2, 402, where the folios
have *always* instead of *also*, and Cæs. II, 1, 329.—Shakespeare's
sparing use of *also* would in itself suffice to disprove the Baconian
theory if any proof were needed beyond the evidence of history
and of psychology. For in Bacon, *also*'s abound, and I have counted
on four successive small pages of Moore Smith's edition of the
New Atlantis 22 instances, exactly as many as are found in the
whole of Shakespeare. *Might* and *mought* seem to be nearly equally
frequent in Bacon, but *mought* is found only once in Shakespeare,
in the third part of *Henry VI*, a play which many competent judges
are inclined not to ascribe to Shakespeare at all. At any rate, this
one instance in one of his earliest works weighs nothing as against
the thousands of times *might* is found. Shakespeare uses *among* and
amongst indiscriminately, Bacon nearly always uses *amongst*.
Bacon frequently employs the conjunction *whereas*, which is not
found at all in the undoubtedly genuine Shakespearian plays, etc.
—Since this was first written, the subject has been investigated
by N. Bøgholm (*Bacon og Shakespeare*, Copenhagen, 1906), who has
succeeded in pointing out an astonishing number of discrepancies
between the two authors.

mouth and so make him at once recognizable for what
he was. I have not, indeed, been able to discover a
single trait in Shylock's language that can be called
distinctly Jewish. And yet Shakespeare has succeeded
in creating for Shylock a language different from that
of anybody else. Shylock has his Old Testament at
his fingers' ends, he defends his own way of making
money breed by a reference to Jacob's thrift in breed-
ing parti-coloured lambs, he swears by Jacob's staff
and by our holy sabbath, and he calls Lancelot 'that
foole of Hagars off-spring.'[1] We have an interesting
bit of Jewish figurative language in 'my houses eares,
I meane my casements' (II, 5, 34). Shylock uses some
biblical words which do not occur elsewhere in Shakespeare : *synagogue, Nazarite* and *publican* ; *pilled* in
'The skilful shepheard pil'd me certain wands' is a
reminiscence from Genesis XXX, 37. But more often
Shylock is characterized by being made to use words
or constructions a little different from the accepted use
of Shakespeare's time.[2] He dislikes the word *interest*
and prefers calling it *advantage* or *thrift* ('my well-
worne thrift, which he cals interrest', I, 3, 52), and
instead of *usury* he says *usance*. Furness quotes
Wylson On Usurye, 1572, p. 32, 'usurie and double
usurie, the merchants termyng it *usance* and double
usance, by a more clenlie name'—this word thus ranks
in the same category as *dashed* or *d–d* for *damned* :
instead of pronouncing an objectionable word in full
one begins as if one were about to pronounce it and
then shunts off on another track (see other examples
below, § 244). Shylock uses the plural *moneys*, which
is very rare in Shakespeare, he says an *equal* pound
for 'exact', *rheum* (rume) for 'saliva,' *estimable* for
'valuable,' *fulsome* for 'rank' (the only instance of
that signification discovered by the editors of the

---

[1] Contrast with this trait the fondness for classical allusions
found in Marlowe's *Barrabas*.

[2] He says *Abram*, but *Abraham* is the only form found in the
rest of Shakespeare's works.

NED.) ; he alone uses the words *eaneling* and *mis-believer* and the rare verb to *bane*. His syntax is peculiar : we *trifle* time ; *rend out*, where Shakespeare has elsewhere only *rend*; I have no mind *of* feasting forth to-night (always *mind to*) ; *and so following*, where *and so forth* is the regular Shakespearian phrase. I have counted some forty such deviations from Shakespeare's ordinary language and cannot dismiss the thought that Shakespeare made Shylock's language peculiar on purpose, just as he makes Caliban, and the witches in *Macbeth*, use certain words and expressions used by none other of his characters in order to stamp them as beings out of the common sort.

232. Shakespeare's vocabulary was not the same in all periods of his life. I have counted between two and three hundred words which he used in his youth, but not later, while the number of words peculiar to his last period is much smaller. Sarrazin[1] mentions as characteristic of his first period a predilection for picturesque adjectives that appeal immediately to the outward senses (*bright, brittle, fragrant, pitchy, snow-white*), while his later plays are said to contain more adjectives of psychological importance. But even apart from the fact that some of the adjectives instanced are really found in later plays (*bright* in *Cæs., Ant., Oth., Cymb., Wint. T.*, etc.), this statement would account for only a small part of the divergencies. Probably no single explanation can account for them all, not even that of the natural buoyancy of youth and the comparative austerity of a later age. It is noteworthy that in some instances he ridicules in later plays words used quite seriously in earlier ones. Thus *beautify*, which is found in *Lucrece, Henry VI B, Titus Andr., Two Gentlemen*, and *Romeo*, is severely criticized by Polonius when he hears it in Hamlet's letter : 'That's an ill phrase, a vilde [i.e. vile] phrase, beautified is a vilde phrase.' Similarly *cranny*, which

---

[1] *Shakespeare-Jahrbuch*, XXXIII, 122.

Shakespeare used in *Lucrece* (twice) and in the *Comedy of Errors*, is not found in any play written later than *Midsummer Night's Dream*, where Shakespeare takes leave of the word by turning it to ridicule in the mouth of Bottom and in the artisans' comedy. The fate of *foeman, aggravate* and *homicide* is nearly the same. Perhaps some of the words avoided in later life were provincialisms (thus possibly *pebblestone, shore*, in the sense of 'bank of a river,' *wood* 'mad', *forefather* 'ancestor,' the pronunciation of *marriage* and of *Henry* in three syllables). In the first period Shakespeare used *perverse* with the unusual signification 'cold, unfriendly, averse to love', later he avoids the word altogether. In such instances he may have been criticized by his contemporaries (we know from the *Poetaster* how severe Ben Jonson was in these matters), and that may have made him avoid the objectionable words altogether.

233. One of the most characteristic features of Shakespeare's use of the English language is his boldness. His boldness of metaphor has often been pointed out in books of literary criticism, and the boldness of his sentence structure, especially in his last period, is so obvious that no instances need be adduced here. He does not always care for grammatical parallelism, witness such a sentence as 'A thought which, quarter'd, hath but one part *wisedom* And ever three parts *coward*' (Hamlet IV, 4, 42). He does not always place the words where they would seem properly to belong, as in 'we send, To know what *willing* ransome he will give' for 'what ransom he will willingly give' (Henry V III, 5, 63), 'dismiss me Thus with his *speechlesse* hand' (Cor. V, 1, 68), 'the *whole* eare of Denmarke Is by a forged processe of my death Rankly abus'd' (the ear of all Denmark, Hamlet I, 5, 36), 'lovers *absent* howres' (the hours when lovers are absent, Othello III, 4, 174), etc. He is not afraid of writing 'wanted lesse impudence' for 'had less impudence' or 'wanted impudence more' (Wint. III, 2, 57) and 'a beggar

without lesse quality' (Cymb. I, 4, 23), nor of mixing
his negatives as he does in many other passages.[1]
Alex. Schmidt, who collects many instances of such
negligence, rightly remarks : 'Had he taken the pains
of revising and preparing his plays for the press, he
would perhaps have corrected all the quoted passages.
But he did not write them to be read and dwelt on by
the eye, but to be heard by a sympathetic audience.
And much that would blemish the language of a
logician, may well become a dramatic poet or an
orator.'[2] There is an excellent paper by C. Alphonso
Smith in the *Englische Studien,* vol. XXX, on 'The
Chief Difference between the First and Second Folios
of Shakespeare', in which he shows that 'the supreme
syntactic value of Shakespeare's work as represented
in the First Folio is that it shows us the English
language unfettered by bookish impositions. Shakespeare's syntax was that of the speaker, not that of the
essayist ; for the drama represents the unstudied
utterance of people under all kinds and degrees of
emotion, ennui, pain, and passion. Its syntax, to be
truly representative, must be familiar, conversational,
spontaneous ; not studied and formal.' But 'the
Second Folio is of unique service and significance in
its attempts to render more 'correct' and bookish
the unfettered syntax of the First. The First Folio is
to the Second as spoken language is to written
language. The 'bad grammar' of the first Folio (1623)
may not *always* be due to Shakespeare himself, but at
any rate we have in that edition more of his own
language than in the 'correctness' of the Second Folio
(1632).

234. Shakespeare's boldness with regard to language
is less conspicuous, though no less real, in the instances
I shall now mention. In turning over the pages of the
New English Dictionary, where every pains has been

---

[1] Besides using such double negatives as were regular in all the
older periods of the language (*nor, never,* etc.).

[2] *Shakespeare-Lexicon,* p. 1420.

taken to ascertain the earliest occurrence of each word
and of each signification, one is struck by the fre-
frequency with which Shakespeare's name is found
affixed to the earliest quotation for words or meanings.
In many cases this is no doubt due to the fact that
Shakespeare's vocabulary has been registered with
greater care in Concordances and in Al. Schmidt's
invaluable *Shakespeare-Lexicon* than that of any other
author, so that his words cannot escape notice, while
the same words may occur unnoticed in the pages of
many an earlier author. But anyhow Shakespeare
uses a great many words which were new in his times,
whether absolutely new or new only to the written
language, while living colloquially on the lips of the
people. My list[1] includes the following words : *aslant*
as a preposition, *assassination* (see above), *barefaced*,
the plural *brothers* (found also in Layamon's *Brut*, but
seemingly not between that and Shakespeare's
youth : Gosson, Lyly, Sidney, Marlowe), *call* 'to pay
a short visit,' *courtship, dwindle, enthrone* (also in
Lyly, earlier enthronize), *eventful, excellent* in the current sense 'extremely good,' *fount* 'spring' (also in
Kyd, Drayton), *fretful, get* intransitive with an
adjective, 'become' (only in 'get clear'), *I have got* for
'I have,' *gust, hint, hurry* (also in Kyd), *indistinguishable, laughable, leap-frog, loggerhead* and *loggerheaded,
lonely* (but Sidney has *loneliness* some years before
Shakespeare began to write), *lower* verb, *perusal,
primy.* Further the following verbs (formed from
nouns that are found before Shakespeare's time) :
bound, hand, jade, and nouns (formed from already
existing verbs) : *control, dawn, dress, hatch, import,
indent.* Among other words which were certainly or
probably new when Shakespeare used them, may be
mentioned *acceptance, gull* 'dupe', *rely,* and *summit.*
I shall give below (§ 238) a list of words and expressions

---

[1] See now also G. Gordon, *Shakespeare's English* (Soc. for Pure
Engl. XXIV, 1928) and G. H. McKnight, *Modern English in the
Making* (New York, 1928), ch. X.

the existence of which in the English language is due to Shakespeare. The words here given would probably have found their way into the language even had Shakespeare never written a line, though he may have accelerated the date of their acceptance. But at any rate they show that he was exempt from that narrowness which often makes authors shy of using new or colloquial words in the higher literary style. Let me add another remark apropos of a list of hard words needing an explanation which is found in Cockeram's *Dictionarie* (1623). Dr. Murray writes:[1] 'We are surprised to find among these hard words *abandon, abhorre, abrupt, absurd, action, activitie* and *actresse,* explained as 'a woman doer,' for the stage actress had not yet appeared.' Now, with the exception of the last one, all these words are found in Shakespeare's plays.

235. Closely connected with this trait in Shakespeare's language is the proximity of his poetical diction to his ordinary prose. He uses very few 'poetical' words or forms. He does not rely for his highest flights on the use of words and grammatical forms not used elsewhere, but knows how to achieve the finest effects of imagination without stepping outside his ordinary vocabulary and grammar. It must be remembered that when he uses *thou* and *thee, 'tis, e'en, ne'er, howe'er, mine eyes,* etc., or when he construes negative and interrogative verbs without *do,* all these things, which are now parts of the conventional language of poetry, were everyday colloquialisms in the Elizabethan period. It is true that there are certain words and forms which he never uses except in poetry, but their number is extremely small. I do not know of any besides *host* 'army', *vale, sire,* and *morn.* As for the synonym *morrow,* apart from its use in the sense of 'next day' and in the salutation *good morrow,* which was then colloquial, it occurs

---

[1] *The Evolution of English Lexicography,* Romanes Lecture (Oxford and London, 1900), p. 29.

only four times, and only in rime. There are some
verb forms which occur in rime only, but the number
of occasions on which Shakespeare was thus led to
deviate from his usual grammar is very small : *begun*
(past tense) eight times, *flee* once (the usual present
is *fly*), *gat* once (in the probably spurious *Pericles*),
sain for *said* once, *sang* once, *shore* participle once,
strown once (the usual form is *strewed*), *swore* participle once—fifteen instances in all, to which must be
added eleven instances of the plural *eyen*. Rhythmical
reasons seem to make *do* more frequent in Shakespeare's verse than in his prose,[1] and rhythm and
rime sometimes make him place a preposition after
instead of before the noun (e.g. go the fools among[2]).
All these things are rare enough to justify the statement that a peculiar poetical diction is practically
non-existent in Shakespeare.

236. In the Old English period the language of
poetry differed, as we have seen (cf. § 53), very considerably from the language of ordinary prose. The
old poetical language was completely forgotten a few
centuries after the Norman Conquest, and a new one
did not develop in the Middle English period, though
there were certain conventional tricks used by many
poets, such as those ridiculed in Chaucer's *Sir Thopas*.
Chaucer himself had not two distinct forms of language, one for verse and the other for prose, apart
from those unavoidable smaller changes which rhythm
and rime are always apt to bring about. We have now
seen that the same is true of Shakespeare ; but in the
nineteenth century we find a great many words and
forms of words which are scarcely ever used outside
of poetry. This, then, is not a survival of an old state
of things, but a comparatively recent phenomenon,
whose causes are well worth investigating. At first it
might be thought that the regard for sonority and

---

[1] W. Franz, *Shakespeare-Grammatik*, 2nd ed., 478, and *Nachtrag*,
p. 590.

[2] Franz, p. 427.

beauty of sound would be the chief or one of the chief
agents in the creation of a special poetical dialect.
But very often poetical forms are, on the contrary,
less euphonious than everyday forms ; compare, for
example, *break'st thou* with *do you break*. Those who
imagine that *gat* sounds better than *got* will scarcely
admit that *spat* or *gnat* sounds better than *spot* or *not* :
non-phonetic associations are often more powerful
than the mere sounds.

237. More frequently it is the desire to leave the
beaten track that leads to the preference of certain
words in poetry. Words that are too well known and
too often used do not call up such vivid images as
words less familiar. This is one of the reasons that
impel poets to use archaic words ; they are 'new' just
on account of their being old, and yet they are not
so utterly unknown as to be unintelligible. Besides
they will often call up the memory of some old or
venerable work in which the reader has met with them
before, and thus they at once secure the reader's
sympathy. If, then, the poetical language of the nineteenth century contains a great many archaisms, the
question naturally presents itself, from what author
or authors do most of them proceed? And many
people who know the pre-eminent position of Shakespeare in English literature will probably be surprised
to hear that his is not the greatest influence on English
poetic diction.

238. Among words and phrases due to reminiscences of Shakespeare may be mentioned the following : *antre* (Keats, Meredith), *atomy* in the sense 'atom,
tiny being,' *beetle* ('the dreadfull summit of the cliffe,
That beetles o'er his base into the sea'), it *beggars all
description*, *broad-blown*, *charactery* (Keats, Browning),
coign of vantage (*coign* is another spelling of *coin*
'corner'), *cudgel one's brain(s)*, *daff* the world aside,
eager 'cold' ('a nipping and an eager ayre'), *eld*
(superstitious eld), nine *farrow*, *fitful* ('Life's fitfull
fever'), *forcible feeble*, a *foregone conclusion*, *forgetive*

(Falstaff : 'of uncertain formation and meaning'. Commonly taken as a derivation of *forge* v., and hence used by writers of the nineteenth century for : apt at forging, inventive, creative'. NED.), a *forthright* (rare), *gaingiving* (Coleridge), *gouts* of blood, *gravel-blind*, *head and front* ('A Shakesperian phrase, orig. app. denoting "summit, height, highest extent or pitch"; sometimes used by modern writers in other senses'. NED.), *hoist with his own petard, lush* (in the sense 'luxuriant in growth'), in my *mind's eye*, the *pink* (of perfection, in Shakespeare only, 'I am the very pinck of curtesie' ; George Eliot has 'Her kitchen always looked the pink of cleanliness', and Stevenson 'he had been the pink of good behaviour'), *silken dalliance, single blessedness, that way madness lies* ('Too kind ! Insipidity lay that way', Mrs. Humphrey Ward), *weird*. The last word is interesting ; originally it is a noun and means 'destiny, fate' ; the three *weird sisters* means the fate sisters or Norns. Shakespeare found this expression in Holinshed and used it in speaking of the witches in *Macbeth*, and only there. From that play it entered into the ordinary language, but without being properly understood. It is now used as an adjective and generally taken to mean 'mystic, mysterious, unearthly'. Another word that is often misunderstood is *bourne* from *Hamlet* (The undiscovered country, from whose borne No traveller returnes) ; it means 'limit', but Keats and others use it in the sense 'realm, domain' (In water, fiery realm, and airy bourne ; quoted NED.). There are two things worth noting in this list. First, that it includes so many words of vague or indefinite meaning, which perhaps were not even clearly understood by the author himself. This explains the fact that some of them have apparently been used in modern times in a different sense from that intended by Shakespeare. Second, that the re-employment of these words nearly always dates from the nineteenth century and that the present currency of some of

them is due just as much to Sir Walter Scott or Keats
as to the original author. *To cudgel one's brains* is
now more of a literary phrase than when Shakespeare
put it in the mouth of the gravedigger (Hamlet V,
1, 63), evidently meaning it to be a rude or vulgar
expression. Inversely, *single blessedness* is now generally used with an ironical or humorous tinge which it
certainly had not in Shakespeare (Mids. I, 1, 78).

239. It must be noted also that none of the words
thus traceable to Shakespeare belong now to what
might be called the technical language of poetry.
Modern archaizing poetry owes its vocabulary more
to Edmund Spenser than to any other poet. Pope and
his contemporaries made a very sparing use of
archaisms, but when poets in the middle of the
eighteenth century turned from his rationalistic and
matter-of-fact poetry and were eager to take their
romantic flight away from everyday realities, Spenser
became the poet of their heart, and they adopted a
great many of his words which had long been forgotten. Their success was so great that many words
which they had to explain to their readers are now
perfectly familiar to every educated man and woman.
Gilbert West, in his work *On the Abuse of Travelling,
in imitation of Spenser* (1739), had to explain in foot-
notes such words as *sooth, guise, hardiment, Elfin,
prowess, wend, hight, dight, paramount, behests, caitiffs*.[1]
William Thompson, in his *Hymn to May* (1740?),
explains *certes* surely, certainly, *ne* nor, *erst* formerly,
long ago, *undaz'd* undazzled, *sheen* brightness, shining,
been are, *dispredden* spread, *meed* prize, *ne recks* nor is
concerned, *affray* affright, *featly* nimbly, *defftly* finely,
glenne a country borough (the real meaning is 'valley';
the wrong sense here given to it is due to E.K.'s notes
to Spenser's *Shepherd's Calendar*), *eld* old age, *lusty-*

---

[1] W. L. Phelps, *Beginnings of the Romantic Movement*, p. 63.
Cf. also K. Reuning, *Das Altertümliche im Wortschatz der Spenser-
Nachahmungen* (Strassburg, 1912). H. G. de Maar, *A History of
Mod. Engl. Romanticism* (Oxford, 1924), ch. IV.

head vigour, *algate* ever, *harrow* destroy, *carl* clown, *perdie* an old word for asserting anything, *livelood* liveliness, *albe* altho', *scant* scarcely, *bedight* adorned.

240. In later times, Coleridge, Scott, Keats, Tennyson, William Morris and Swinburne must be mentioned as those poets who have contributed most to the revival of old words. Coleridge in the first edition of the *Ancient Mariner* used so many archaisms in spelling, etc., that he had afterwards to reduce the number in order to make his poem more palatable to the reading public. Sometimes *pseudo*-antique formations have been introduced ; *anigh,* for instance, which is frequent in Morris, is not an old word, and *idlesse* is a false formation after the legitimate old *noblesse* and *humblesse* (OFr. noblesse, humblesse). But on the whole, many good words have been recovered from oblivion, and some of them will doubtless find their way into the language of ordinary conversation, while others will continue their life in the regions of higher poetry and eloquence. On the other hand, many pages in the works of Shakespeare, of Shelley, and of Tennyson show us that it is possible for a poet to reach the highest flights of eloquent poetry without resorting to many of the conventionally poetical terms.

241. As for the technical *grammar* of modern poetry, the influence of Shakespeare is not very strong, in fact not so strong as that of the Authorized Version of the Bible. The revival of *th* in the third person singular was due to the Bible, as we have seen above (§ 205).[1] *Gat* is more frequent than *got* in the Bible, while Shakespeare's ordinary form is *got* ; the solitary instance of *gat* (see § 235) only serves to confirm the rule.[2] The past tense of *cleave* 'to sever' in Shake-

---

[1] When modern clergymen in reading the Bible pronounce *lovèd,* *dancèd,* etc., they are reproducing a language about two hundred years earlier than the Authorized Version.

[2] *Gat* is the only form of this verb admitted by some modern poets, who avoid *get* and *got* altogether. Shakespeare uses the verb hundreds of times. In the Authorized Version *get* is pretty frequent, but *got* is avoided in the New Testament, while it is found seven

speare is *clove* or *cleft*; *clave* does not occur in his writings at all, but is the only biblical past of this verb. *Brake* is the only preterit of *break* found in the Bible; in Shakespeare *brake* is rarer than *broke*; Milton and Pope have only *broke*; Tennyson, Morris, and Swinburne prefer *brake*.

242. On the whole, however, modern poets do not take their grammar from any one old author or book, but are apt to use any deviation from the ordinary grammar they can lay hold of anywhere. And thus it has come to pass in the nineteenth century that while the languages of other civilized nations have the same grammar for poetry as for prose, although retaining here and there a few archaic forms of verbs, etc., in English a wide gulf separates the grammar of poetry from that of ordinary life. The pronoun for the second person is in prose *you* for both cases in both numbers, while in many works of poetry it is *thou* and *thee* for the singular, *ye* for the plural (with here and there a rare *you*); the poetical possessives *thy* and *thine* never occur in everyday speech. The usual distinction between *my* and *mine* does not always obtain in poetry, where it is thought refined to write *mine ears*, etc. For *they sat down* the poetical form is *they sate them down*; for *it's* poets write *'tis*, and for *whatever* either *whatso* or *whatsoever* (or *whate'er*), for *does not mend* they often write *mends not*, etc. Sometimes they gain the advantage of having at will one syllable more or less than common people : *taketh* for *takes*, *thou takest*

---

times in the Old Testament (in five of these places the revisers of 1881 substituted other words : gathered, bought, come) ; *gat* is used 20 times, all of them in the O.T. (three of these were changed in 1881) ; *gotten* is found 23 times in the O.T., and twice in the N.T. (five of these, among them both the instances in the N.T., were changed in 1881). Milton makes a very sparing use of the verb (which he inflects *get, got, got*, never *gat* in the past or *gotten* in the participle) ; all the forms of the verb only occur 19 times in his poetical works, while, for instance, *give* occurs 168 times and *receive* 73 times. The verb is rare in Pope too. Why is this verb tabooed in this way?

for *you take, movèd* for *moved, o'er* for *over*, etc.; compare also *morn* for morning. But in other cases the only thing gained is the impression, produced by uncommon forms, that we are in a sphere different from or raised above ordinary realities. As a matter of course, this impression is weakened in proportion as the deviations become the common property of any rimer, when a reaction will probably set in in favour of more natural forms. The history of some of the poetical forms is rather curious : *howe'er, e'er, e'en* were at first vulgar or familiar forms, used in daily talk. Then poets began to spell these words in the abbreviated fashion whenever they wanted their readers to pronounce them in that way, while prose writers, unconcerned about the pronunciation given to their words, retained the full forms in spelling. The next step was that the short forms were branded as vulgar by schoolmasters with so great a success that they disappeared from ordinary conversation while they were still retained in poetry. And now they are distinctly poetic and as such above the reach of common mortals.

243. Among the elements of ordinary language, some can be traced back to individual authors. Besides those already mentioned I shall cite only a few. *Surround* originally meant to overflow (Fr. sur-onder, Lat. super-undare) ; but according to Skeat, both the modern signification, which implies an erroneous reference to *round,* and the currency of the word are due to Milton. *The soft impeachment* is one of Mrs. Malaprop's expressions (in Sheridan's *Rivals,* act V, sc. 3). *Henchman* was made generally known by Scott, and *to croon* by Burns. Burke originated the expression *the Great Unwashed.* A certain number of proper names in works of literature have been popular enough to pass into ordinary language as appellatives,[1] as for instance *pander* or *pandar* from Chaucer's

---

[1] Aronstein, *Englische Studien,* XXV, p. 245 ff., Josef Reinius, *On Transferred Appellations of Human Beings* (Göteborg, 1903), p. 44 ff.

Troilus and Criseyde, Abigail 'a servant-girl' from Beaumont and Fletcher's *Scornful Lady, Mrs. Grundy* as a personification of middle-class ideas of propriety from Morton's *Speed the Plough, Paul Pry* 'a meddlesome busybody' from Poole's comedy of that name, *Sarah Gamp* 'sick nurse of the old-fashioned type' and 'big umbrella' from Dickens's *Martin Chuzzlewit, Pecksniff* 'hypocrite' from the same novel, *Sherlock Holmes* 'acute detective' from Conan Doyle's stories.

244. Ordinary language sometimes makes use of the same instruments as poetry. Above (§ 56) we have seen a number of alliterative formulas ; here I shall give some instances of riming locutions : *highways* and *byways, town* and *gown*, it will neither *make* nor *break* me (cf. the alliterative *make . . . mar*), *fairly* and *squarely, toiling* and *moiling*, as *snug* as a *bug* in a *rug* (Kipling), *rough* and *gruff*, 'I mean to take that girl— *snatch* or *catch*' (Meredith), *moans* and *groans*.[1] Compare also such popular words as *handy-dandy, hanky-panky, namby-pamby, hurly-burly, hurdy-gurdy, hugger-mugger, hocus pocus, hoity toity* or *highty tighty, higgledy-piggledy* or *higglety-pigglety, hickery-pickery. Hotchpot* (from French *hocher* 'shake together' and *pot*) was made *hotch-potch* for the sake of the rime ; then the final *tch* was changed into *dge* (cf. *knowledge* from *knowleche*) : *hotchpodge*, and the rime was re-established : *hodge-podge*.

245. Rhythm undoubtedly plays a great part in ordinary language, apart from poetry and artistic (or artificial) prose. It may not always be easy to demonstrate this ; but in combinations of a monosyllable and a disyllable by means of *and* the short word is in many set phrases placed first in order to make the rhythm into the regular ˈaa ˈaa instead of ˈaaa ˈa (ˈ before the *a* denotes the strongly stressed syllable).

---

[1] As Old English has *mœnan* 'moan', the modern verb may have derived its vowel from the frequent collocation with *groan*, OE. *granian. Square* may owe one of its significations to the collocation with *fair*.

Thus we say 'bread and butter,' not 'butter and bread'; further : bread and water, milk and water, cup and saucer, wind and weather, head and shoulders, by fits and snatches, from top to bottom, rough and ready, rough and tumble, free and easy, dark and dreary, high and mighty, up and doing.[1] It is probable that rhythm has also played a great part in determining the order of words in other fixed groups of greater complexity.[2]

---

[1] Compare also such titles of books as Songs and Poems, Men and Women, Past and Present, French and English, Night and Morning. In some instances, rhythm is obviously not the only reason for the order, but in all I think it has been at least a concurrent cause. F. N. Scott, in *Modern Language Notes*, 1913, has collected a number of combinations in which this rhythmical rule is not observed, but in many of these the word-order is obviously determined by other causes.

[2] P. Fijn van Draat, *Rhythm in English Prose* (Heidelberg, 1910), has many interesting observations on the influence of rhythm, though I would not subscribe to all his conclusions. Much of what he has written on the subject in later papers in the *Anglia* also appears to me very doubtful.

Chapter XI

Conclusion

246. In the preceding chapters we have considered the early vicissitudes of the English language, the various foreign influences brought from time to time to bear on it, its inner growth, lexical and grammatical, and the linguistic tendencies of its poets. It now remains to look at a few things which have contributed towards shaping the language, but which could find no convenient place in any of the preceding chapters, and then to say something about the spread and probable future of the language.[1]

247. Aristocratic and democratic tendencies in a nation often show themselves in its speech ; indeed, we have already regarded the adoption of French and Latin words from that point of view. It is often said, on the Continent at least, that the typical Englishman's self-assertion is shown by the fact that his is the only language in which the pronoun of the first person singular is written with a capital letter, while in some other languages it is the second person that is honoured by this distinction, especially the pronoun of courtesy (German *Sie*, often also *Du*, Danish *De* and in former times *Du*, Italian *Ella*, *Lei*, Spanish *V.* or *Vd.*, Finnish *Te*). Weise goes so far as to say that 'the Englishman, who as the ruler of the seas looks down in contempt on the rest of Europe, writes in his language nothing but the beloved *I* with a big letter'.[2] But this is little short of calumny. If self-assertion

---

[1] On some recent tendencies in English, I may refer to Stuart Robertson, *The Development of Modern English*, 1934, besides the works mentioned above (§1 61).

[2] *Charakteristik der lateinischen Sprache*, 1889, p. 21.

had been the real cause, why should not *me* also be written *Me*? The reason for writing *I* is a much more innocent one, namely, the orthographic habit in the middle ages of using a 'long i' (that is, j or I) whenever the letter was isolated or formed the last letter of a group; the numeral 'one' was written j or I (and three, iij, etc.), just as much as the pronoun. Thus no sociological inference can be drawn from this peculiarity.

248. On the other hand, the habit of addressing a single person by means of a plural pronoun was decidedly in its origin an outcome of an aristocratic tendency towards class-distinction. The habit originated with the Roman Emperors, who desired to be addressed as beings worth more than a single ordinary man; and French courtesy in the middle ages propagated it throughout Europe. In England as elsewhere this plural pronoun (*you*, *ye*) was long confined to respectful address. Superior persons or strangers were addressed as *you*; *thou* thus becoming the mark either of the inferiority of the person spoken to, or of familiarity or even intimacy or affection between the two interlocutors. English is the only language that has got rid of this useless distinction. The Quakers (the Society of Friends) objected to the habit as obscuring the equality of all human beings; they therefore *thou*'d (or rather *thee*'d) everybody. But the same democratic levelling that they wanted to effect in this way was achieved a century and a half later in society at large, though in a roundabout manner, when the pronoun *you* was gradually extended to lower classes and thus lost more and more of its previous character of deference. *Thou* then for some time was reserved for religious and literary use as well as for foul abuse, until finally the latter use was discontinued also and *you* became the only form used in ordinary conversation.

249. Apart from the not very significant survival of *thou*, English has thus attained the only manner of address worthy of a nation that respects the elementary rights of each individual. People who express regret at not having a pronoun of endearment and who insist how pretty it is in other languages when, for instance, two lovers pass from *vous* to the more familiar *tu*, should consider that no foreign language has really a pronoun exclusively for the most intimate relations. Where the two forms of address do survive, *thou* is very often, most often perhaps, used without real affection, nay very frequently in contempt or frank abuse. Besides, it is often painful to have to choose between the two forms, as people may be offended, sometimes by the too familiar, and sometimes by the too distant mode. Some of the unpleasant feeling of Helmer towards Krogstad in Ibsen's *Dukkehjem* (*A Doll's House* or *Nora*) must be lost to an English audience because occasioned by the latter using an old schoolfellow's privilege of *thou*-ing Helmer. In some languages the pronoun of respect often is a cause of ambiguity, in German and Danish by the identity in form of *Sie* (*De*) with the plural of the third person, in Italian and Portuguese by the identity with the singular (feminine) of the third person. When all the artificialities of the modes of address in different nations are taken into account— the *Lei*, *Ella*, *voi* and *tu* of the Italians, the *vossa mercê* ('your grace', to shopkeepers) and *você* (shortened form of the same, to people of a lower grade) of the Portuguese (who in addressing equals or superiors use the third person singular of the verb without any pronoun or noun), the *gij*, *jij*, *je* and *U* of the Dutch, not to mention the eternal use of titles as pronouns in German and, still more, in Swedish ('What does Mr. Doctor want?' 'The gracious Miss is probably aware,' etc.)—the English may be justly proud of having avoided all such mannerisms and ridiculous extravagances, though the simple Old English way of using *thou* in addressing one person and *ye* in addressing more than one would have been still better.

250. Religion has had no small influence on the

English language. The Bible has been studied and quoted in England more than in any other Christian country and a great many Biblical phrases have passed into the ordinary language as household words. The style of the Authorized Version has been greatly admired by many of the best judges of English style, who—with some exaggeration—recommend an early familiarity with and a constant study of the English Bible (and of that great imitator of Biblical simplicity and earnestness, John Bunyan) as the best training in the English language.[1] Tennyson found that parts of *The Book of the Revelation* were finer in English than in Greek, and he said that 'the Bible ought to be read, were it only for the sake of the grand English in which it is written, an education in itself'.[2] The rhythmical character of the Authorized Version is seen, for instance, in the well-known passage (Job III, 17), 'There the wicked cease from troubling : and there the wearie be at rest', which Tennyson was able to use as the last line of his *May Queen* with scarcely any alteration : 'And the wicked cease from troubling, and the weary are at rest'.

251. C. Stoffel has collected quite a number of scriptural phrases and allusions used in Modern English.[3]

---

[1] See the long series of quotations given in Albert S. Cook's little book, *The Bible and English Prose Style* (Boston, 1892). On the other hand, Fitzedward Hall says, 'To Dr. Newman, and to the myriads who think as he does about our English Bible, one would be allowed to whisper, that the poor "Turks" of the Prayer Book talk exactly in their own fashion, and for reasons strictly analogous to theirs, about the purity of diction, and what not, of "the Blessed Koran". . . . Ever since the Reformation, the ruling language of English religion has been, with rare exception, an affair either of studied antiquarianism or of nauseous pedantry. Simplicity, and little more, was aimed at, originally ; and it sufficed for times of real earnestness. But the very quaintness of phrase which King James countersigned has attained to be canonized, till a *hath*, or a *thou*, delivered with conventional unction, now well nigh inspires a sensation of solemnity in its hearer, and a persuasion of the sanctanimity of its utterer.' (*Modern English*, p. 16–17).

[2] *Life and Letters*, II, 41 and 71.

[3] *Studies in English, Written and Spoken*, 1894, p. 125.

such as 'Tell it not in Gath', 'the powers that be', 'olive branches' (children), 'strain at (or out) a gnat', 'to spoil the Egyptians', 'he may run that readeth it', 'take up his parable', 'wash one's hands of' something, 'a still small voice', 'thy speech bewrayeth thee'. Some which Stoffel does not mention may find their place here. The modern word a *helpmate* is a corruption of the two words in Gen. II, 18 : 'I will make him an *helpe meet* for him' (*meet* 'suitable') ; the slang word a *rib* 'a wife' is from Genesis, too, and so is the expression 'the lesser lights'. 'A howling wilderness' is from Deuteron. XXXII, 10. 'My heart was still hot within me ; then spake I with my tongue' (used, for instance in Charlotte Brontë's *The Professor*, p. 161) is from Psalms XXXIX, 3, and 'many inventions' from Ecclesiastes VII, 29. From the New Testament may be mentioned 'to kill the fatted calf',[1] 'whited sepulchres', 'of the earth, earthy', and 'to comprehend with all saints, what is the breadth, and length, and depth and height'. But people now begin to complain that scriptural allusions are to a great extent lost to the younger generation.

252. The scriptural 'holy of holies', which contains a Hebrew manner of expressing the superlative,[2] has given rise to a great many similar phrases in English, such as 'in my heart of hearts' (Shakespeare, Hamlet III, 2, 78 ; Wordsworth, *Prelude* XIV, 281), 'the place of all places' (Miss Austen, *Mansfield P.* 71), 'I remember you a buck of bucks' (Thackeray, *Newcomes*, 100), 'every lad has a friend of friends, a crony of cronies, whom he cherishes in his heart of hearts' (ib. 148), 'the evil of evils in our present politics' (Lecky, *Democr. and Lib.* I, 21), 'the woman is a horror of horrors' (H. James, *Two Magics*, 60), 'that mystery of mysteries, the beginning of things' (Sully, *Study of Childhood*, 71), 'she is a modern of

---

[1] While the phrase *prodigal son* is not found in the text of the Bible, it occurs in the heading of the chapter (Luke XV).

[2] Cf. I Timothy VI, 15, 'the King of kings, and Lord of lords'.

the moderns' (Mrs. H. Ward, *Eleanor*, 265), 'love like yours is the pearl of pearls, and he who wins it is prince of princes' (Hall Caine, *Christian*, 443), 'chemistry had been the study of studies for T. Sandys' (Barrie, *Tommy and Grizel*, 6). Compare also 'I am sorrowful to my tail's tail' (Kipling, *Sec. Jungle B.* 160).

253. Some scriptural proper names have often been used as appellatives, such as *Jezebel* and *Rahab* ; when a driver is called a *jehu* in slang, the allusion is to 2 Kings IX, 20, where Jehu's furious driving is mentioned. There is an American slang expression 'to give a person *jessie*' meaning 'to beat him soundly' which is not explained in the dictionaries (quotations may be found in Bartlett and in Farmer and Henley). Is it not in allusion to the *rod* mentioned in Isaiah II, 1 ? ('There shall come forth a rod out of the stem of Jesse.') The NED. has the spelling *jesse* with the meaning 'a genealogical tree representing the genealogy of Christ . . . a decoration for a wall, window, vestment, etc., or in the form of a large branched candlestick'.

254. The influence of Puritans, though not strong enough to proscribe such words as *Christmas,* for which they wanted to substitute *Christtide* in order to avoid the Catholic *mass,* was yet strong enough to modify the custom of swearing. In Catholic times all sorts of fantastic oaths were fashionable :

> Hir othes been so grete and so dampnable,
> That it is grisly for to here hem swere ;
> Our blissed lordes body they to-tere ;
> Hem thoughte Jewes rente him noght ynough.[1]

This practice was continued after the Reformation, and all sorts of alterations were made in the name of *God* in order to soften down the oaths : *gog, cocke, gosse, gosh, gom, Gough, Gad,* etc. Similarly instead of (the) *Lord* people would say something like *Law, Lawks, Losh,* etc. Sometimes only the first sound was left out ('Odd's lifelings,' Shakespeare, Tw. V, 187),

---

[1] Chaucer C. T., C. 472 ff., also see Skeat's note to this passage, *Chaucer's Works*, V, p. 275.

more often only the genitive ending survived :
'Sblood (God's blood), 'snails, 'slight, 'slid, 'zounds
(God's wounds). The final sound of the nominative
is kept in *'drot it* (God rot it), which was later made
drat it (or with a playful corruption *rabbit it*). Many
of these disguised oaths were extremely popular, and
some survive to this day. *Goodness gracious me*,
which defies all grammatical analysis, is one among
numerous compromises between the inclination to
swear and the fear of swearing ; note also Rosalind's
words : 'By my troth, and in good earnest, and so
God mend mee, and by all pretty oathes that are not
dangerous.' (As IV, 1, 192).

255. The Puritans caused a law to be enacted in
1606 by which profane language was prohibited on the
stage (3 James I, chap. 21), and consequently words
like *'zounds* were changed or omitted in Shakespearian
plays, as we see from a comparison of the folio of 1623
and the earlier quartos ; *Heaven* or *Jove* was substituted for *God*, and *'fore me* (*afore me*) or *trust me* for
(*a*)*fore God* ; 'God give thee the spirit of persuasion'
(H 4 A I, 2, 170) was changed into 'Maist thou have
the spirit of perswasion', etc. But in ordinary life
people went on swearing, and from the comedies of the
Restoration period a rich harvest may be reaped of
all sorts of curious oaths. By little and little, however,
the Puritan spirit conquered, and the English came to
swear less than other European nations. Even the
usual terms for oaths—'profane language' and
'expletives'—point to a greater purity in this respect.
Instead of *My God*, an Englishwoman will often say
Dear me! or *Oh my!* or *Good gracious!* Note also
euphemisms like 'deuce' for devil and 'the other
place' or 'a very uncomfortable place' for hell.[1]
Among words that used to be tabooed in England one
finds a great number which in other countries would
be considered quite innocent, and the English have
shown a really astonishing inventiveness in 'apologies'

---

[1] Compare also 'I will see you *further*'.

for strong words of every kind. *Damn* was considered
extremely objectionable, and even such a mild substitute for it as *confound* was scarcely allowed in polite
society.[1] In Bernard Shaw's *Candida*, Morell is provoked into exclaiming 'Confound your impudence !'
whereupon his vulgar father-in-law retorts, 'Is that
becomin' language for a clorgyman?' and Morell
replies, 'No, sir, it is not becoming language for a
clergyman. I should have said damn your impudence :
that's what St. Paul or any honest priest would have
said to you.' Other substitutes for *damned* are *hanged*,
somethinged (much rarer)[2] and a few that originate in
the manner in which the objectional word is — *not*
printed : *dashed* (a — or 'dash' being put instead of
it), *blanked* or *blanky* (from the same manner), *deed*
(from the abbreviation d—d ; sometimes the verb is
printed *to D*). *Darned* is perhaps nothing but a purely
phonetical development of *damned*, which is not without analogies, while *danged*, which occurs in Tennyson,
is a curious blending of *damned* and *hanged*.[3] Thus we
have here a whole family of words with an initial *d*,
allowing the speaker to begin as if he were going to
say the prohibited word, and then to turn off into
more innocent channels.[4] The same is the case with
the *bl*-words. *Blessed* by a process which is found in
other similar cases[5] came to mean the opposite of the
original meaning, and became a synonym of cursed ;
blamed had the same signification.[6] Instead of these
strong expressions people began to use other adjec-

[1] In the original sense it has often to be accompanied by *together*
to avoid misunderstanding.

[2] Cf. the similar use of *something* in 'Where the something are
you coming to?' (Pett Ridge, *Lost Property*, 167).

[3] 'I'm doomed!' Corp muttered to himself, pronouncing it in
another way. (Barrie, *Tommy and Grizel*, p. 122). This shows
another way of disguising the word *in print*.

[4] Cf. also the expression : 'Kingsley's struggles with the fourth
letter of the alphabet' (a little swearing was thought no blemish
in your muscular Christian), *Life of Leslie Stephen*, 138.

[5] Cf. *silly*, French *benêt*, etc.

[6] There exists also a word *blarned*, a blending of *blamed* and

tives, shunting off after pronouncing *bl-* into some innocent word like *bloody*, which soon became a great favourite with the vulgar and therefore a horror to ears polite, or *blooming*, which had the same unhappy fate in the latter half of the nineteenth century. Few authors would now venture to term their heroines 'blooming young girls' as George Eliot does repeatedly in *Middlemarch*. Similarly Shakespeare's expression 'the bloody book of law' is completely spoilt to modern readers, and lexicographers now have to render Old English *blodig* and the corresponding words in foreign languages by 'bleeding', 'blood-stained', 'sanguinary' or 'ensanguined'; but even *sanguinary* is often made a substitute for 'bloody' in reporting vulgar speech.

256. This is the usual destiny of euphemisms; in order to avoid the real name of what is thought indecent or improper people use some innocent word. But when that becomes habitual in this sense it becomes just as objectionable as the word it has ousted and now is rejected in its turn. *Privy* is the regular English development of French *privé*; but when it came to be used as a noun for 'a privy place' and in the phrase 'the privy parts', it had to be supplanted in the original sense by *private*, except in 'Privy Council', 'Privy Seal' and 'Privy Purse', where its official dignity kept it alive. The plural *parts* was an ordinary expression for 'talents, mental ability', until the use of the word in veiled language made it impossible.[1]

257. The twentieth century, and especially the time after the Great War, has put a stop to many of the linguistic prohibitions that flourished in the Victorian era. People are not now so afraid of saying *damn* and *bloody* as their ancestors were, and many sexual

---

damned (darned). Cf. also *I swan, I swow*, and other similar ways of not saying *I swear*.

[1] Cf. from America 'He-biddy—a male fowl. A product of prudery and squeamishness'. Farmer, *Americanisms*, p. 293. Cf. also Storm, *Engl. Philologie*, p. 887 (roosterswain).

things are now spoken of quite openly. The present
generation shake their heads at the prudery of Boston
ladies who would speak of the *limbs* of a piano or their
own *benders* instead of *legs*.[1] Many absurd names
(inexpressibles, inexplicables, indescribables, unmen-
tionables, unwhisperables, my mustn't mention-'em,
etc.) were used to avoid the simple word *trousers*, at
which no one takes offence nowadays. According to
F. T. Elworthy[2] even Somerset peasants thought
such names as *bull, stallion, boar, cock, ram* indelicate.
All this now belongs to ancient history.

258. This volume has in so far been one-sided as it
has dealt chiefly with Standard English, and has left
out of account nearly everything that is not generally
accepted as such, apart from here and there a nonce-
formation or a bold expression which is not recognized
as good English though interesting as showing the
possibilities of the language and perhaps in some cases
deserving popularity just as well as many things that
nobody finds fault with. I have had no space in this
little volume for the question how one form of English
came to be taken as standard in preference to dialects,[3]
nor for chapters on provincialisms, cockneyisms and
vulgarisms, on American and Colonial English, on
slang[4] and cant,[5] on Pidgin-English and other exotic
forms of English,[6] etc. I have also deliberately
omitted all the problems connected with that pseudo-
historical and anti-educational abomination, the
English spelling.[7] At present I shall conclude with a

---

[1] Cf. Opie Read, *A Kentucky Colonel*, p. 11. 'He was so delicate
of expression that he always said limb when he meant leg.'

[2] *Transactions of the Philological Society*, 1898.

[3] See now *Mankind, Nation and Individual* (Oslo, 1925), ch.
III and IV, where the development of common languages in general
is discussed.

[4] Ibid. ch. VIII.

[5] Ibid. ch. X.

[6] Cf. *Language*, ch. XII, on Beach-la-Mar and Pidgin.

[7] An historical account of the English sound-system and English
spelling may be found in my *Modern English Grammar* I (Heidel-

few remarks on what might be called the Expansion of English.

259. Only two or three centuries ago, English was spoken by so few people that no one could dream of its ever becoming a world language. In 1582 Richard Mulcaster wrote, 'The English tongue is of small reach, stretching no further than this island of ours, nay not there over all'. 'In one of Florio's Anglo-Italian dialogues, an Italian in England, asked to give his opinion of the language, replied it was worthless beyond Dover. Ancillon regretted that the English authors chose to write in English as no one abroad could read them. Even such as learned English by necessity speedily forgot it. As late as 1718, Le Clerc deplored the small number of scholars on the Continent able to read English.'[1] Compare what Portia replies to Nerissa's question about Fauconbridge, the young baron of England (Merch. I, 2, 72) : 'You know I say nothing to him, for hee understands not me, nor I him : he hath neither Latine, French, nor Italian, and you will come into the Court and sweare that I have a poore pennie-worth in the English. Hee is a proper man's picture, but alas, who can converse with a dumbe show?' In 1714 Veneroni published an Imperial Dictionary of the four chief languages of Europe, that is, Italian, French, German and Latin.[2] Nowadays, no one would overlook English in making even the shortest possible list of the chief languages, because in political, social and literary importance it is second to none, and because it is the mother-tongue of a greater number of human beings than any of its competitors.

---

berg, Carl Winter, 1909). A later, but unfortunately only half-finished treatment is Karl Luick, *Historische Grammatik der englischen Sprache* (Leipzig, 1914–1929).

[1] Ch. Bastide, *Huguenot Thought in England*, Journal of Comparative Literature I (1903), p. 45.

[2] Das kayserliche Spruch- und Wörterbuch, darinnen die 4 europäischen Hauptsprachen, als nemlich : das Italiänische, das Frantzösische, das Teutsche und das Lateinische erklärt werden.

260. It would be unreasonable to suppose, as is sometimes done, that the cause of the enormous propagation of the English language is to be sought in its intrinsic merits. When two languages compete, the victory does not fall to the most perfect language as such. Nor is it *always* the nation whose culture is superior that makes the nation of inferior culture adopt its language. It sometimes happens in a district of mixed nationalities that the population which is intellectually superior give up their own language because they can learn their neighbours' tongue while these are too dull to learn anything but their own. Thus a great many social problems are involved in the general question of rivalry of languages, and it would be an interesting but difficult task to examine in detail all the different reasons that have in so many regions of the world determined the victory of English over other languages, European and non-European. Political ascendancy would probably be found in most cases to have been the most powerful influence.

261. However that may be, the fact remains that no other European language has spread over such vast regions during the last few centuries, as shown by the following figures, which represent the number of millions of people speaking each of the languages enumerated[1] :

Year	*English*	*German*	*Russian*	*French*	*Spanish*	*Italian*
1500	4(5)	10	3	10(12)	$8\frac{1}{2}$	$9\frac{1}{2}$
1600	6	10	3	14	$8\frac{1}{2}$	$9\frac{1}{2}$
1700	$8\frac{1}{2}$	10	3(15)	20	$8\frac{1}{2}$	$9\frac{1}{2}$(11)
1800	20(40)	30(33)	25(31)	27(31)	26	14(15)
1900	116(123)	75(80)	70(85)	45(52)	44(58)	34(54)
1926	170	80	80	45	65	41

---

[1] The numbers given are necessarily approximate only, especially for the older periods. Where my authorities disagree, I have given the lowest and in parenthesis the highest figure. The figures for 1926 are from L. Tesnière's *Appendice* to A. Meillet's *Les Langues dans l'Europe Nouvelle* (Paris, 1928).

The latest figures that have come to hand are those
in H. L. Mencken, *The American Language*, 4th ed.,
1936, p. 592 : 'First, let us list those to whom English
is their native tongue. They run to about 112,000,000
in the continental United States, to 42,000,000 in the
United Kingdom, to 6,000,000 in Canada, 6,000,000
in Australia, 3,000,000 in Ireland, 2,000,000 in South
Africa, and probably 3,000,000 in the remaining
British colonies and in the possessions of the United
States. All these figures are very conservative, but
they foot up to 174,000,000. Now add the people who,
though born to some other language, live in English-
speaking communities and speak English themselves
in their daily business, and whose children are being
brought up to it—say 13,000,000 for the United States,
1,000,000 for Canada, 1,000,000 for the United Kingdom and Ireland, and 1,000,000 for the rest of the
world—and you have a grand total of 191,000,000.'
Mencken gives the figures for Spanish as 100, for
Russian as 80, and for German as 85 millions, and
adds : 'Thus English is far ahead of any competitor.
Moreover, it promises to increase its lead hereafter, for
no other language is spreading so fast or into such
remote areas . . . Altogether, it is probable that English
is now spoken as a second language by at least
20,000,000 persons throughout the world—very often,
to be sure, badly, but nevertheless understandably.'

Whatever a remote future may have in store, one
need not be a great prophet to predict that in the near
future the number of English-speaking people will
increase considerably. It must be a source of gratifica-
tion to mankind that the tongue spoken by two of the
greatest powers of the world is so noble, so rich, so
pliant, so expressive, and so interesting as the language
whose growth and structure I have been here en-
deavouring to characterize.

Phonetic Symbols

' stands before the stressed syllable.

· indicates length of the preceding vowel.

[a·]	as in *alms*.	[ʌ]	as in *hut*.
[ai]	as in *ice*.	[u·]	as in French *épouse*.
[au]	as in *house*.	[uw]	as in *who* ; practically
[æ]	as in *hat*.		= [u·].
[ei]	as in *hate*.	[y]	as in French *vu*.
[ə]	as in *about, colour*.	[þ]	as in *thin*.
[i·]	as in French *dise*.	[ð]	as in *this*.
[ij]	as in *heat* ; practically	[s]	as in *seal*.
	= [i·].	[z]	as in *zeal*.
[ou]	as in *so*.	[ʃ]	as in *shin* ; [tʃ] as in *chin*.
[ɔ]	as in *hot*.	[ʒ]	as in *vision* ; [dʒ] as in *gin*.
[o·]	as in *hall*.		

See my *Modern English Grammar* I (1909).

Abbreviations

OE. = Old English ('Anglo-Saxon').

ME. = Middle English.

ModE. = Modern English.

OFr. = Old French.

ON. = Old Norse.

OHG. = Old High German.

NED. = A New English Dictionary, by Murray, Bradley, Craigie, and Onions.

The titles of Shakespeare's plays are abbreviated as in Al. Schmidt's *Shakespeare-Lexikon*, thus Ado = *Much Ado about Nothing*, Gent.= *The Two Gentlemen of Verona*, H4A = *First Part of Henry the Fourth*, Hml. = *Hamlet*, R2 = *Richard the Second*, Tp. = *Tempest*, Tw. = *Twelfth Night*, Wiv. = *The Merry Wives of Windsor*, etc Acts, scenes and lines as in the Globe edition.

INDEX

References are to sections, not to pages.

Only the more important words used as examples are included.